Delivering Successful Projects with TSP℠ and Six Sigma

A Practical Guide to Implementing Team Software Process℠

Delivering Successful Projects with TSP^{SM} and Six Sigma

A Practical Guide to Implementing Team Software Process^{SM}

Mukesh Jain

CRC Press
Taylor & Francis Group
Boca Raton London New York

CRC Press is an imprint of the
Taylor & Francis Group, an **informa** business

AN AUERBACH BOOK

CRC Press
Taylor & Francis Group
6000 Broken Sound Parkway NW, Suite 300
Boca Raton, FL 33487-2742

First issued in paperback 2019

ISBN-13: 978-1-4200-6143-7 (hbk)
ISBN-13: 978-0-367-38637-5 (pbk)

Library of Congress Cataloging-in-Publication Data

Jain, Mukesh.
    Delivering successful projects with TSP SM and Six Sigma : a practical guide to implementing Team / Mukesh Jain.
        p. cm.
    Includes bibliographical references and index.
    ISBN 978-1-4200-6143-7 (alk. paper)
    1. Computer software--Development. 2. Computer software--Quality control.
3. Six sigma (Quality control standard) 4. Teams in the workplace. I. Title.

QA76.76.D47J352 2008
005.1--dc22   2008043060

Visit the Taylor & Francis Web site at
http://www.taylorandfrancis.com

and the CRC Press Web site at
http://www.crcpress.com

Contents

Preface

This book gives an overview of Team Software Process^{SM} (TSP^{SM}) and real-world details about my experience in successfully implementing TSP and Six Sigma in Microsoft. It also shows how geographically widely distributed new teams were able to deliver on time a very high quality product (two thirds of them with zero defects) with a decent work–life balance. This book highlights real-world scenarios that I experienced while coaching development teams on TSP. It also gives some tips and techniques to follow while implementing TSP.

This will be a handy book on understanding how some of the problems faced by the software industry can be solved using TSP. It gives an overview of TSP and shares actual real-world experience in implementing TSP, telling how some mistakes can be avoided to get the best out of a TSP implementation.

In this book, you will see how to effectively manage the development of a software project and deliver it successfully in line with expectations.

When I mention quality to software engineers, they talk about how impossible it is to eliminate defects from software: "Software will have defects no matter what process you follow." It's taken for granted, and since nobody acts to improve the situation, we make it horribly true. This goes, too, for software projects; I get the same reaction from project managers and a lot of time it's the blame game: "Software project got delayed because software engineers did not do a good job in development" or "Software project timeline was unrealistic—it's the project manager's fault." It's time we review the situation and enable software engineers and project managers to be effective in software development process—end-to-end.

Delivering successful projects means "the ability to produce high quality software within budget and on time—consistently." Clients expect the software applications to meet their expectations, to be delivered within budget and expected timeline. The project team strives to delight the clients by meeting or exceeding the expectations, attracting new business, and at the same time making a reasonable profit. If you are able to deliver a project that meets both clients' and project team's goals, the project can be considered successfully delivered.

Why I Wrote This Book

In my career, I had the opportunity to work in various areas including ISO 9001, CMM/CMMi level 3,4,5, and Six Sigma with software developers, testers, and project managers, finding that the problems are pretty much the same for any organization, groups, teams, or individuals. We needed something to do at the grassroots level to prevent recurring problems. I tried coaching people with some of the techniques of Six Sigma and blending these with software engineering. I started seeing dramatic results. It was the mind set for change and the passion for improvement and excellence that made the difference. This was not possible without the measurement system and framework.

Then I was exposed to TSP/PSP, and I could relate it to what I was doing. It had a good measurement framework and process to achieve a high-quality product and project management. I then started evangelizing it within Microsoft India, and we began seeing good results.

The knowledge I had from implementing TSP/PSP and Six Sigma was with me and a few of my colleagues, then I started doing presentations in several international conferences. I got a good response and several requests for sharing my knowledge. That is when I thought of writing a book to offer these ideas to a wider audience. With the help of John Wyzalek and Auerbach Publications I was able to get this moving, and put my thoughts onto paper in this book.

How Is the Book Organized?

The book is organized in a natural flow starting with current challenges in the software industry, software project management, and then giving an overview of PSP and TSP.

Next, it goes in depth into the TSP launch process and talks about how to go about a launch, with notes on points needing attention—do's and don'ts, etc. It can be used as a ready reference along with the TSP material provided by SEI.

Within the appropriate chapters, I have also added images and details for using the TSP tool. This can be used as a user guide for working with the TSP tool.

Toward the end of the book the chapter on Six Sigma gives an overview of the methodology and how to blend Six Sigma with the software development processes.

Who Should Read This Book?

This book is intended for professionals who are involved with software development and software process improvement. It will be useful for the following audience: developers, testers/QA, program managers, project managers, TSP coaches, quality assurance engineers, improvement specialists, process champions, etc. With this book, they will be able to look at their development process from a different angle and will be able to relate TSP concepts to the problems they are facing. This book will serve as a guiding document for them to implement TSP, to avoid mistakes others have made, and to get the best out of TSP. Organizations will be able to save time and money, and at the same time improve the quality of the output and customer satisfaction, driving more business.

There is no prereading required to understand this book. It covers all the basic concepts related to PSP and TSP. This book is not a replacement for formal training related to PSP and TSP, and is not intended to show a radically different approach to software development.

Acknowledgments

I started using Personal Software Process^{SM} (PSP^{SM}) and Team Software Process^{SM} (TSP^{SM}) in mid 2004, and received good support and guidance from SEI, especially from Watts Humphrey. In 2005, I had the opportunity to host Watts Humphrey in India during his trip there, learning much from his perspective on PSP and how to implement it successfully in large organizations like Microsoft. Several opportunities came up to review our TSP implementation approach with him, and I was able to fine tune it to be more effective. Today, TSP is implemented in a majority of the projects in Microsoft India; it would not have been possible without continued support and guidance from him. Thank you, Mr. Humphrey!

While writing this book, I have referred to SEI's TSP Launch Material and the SEI's (James Over) TSP tool.

TSP Launch and TSP Tool are copyrighted material from SEI. For more information please contact SEI directly. http://www.sei.cmu.edu/tsp/get-started.html

PSP and Personal Software Process are service marks of Carnegie Mellon University. TSP and Personal Software Process are service marks of Carnegie Mellon University.

Capability Maturity Model® (CMM®) and Capability Maturity Model Integration® (CMMI®) are registered in the U.S. Patent and Trademark Office by Carnegie Mellon University.

Acknowledgments

About the Author

Mukesh Jain is a principal quality manager at Microsoft, driving quality of service strategy and continuous improvement in online services. This represents over 200,000 servers for over 700 million users worldwide. He has been with Microsoft for more than nine years, implementing Six Sigma, TSP^SM/PSP^SM, Mistake Proofing (Poka-Yoke), and driving a quality-focused culture. He is a recipient of Microsoft's most prestigious individual excellence award, the "Gold Star," for four consecutive years. He recently received an honorarium mention from Microsoft's Chief Strategy Officer, Craig Mundie, for his contribution to building the Quality of Service Program and achieving outstanding results. He is a recipient of the Asia Pacific Leadership award (runner-up), Role-Model, Great People—Leadership award (IGNITE Category), Innovation Award, Solution Excellence, and several quality of service focus awards.

He has authored two "Thinkweek" papers for Bill Gates on performance monitoring and quality management. In 2001, Jain initiated and led Microsoft's first-of-its-kind Six Sigma project to improve the user's experience with Outlook performance. Since then he has mentored 14 Six Green Belt Sigma projects, 4 Black Belt projects, and 27 software projects on TSP, achieving a cumulative savings of $3.1 million.

For the past 13 years, Mukesh has worked at key positions as a developer, business analyst, program manager, solutions architect, coach, process and quality manager, and head of quality. He is an experienced coach and has directed and coached programmers and engineering teams to deliver projects on time, with high quality, and within budget. Prior to Microsoft, Mukesh was associated with several multinational corporations, among them Datamatics, Syntel, and Atos Origin, leading project, quality, and program management. His core expertise focuses on managing quality, leading organizations with process maturity, driving predictability (TSP/PSP, CMM, ISO 9000), measurement/metrics programs, guiding continuous improvements (Six Sigma), and shipping world-class products in multi-national organizations. In the industry, he is recognized as a leader and coach and has made significant differences in the careers of several people.

Along with a bachelor's degree in computer engineering and science, he has achieved various certifications that include Certified Standards Professional, TSP Coach, PSP Developer, PSP Engineer, PSP Instructor, CSTE, CSQA, CQM, CQIA, CQA, CTFL, CPD, CPE, Six Sigma Black Belt, Microsoft Office Specialist, ISO 9000 Auditor, MOF, and ITIL. In 2006, he was honored as "Best Six Sigma Black Belt" by *iSixSigma* magazine.

Mukesh's work in process improvements, defect prevention, Six Sigma, and TSP/PSP has been recognized at various international conferences, including

- "Quality of Service: Measuring and Improving User Experience the Right Way," Microsoft (Engineering Excellence/Trustworthy Computing Conference), United States (June 2008)
- "SCRUM Management: An Offshore Perspective," QAI's Project Management Leadership Conference, India (May 2008)
- "Delivering Successful Projects with TSP and Six Sigma: A Practical Guide to Implementing Team Software," QAI Quest Quality Engineered Software and Testing Conference, United States (April 2008)
- "Improving Web Application Performance Using Six Sigma," BZMedia Software Performance Conference, United States (April 2008)
- "Blending Inspections With Agile and TSP—What's in it?" SEI SEPG 2008, USA (March 2008)
- "Improving Web Application Performance Using Six Sigma," BZMedia Software Performance Conference, Boston (October 2007)
- "Avoiding Software Failures Using TSP/PSP and Six Sigma Methods," SQE/Better Software Conference, United States (2007)
- "Improving Web Application Performance Using Six Sigma," BZMedia Software Performance Conference, United States (April 2007)
- "Planning for Highly Predictable Results with TSP/PSP, Six Sigma, and Poka-Yoke," Microsoft Engineering Excellence (November 2006)
- "Planning for Highly Predictable Results with TSP/PSP, Six Sigma, and Poka-Yoke," PNSQC conference, United States (October 2006)
- "Delivering Successful Projects with Challenges of New Teams," SEI TSP User Group Conference, United States (September 2006)
- "Personal Productivity Improvement with TSP/PSP, Six Sigma, and Poka-Yoke," NASSCOM, India (September 2006)
- "Maturing Your Estimation Process Through Six Sigma and TSP," QAI Software Estimation Colloquium, India (August 2006)
- "Improving Product Usability Through Six Sigma," STeP-In Usability Conference (May 2006)

- "Can Your Software Project Deliver High Quality Results Within Budget, On-Time–Every Time?" STeP-Automation Conference, India (June 2006)
- "Test Process Maturity thru PSP/TSP," QAI, India (December 2005)
- "TSP in Global Model," SEI TSP Conference, Pittsburgh (September 2005)
- "TSP/PSP," Microsoft (Trustworthy Computing Conference) (June 2005)
- "Six Sigma and TSP," Microsoft (Corporate Business Excellence Conference) (June 2005)
- "TSP—The Road Towards Successful Project Management," Gyan Lahari, PMI, India (April 2005) (Award: *Best Paper*)
- "Planning for Success with TSP, Six Sigma," SEI TSP User Group Conference, India (November 2004)
- "Zero Defects Through Poka-Yoke," Seattle IT E-Commerce Applications Testing Conference, QAI, (2002)
- "Reducing Defects by Eliminating Mistakes at Source," ASQ, United States (March 2002) (Award: *Quality Laureate*)

Jain has published articles and white papers in several notable magazines including Microsoft, Satyam, ICFAI, and iSixSigma. He has been on the advisory boards for Keynote Systems, PNSQC, IEEE, ISPI, ASQ, SEI, SPIN, and CAI, among others.

Please visit http://www.MukeshJain.org for his latest profile, articles, and white papers .

Chapter 1

Introduction

Today, our global competitive marketplace demands the best of everything. A defect-free product delivered on time at minimal cost is the new standard that demanding customers expect and good suppliers continually strive to meet. In addition to ever more technical challenges, projects are more complex because of geographically distributed teams, time differences, language, and cultural differences. Project members do not have an easy task in meeting these challenges while still delivering high levels of quality, meeting schedules, and managing costs, as well as balancing professional and personal lives. There is no silver bullet, but we can meet all these goals by embracing a disciplined software development process and managing the project with the right set of metrics.

In the current economy, the majority of the products and services we consume interact with or use software. Software is so common in everything that we hardly notice its presence. It is, however, important to remember that a lot of hard work by hundreds to thousands of people goes into the development of these software products.

Often, projects are planned by managers and executed by a team; if things go wrong, it becomes the team's failure. It is easy to be reactive at work, but much harder and very necessary to be proactive and to plan teamwork. Historically, application development is often estimated and tracked based on a gut feeling. A schedule is developed from the rough estimate and, as the team tries to meet its schedule, it struggles to meet deadlines. Corners get cut, and the last phase—testing and stabilization—usually suffers the full effect of poor planning and estimating. Engineers often have to spend endless evenings and weekends in the office to get the project out, and their work and life become unbalanced, which is not healthy for any organization from any angle, including money, time, and staffing. In the end, customers are most likely dissatisfied, teams are exhausted, and quality may have been compromised in the drive to meet the promised date.

I analyzed several projects and found that more than two-thirds of the effort and money is spent in testing and stabilizing the product. This is a non-value-added activity, and managing it properly can be a great opportunity to help organizations save time and money.

The software engineering's Team Software Process^{SM} (TSP^{SM}) really shifts the focus from testing as the "find it and fix it" stage. With TSP, each individual engineer acts to prevent defects throughout the project life cycle. Team members record data during project execution, track key metrics, and take corrective action as soon as the project deviates from the plan. Each engineer performs a self review to ensure the quality of their own output before it goes to the next phase. This brings about a high level of predictability in schedule, effort, and quality.

Instead of managers, the TSP team plans the project, tracks all the important metrics on a weekly basis, and takes corrective action as needed. It becomes the team's project plan, and every member is committed to it. Using Six Sigma along with TSP makes future planning even better. Senior management will be able to strategize more accurately and confidently with a TSP project plan and estimates based on historical data (rather than guesstimates).

This book will detail how TSP techniques can be followed to plan the right thing, do the right thing, and expect the right thing at the right time—every time. I have shared real-world experience in implementing TSP at Microsoft, and now share the success stories on how the newly formed teams had a better work–life balance, delivering very high quality products on schedule and within budget. The projects delivered significant benefits in predictability, and two-thirds of them delivered zero defects. Also, I have highlighted some common pitfalls to avoid while implementing TSP and coaching TSP teams.

Chapter 2

Current Challenges in the Software Industry

Today, the competitive marketplace demands the best of everything—the best quality, reduced costs, and a perfect schedule. A defect-free product delivered on time at minimal cost is the new standard that demanding customers expect and good suppliers continually strive to meet.

Often, projects are planned by managers and executed by the team, and if things go wrong, it becomes the team's failure. It is easy to be reactive at work but harder and necessary to be proactive and plan your team's work. Sometimes your manager will grab you in the hall and say, "Hey, can you do this project now and finish it in two months?" Or, a senior management planning committee will call you into its meeting and say, "We need this project now. Can you commit to it?" It is very tempting to say "Yes." However, saying yes is exactly the wrong thing to do, and your initial "gut feel" estimate will be taken as commitment and the project will be in trouble. Nobody wants to set you and the project up for failure, but, in the rush to get the project done and delight the customer, we all miss the very important step—planning. You could have said, "Let me check to see if my previous estimate is still accurate, and I'll get back to you within the next two hours."

It is not an easy task to meet these challenges without compromising the high-quality levels or the schedule or the cost. There is no silver bullet; we can meet all these goals by having a disciplined process, planning it the right way, and managing with the right set of matrices.

In this book, you will learn how sound software engineering principles, project management techniques, and continuous improvement processes can be applied to streamline your development process and overcome the crisis that people face due to ad hoc software development processes.

2.1 The Software Crisis

The rapid evolution of the software industry has led people to focus more on project management. Software development, on the other hand, was left to the developers, whose main focus was to deliver the features of the project. Such an approach resulted in an ad hoc approach to software development and no focus on software design concepts or software development methodology. This hampered the application of systematic processes, and can also be referred to as the software crisis.

Some of the major reasons to which you can attribute the software crisis include

- Software developers used multiple programming languages and multiple variations of the languages.
- Most of the requirements were vague and complex and were developed by people who had little or no exposure to software.
- Software developers focused more on technology rather than solution.
- Software engineering education did not give enough emphasis on software quality.
- Software developers poorly mapped requirements to the actual product.
- Getting multiple software systems to work together was a nightmare (very low interoperability).
- Software maintenance was costly.
- Documentation was never given adequate emphasis, which resulted in loss of knowledge and continuity.

2.2 Software Project Management

In the beginning, the focus of software was just to have some program consisting of a set of instructions that would enable the hardware to perform some activity. Most of the commands were mathematical in nature, which the users create themselves for their own use. As the software product grew in importance within organizations, the expectations increased, and more and more people were required to build it. There was a strong need for managing the project and making it more scalable. A project manager was assigned a role to plan the project, manage resources, manage client interaction, and drive software project completion and delivery on time.

The process of software and product development is different from any other project. Traditional methods of measuring size, effort, and productivity cannot be applied to software development. Moreover, techniques to identify, define, and measure the software development process and product are comparatively new and are not mature enough to be used without problems.

Typical software project management activities are

- Understanding and dissipating client requirements
- Determining the scope
- Estimating the cost, effort, expertise and resource requirements
- Identifying and selecting resources with appropriate skills and allocating them
- Identifying the software development life-cycle model
- Identifying risk, creating a mitigation plan, and managing them
- Estimating the project cost and effort required
- Creating project schedule, milestones, deliverables, and overall project plan
- Tracking project schedule and taking necessary action to ensure it would be on track
- Maintaining all versions of the software product
- Managing software product quality, configuration, and changes
- Implementing project tracking, team meetings, communication, and reporting
- Identifying appropriate metrics
- Ensuring project delivery, closure, and post-mortem assessment
- Sharing project learnings with other teams and using them for future projects

Managing a software project is different from managing any other engineering projects due to the complexity and uniqueness of its development process. Although, some of the traditional project management concepts can be applied to software projects, in last 15 years, software project management has evolved as a separate area of expertise.

Typically, a software product is composed of tightly integrated functions, programs, platforms, databases, user interfaces, etc. Several people or teams work together for months and years to develop it. Matters such as cross-group collaboration, attrition, talent-management, people conflicts, managing priorities, and offshore/outsource model add to the complexity, which brings more challenges to project management and chaos in delivering the product successfully. Just having the software that works is not enough; we need to have a quality product that is reliable (that does not have a lot of defects, is resilient to failures, secure, fast, usable, predictable, etc.).

As more and more software applications are being used in financial, medical, and other critical systems, the margin of error is not tolerable, and getting a product to meet this type of quality bar becomes more and more impossible with the traditional approach of software development and project management. You can see, as we move towards more sophisticated systems, expectations are growing, and what worked 5 years back may not work now.

Figure 2.1   The Iron Triangle.

2.3 The Iron Triangle—Scope, Schedule, Resources

Any projects, similar to any other endeavor, will have one or more important factors regarding successful delivery. Project constraints are scope, schedule, and resources. The iron triangle has these constraints represented as edge (side) of the triangle with quality as a central theme. This is also called Project Management Triangle or Project Management "Triple Constraint," and is shown in Figure 2.1.

These three constraints are often competing constraints or demands; increased scope typically means increased time and increased cost, a tight time constraint could mean increased costs and reduced scope, and a tight budget could mean increased time and reduced scope. If you change any side of the triangle, one or both of the others will have to change as well. So, if the scope changes, either schedule or resource requirements need to change, or both. One side of the triangle cannot be changed without impacting the others. In this book, you will see the tools and techniques that enable members of the project team (not just the project manager) to organize their work to meet these constraints.

Together, the team can accomplish the project "Right Quality, On Time, On Budget, On Spec."

2.3.1 Scope

The scope constraint refers to what must be done to produce the project's end result. *Scope* is the set of requirements from the user that is agreed and planned for a particular release (user expectations from a particular system release). It is the overall definition of what the project is supposed to accomplish, and a specific description of what the end result should accomplish. Even though quality may not have been explicitly specified as a requirement, it is a major component of scope of the final product. There are always a set of stated and implied needs from the users. Over the course of a large project, quality can have a significant impact on schedule and cost (or vice versa).

Scope changes are pretty common during the project. In several cases, we need to accommodate the scope changes, as the purpose of the project is the deliver value to the client. Scope changes are of three kinds: new feature, change to a feature, and remove any feature. In any case, the cost is not the same as the original. That is, if a feature requires 100 hours to design and code, changes to it may need more than 100 hours.

2.3.2 Schedule

The schedule constraint refers to the amount of time available to complete a project. For all practical purposes, the time required to develop/deliver a project component is estimated using several techniques. One method is to identify tasks/steps needed to produce the deliverables documented in a work breakdown structure (WBS). The work effort for each task is estimated, and those estimates are rolled up into the final deliverable estimate for the project. The tasks are prioritized based on the dependencies between tasks and delivery schedule/milestones. The dependencies between the tasks can affect the length of the overall project, as can the availability of resources. Time or schedule is not considered a cost or a resource because the project manager cannot control the rate at which it is expended. This makes it different from all other resources and cost categories.

2.3.3 Resources/Cost

The resources constraint refers to the budgeted amount, machines/equipment, people/consultants, and other resources available for the project. When hiring an independent consultant for a project, cost will typically be determined by the consultant's or firm's per diem rate multiplied by an estimated quantity for completion. If you need to finish a job in a shorter time, you can throw more people at the problem, which in turn will raise the cost of the project, unless by doing this task quicker we will reduce costs elsewhere in the project by an equal amount.

2.4 Software Quality

The quality of the project end result is not really a constraint but a collective output. The quality of the deliverable is a function of all sides of the triangle. Whenever there is a change in any of the sides, it impacts the overall quality of the deliverable.

There is no point in delivering something very fast and not meeting customer expectations. We cannot take forever either to deliver something that is of exceptional quality. Quality is a subjective measure. If a defect is not encountered, quality is considered high, and yet there may be a defect. So, our goal should be that our users should not encounter any defects. Quality is something that is hard to notice, but its absence/shortcoming is very easily felt.

Software projects rarely follow the planned schedule. Delays happen, and the schedule starts slipping one day at a time. Some of the projects do not have the right level of project tracking, which brings lot of surprises to the development teams towards the end, engineers start cutting corners to meet the date, and the chaos starts. Developers and testing are typically separated; shifting responsibility is illustrated by the attitude that "A test should have caught this problem."

A prevention mindset is not common; instead of analyzing why a bug occurred and finding means to reduce it in the future, the attitude is more often, "The bug is fixed, get a new build." No effort is expended on finding the root cause of a problem and thinking about preventing this problem in future. By the time the project moves to the testing phase, the project is already in a difficult situation, and managing the project becomes a challenge. The test team is under pressure to complete the test pass and get the project shipped.

Often people have the mindset of testing quality into the project deliverable, the assumption being "Let's get the coding done, we will put more people to test it and ship it." Putting more effort in testing does not guarantee better quality. The project should take care of quality right from the planning phase. I will talk more about this in the next few chapters.

I have seen people saying, "Faster, cheaper or better—choose two." People often think that if you have a tight schedule and a low budget, you will have poor quality, and I have also seen people saying, "Spend more time in testing to get higher quality." Both are not totally true. It's like saying, "I can deliver this fast and at a low cost, but it will not meet your needs or may not work." It is clear that quality should not be part of the constraint, and it can never be an optional component.

If you get your things done right the first time, take all the right measures to ensure quality, you can have an excellent quality product with low budget and a short schedule. On the other extreme, testing can only find certain number of bugs. If you have 100 bugs, and the test process efficiency is 90%, you will still slip 10 bugs. By extending the testing period you might be able to take the test process efficiency to 92–95%, but then you might still have bugs in the end product. The math is clear: to get better quality, focus on the input. If the number of bugs entering the testing phase is 10 (instead of 100), with 90% efficiency you can pretty much ship a world-class product.

People have the misconception that high quality will cost more or will take more time because of variation in its definition. Quality is referred to in multiple ways. It can be broadly classified into three major categories: reliability, usability/aesthetics, and grade. Once the requirements for the product have been agreed upon, its quality refers to the degree to which it meets those requirements.

2.4.1 Reliability

Reliability is the ability of a product to perform a required function under stated conditions for a stated period of time. A reliable product will have the attributes of being accurate, predictable, dependable, secure, maintainable, resilient, and having low or no defects. As you can see, these attributes are important to everybody, and if the product is not able to meet one or more of these attributes and it impacts the customer/user, the product is tagged as a not reliable or poor-quality product.

If the product has defects, unexpected behavior, or raises security or privacy concerns, it will have reliability issues. You can build a reliable product, but not provide good/intuitive UI to access—and your users may not be able to access some of its functionalities at all. So, you can see that all of these aspects are reasonably important, and we need to make sure that they are all there when we talk about quality. Depending on the product and the intended users or customers, we might have different levels of expectations in each of these categories.

In most of the discussion in this book, we will refer to "reliability" when I use the term quality.

2.4.2 Usability/Aesthetics

Just having a good set of functionalities is not enough for a product. The UI needs to be decent and should be intuitive enough to get to this functionality from the main UI. For power users, this may not be very important, but if you are targeting your product to the masses, it assumes considerable significance. Good usability is important for enabling the accessibility features of the product. We want to make sure that the product can be used by everybody, including those who are physically challenged.

If the product usability is not good, people will have difficulty accessing the functionality, and this will increase the support call volume and in turn impact the cost. It might also impact your market share when people find it difficult to use the product. They will tag the product as of poor quality and will seek a better option elsewhere, thus impacting your revenue.

2.4.3 Grade

Grade refers to the set of attributes on which the quality of a product will be judged by some people. For example, you can buy milk in various grades (such as "fat-free," "1%," "2%," "whole," etc.). The industry has defined a set of attributes for each grade for fat content. The quality of "fat-free" milk will be similar to that of "whole" milk. The grade of the product is based on the scope, and if it meets that need, it will satisfy the appropriate grade quality expectations.

If you want a software product with lot of customization options, then it will cost you more time or money, whereas the same functionality with only a few customization options might be significantly cheaper. An example would be the version of Microsoft Windows Vista or Microsoft Office system; these applications comes in multiple flavors (home, standard, professional, enterprise, ultimate, etc.).

Producing a poor-quality product does not save time or money. In fact, as we will discuss later, quality problems actually cost us time and money.

2.5 Cost of Quality

It is important for us to know and understand the cost of quality and what it covers. Overall, the cost of quality has three components: prevention, detection, and correction.

2.5.1 Prevention

Prevention includes all the activities that can prevent defects from being put in the product in the first place. This includes training, standards and processes, and design activities. For example, requirements engineering, architecture and design activities, design templates, guidelines, automation, coding standards, standard processes, project postmortem, etc., are considered prevention activities.

Most organizations look at these activities as overhead that are not related to delivery of the project, and so they try to minimize them or avoid them altogether. If these activities are correctly included as costs of quality, then they could easily be planned, tracked, and managed to ensure that they are adding value.

2.5.2 Detection

Detection is the set of activities that normally find any defect. Activities such as test planning, test environment setup, test execution, test automation, and reviews and inspection are counted as detection cost. They typically constitute the costs that the organization reports as quality cost. These costs show up in the project budget as the cost of quality.

The usual behavior is, if you want to increase focus on quality, spend more money in the detection area, that is, allocating more resources and time to these activities. I have seen some organizations take pride in saying that they spent more dollars in testing than in development. As you can see, detection activities can only find the defects; you will still need somebody who will have to fix them. You can put more resources in this and find more bugs, but if you do not have adequate budget and time to fix them, you won't get the benefits of this phase. Also, think about it—if these defects were never there in the product, there would be a huge opportunity to reduce the effort around them.

That is why it is important to consider the other two components of the cost of quality to determine how each of these components interact with each other and how you can drive a positive attitude change in the organization in understanding and appreciating the cost of quality.

2.5.3 Correction

Correction is the set of activities that are triggered by the discovery of defects. It includes defect reporting, and investigating, fixing, retesting, and managing the defect reports. The major defect correction cost is incurred by development engineers who must investigate and diagnose the problems, devise appropriate fixes, and rework the product to remove the defects. In addition to this, correction includes the cost to test the fix and regression test the system to ensure that the fix did not introduce other problems. Further, if the problem was reported from the field by the customer or user, it includes the cost of distributing the fix and supporting the customers who encounter the problem.

Every time the developer fixes a defect, the overall cost of the project increases and potentially impacts the schedule. However, the increase in project cost and schedule is not tracked as a cost of quality. Instead, retesting is counted as a defect detection cost, hiding it in the wrong part of the cost of quality. To get the correct metrics around this, the process should be in place to mark any rework activity as the correction cost of quality.

I have seen many organizations measure only the cost of detection, and only some organizations measure correction cost. Having a good understanding of the effort in each of the cost-of-quality components is required to make sound decisions for the project and to accurately plan for future projects.

2.6 Global Competition and Market Challenge

With more and more companies adopting the global model, they choose to outsource or set up offshore development offices in countries such as India and China. Some of the reasons for this are cost difference, talent pool, visa restrictions, new and developing market penetration, etc.

New markets bring in a unique set of challenges. Some of them are time difference, cultural difference, language, protocol, and high attrition rate. It becomes more and more challenging to consider these challenges while planning. Just adding more time and people will not help. Acknowledging the differences, and planning for handling these challenges and tracking them is key to success of the project.

2.7 Managing Project Constraints

Different people involved in the project will have different views about the constraints. The QA team considers that quality is the most important attribute to achieve. The marketing team will talk about "feature set," and hitting a date is a top priority to sustain or capture market share. Management would think that being within budget is very important. So, in the end, everybody is focusing on a different priority, which could result in chaos and impact the shipping of the product. It is very essential to understand what is the right set of priorities for the project and why. The project team needs to be informed about this and empowered to plan the project according to its needs.

A project can be date driven because it needs to

1. Synchronize with another product's release.
2. Meet competitive threats.
3. Coincide with corporate or consumer buying seasons.

At the beginning of the project, determine if the release date is tied to some external event, and schedule milestone dates accordingly.

A project can be feature-set driven because it needs to

1. Address specific customer requirements and needs that require a minimum set of functionality. This is especially true of version 1.0 products.
2. Address competitive threats.

Whether date-driven or feature-driven, quality is critical and should be considered during the planning stage.

2.8 Project Failures

As said earlier, often projects are planned by managers, executed by the team and, if things go wrong, it becomes the team's failure. It is easy to be reactive at work. It is harder and necessary to be proactive and plan your team's work. Sometimes your manager will grab you in the hall and say, "Hey, can you do this project now, and finish it in two months?" Or, a senior management planning committee will call you into its meeting and say, "We need this project now. Can you commit to it?" It is very tempting to say yes. However, saying yes is exactly the wrong thing to do.

Unfortunately, project management is a weak link in the overall software development life cycle. Problems in project management lead to more delays and failures of large software projects than any other known factor. This chapter talks about some of the common causes of project failures and the essential skills for successful software project management and delivery. These skills include budgeting, planning, estimating, measurement, tracking, reporting, and quality assurance and control. Improving the project management process and focusing on sound engineering practices is a critical step towards successful project delivery.

Big projects are usually difficult to control because of the following challenges:

■ Hardly anyone has personal plans that provide details of what development will be undertaken, and its measurements and tracking.
■ Without such a plan, it is almost impossible for you to find out the status of the work and gain an accurate insight into its schedule.

- If we don't know where you are, we cannot predict or commit to the completion date, and nobody will know the status of the project until it is too late.
- If management cannot find the current progress of the project and its status, it cannot manage the project.

2.9 Geographically Distributed Teams and Attrition

The majority of the software projects now-a-days spans multiple locations; typically, teams are geographically distributed across the globe. Achieving success with geographically distributed teams is quite a challenge for project managers. As more organizations adopt offshore development, telecommuting, and "going virtual," this challenge becomes more apparent.

There are benefits and challenges in geo-distributed teams.

Benefits

- More flexibility
- Employee retention
- Wider talent pool
- Cost effective—cost-of-living/salary difference
- Regional knowledge
- Wide range of experience

Challenges

- Communication
- Cultural difference
- Team interaction
- Time difference

Here are some of the characteristics needed for a successful geo-distributed/virtual team.

- A detailed project plan and rigorous project management. All the team members need to have a clear sense of vision, mission and priorities. They know who is responsible for what, and when.
- Ongoing communication. Team members communicate regularly using the phone, conference calls, video teleconference, e-mail, instant messenger, voice/video chat, common databases, SharePoint, Wiki, and other technical methods as appropriate. They must be able to communicate effectively without the benefit of nonverbal cues.
- Free-flowing information. All the team members (new and old, irrespective of the work location) willingly share what they know and what they learn

with everyone else. They also acknowledge or ask about what they don't know.

■ Trust. Team members respect and understand one another as people, not just professionals.
■ Cultural factors. Understanding and respecting cultural differences.
■ Office visits. The plan should consider regular visits (once every 3–5 months) for team members to be able to spend 1–2 weeks together at one of the locations. This helps in building effective teams, and people can attach faces to names and understand each other better.

Chapter 3

Delivering a Successful Project

3.1 Overview

As the software industry matures, the expectations around software engineering projects can be categorized as follows:

Trustworthy: Systems that people can trust for quality, reliability, security, and privacy

Predictability and Agility: Ability to deliver high-quality products on time and within budget, and to rapidly adapt to evolving and changing global business needs

Integration: Ability to build flexible and adaptable systems that can integrate with multiple systems—from legacy mainframes to PC devices, and mobile and global Web

The key challenge would be to mature software engineering processes to meet these expectations and deliver on them.

3.2 Software Projects

A project is a temporary endeavor undertaken to create a unique product or service. The word *temporary* is used to signify that there will be a start date and end date. Things that go on forever cannot be considered as projects (e.g., support, maintenance, etc., are not projects).

Here is a list of attributes that the projects can typically have:

- Have a defined start and end date
- Requires resources and time
- Focus on getting things done
- Solve business or technical problems
- Seize opportunities
- Different from other work/activities/product
- Are challenging

3.3 Project Management

Project management is the discipline of the organization, management, and delivery of all aspects of a specific project throughout its duration, from initial concept to final delivery, in such a way that the project is completed within defined scope, quality, time, and cost constraints. The final output product should achieve the overall objectives of the project with respect to the following:

- Successfully fulfill the project scope and quality requirements
- Deliver within the schedule
- Completion within the agreed-upon cost and effort parameters

Effective project management is getting high-quality work done on time and within budget that meets customer expectations and keeps the team happy. It is about accomplishments, leadership, and results. Project management needs excellent communication skills, leadership skills and, most important, the skill for working with people.

The awareness of project management's role as a special skill set and competency that is learned and applied, similar to engineering, has been growing. Project management is evolving as a separate and distinct function that is performed independently of, but in conjunction with, architects, developers, engineers, and testers, each executing its respective project role.

Software project management is one that focuses specifically on creating or updating software. It has some key differences and distinctions from project management in other fields. The majority of the aspects is connected with the maturity of the field, tangible versus nontangible components, etc. For example, in a software project, the scope is hard to see and equally difficult to explain, and similarly, quality is hard to see or measure. It is thus difficult to define these aspects clearly.

Here is a list of other major differences and distinctions:

1. The majority of the costs in an IT project is people cost, and it varies based on the specialization.
2. Even in the same job category and at the same experience level, there is a huge difference in the productivity rates of the people.
3. The quality of output varies between people.
4. Software projects typically are more complex.

5. Estimation is more complex.
6. Software projects typically involve a large number of changes to the requirements.
7. There is a high degree of risks.
8. Attrition is very high.
9. There is no consistent criteria or definition of quality.
10. There are multiple ways to do the same thing—architecture, methodology, algorithms, tools, etc., and they are constantly changing from project to project and sometimes within a project.
11. The software industry is still evolving—there are new technologies, languages, platforms, operating systems, architecture, telecommunications, interfaces, tools, etc.
12. Return on investment (ROI) is almost impossible to measure.
13. Fairly young people work in this industry, with comparatively less experience.
14. Unrealistic pressure from management is placed on the project manager and teams for delivering projects better, cheaper, and faster.
15. Software projects typically involve offshore resources.

Projects usually have multiple teams, which bring in more challenges. Here is a list of typical teams a project might have:

1. Software engineering
2. Hardware engineering
3. Systems engineering
4. Project management
5. Operations engineering
6. Marketing
7. Product management
8. Support

With multiple teams comes multiple processes, and when each team uses its own process for planning and execution, you can imagine the variation in the plans and project output. With all these differences and challenges in delivering successful projects, project management is considered very important.

Project management has the following eight key expectations:

■ People
■ Quality
■ Scope
■ Time
■ Cost
■ Communication
■ Risks
■ Integration

People: People are very important to the success of any project; without dedicated and motivated people, it might be almost impossible to deliver the project successfully. While delivering the project, the project managers need to make sure they don't deliver the project at the cost of the people. Work–life balance and career growth should always be in focus.

Quality: Quality should not be an afterthought; it should be well thought out throughout the project. There is no value delivering something that does not work, even if all other expectations are met. Quality is not just about defects in the software. It's about the overall experience, and reliability.

Scope: It is natural for the business and customer to ask for more features and changes to the project scope to meet their business needs. The project manager needs to maintain a balance here to ensure that the team does get randomize with every change and at the same time need to adapt few critical business needs. Essentially, the project and product scope need to be very well managed to ensure that you still deliver the high quality software on time that meet majority of the business needs.

Time: Delivering on time is very crucial for the team and the organization to call the project successful. If you deliver tax software late—after April 15—not many people will buy that. If we wait forever to deliver high-quality software, the market might not be there. The timely delivery of the project is very critical for the organization to remain competitive.

Cost: Every project needs money, and the majority of the cost is around people. The project manager needs to ensure cost estimating, budgeting, tracking, reporting, and control. One cannot have all the money for the project, so, managing the budget for the project is equally important. Cost overruns for the projects are typical issues that hurt an organization's performance.

Communication: A project needs multiple levels of communication—within the team, with stakeholders, customers, etc. A regular and predictable communication rhythm keeps everybody informed with good news, bad news, project progress, and estimated date of completion.

Risk: If anything can go wrong, it will—that's Murphy's law. In day-to-day project management, there are several things that might go wrong. Identifying risks, tracking, and mitigation planning are important areas. If the risks are not planned for and mitigated, the project might be in danger.

Integration: Integration needs to happen at the project level and at the organizational systems level. Both need to happen early in the cycle to effectively identify issues and fix them as soon as possible.

3.4 Project Management Myths

In most cases, you learn the skills required to manage a software project while on the job. Unfortunately, this skill is not taught in engineering school. As a result, most software project managers practice a lot of management techniques that are of doubtful authenticity. Many software project managers learn about so-called management skills and concepts that are actually myths.

3.4.1 Clarifying the Project Management Myths

The following list aims to clarify some of the more prevalent myths in software project management.

Myth 1: Combining the best resources with the worst resources available for a software project helps to complete the project successfully.

In software projects, combining the best resources with the worst resources drags down the efficiency and productivity of the good resources. This invariably decreases the speed of the software project, and the project ends much later than the specified deadline.

Myth 2: A general statement of objectives is sufficient to begin work on the software project.

Many software project managers and customers believe that a general statement of objectives gives a reasonable idea of the requirements. However, a formal and detailed description of customer requirements is needed before the project commences. The software project manager must ensure that all information regarding the software project, such as the function, performance, interfaces, constraints, assumptions and validation criteria, is gathered.

Myth 3: Allocating extra resources to a late project allows it to catch up with the project schedule.

A software project is not a mechanical process such as, say, building a road. In the case of building a road, adding more people to the job can help build the road in a shorter period of time. However, in a software project, adding more people actually increases the time required to finish the project. This happens because a new person joining the project requires time to understand the requirements of the client, software design, and standards. Moreover, the existing people in the project need to devote time and effort to train the new people on the software project. Therefore, allocating additional resources to a risky situation increases the risk to the software project.

Myth 4: As software by itself is flexible, you can change the requirements at any point in the software project life cycle.

Requests for changes are common with all projects. However, the timing of the changes for requests is critical. This is because an untimely change adversely impacts the cost of the software project. For example, a change request during the software construction stage can be extremely expensive to incorporate.

The software project manager must decide with the customer upon a set of objectives that must be achieved at the end of the project. In addition, the project manager and the customer must decide on a specific phase, beyond which only critical change requests are accepted.

Myth 5: The management and the customer always impose an unrealistic deadline for the software project.

The management and customer usually believe that project managers prepare cost, effort, and time estimates inclusive of buffers. The management and customers rationalize that, if they can cut the buffers by imposing a tight deadline or a low budget on a project, the project manager would still complete the project on time.

Myth 6: A software project that meets all the stated objectives is a success.

Customer requirements for a software project are always in two forms: spoken and unspoken. Usually, the objectives formed from customer requirements are based on spoken requirements. The software project manager must be aware of unspoken requirements and ensure that these are met.

Myth 7: Software maintenance is an easy task and requires less effort than actual software development.

If change requests are made toward the end of the project, then maintenance activities can contribute to large cost-and-effort overruns. Moreover, contrary to the popular view, implementing changes in the software product at the maintenance stage is a painstaking task.

Myth 8: Identifying and reporting errors during the reviews makes the software developer unhappy and spoils the work environment.

If a developer makes an error, it is important to point it out so that the error is fixed in time. A project manager must communicate assertively so that the team does not lose focus on quality. In addition, letting an error pass may have ripple effects on the quality of the software product, frustrating the entire team.

Myth 9: Web-enabling an application or adopting client/server architecture helps to run software projects smoothly.

No single technology platform, language, or architecture is a one-point solution for all software projects. All approaches to software development have unique merits and demerits. For example, if a marketing firm needs to make information accessible to people at remote locations, then a Web-based application is a good option. However, mainframes are still preferred for application created for the banking industry.

Myth 10: A dedicated team for testing will take care of the software quality.

This is the most common myth; when it comes to quality, the first thing that comes to people's minds is testing. Quality is not dependent on testing and is not directly proportional. Testing does not produce quality; it ensures the quality of the product. Testing is not to find defect; its job is to ensure there are no defects. Testing has its own limitation; it cannot find 100% of defects, and it is also costly. If you have a low-quality product entering the testing phase, you cannot expect high-quality output from it.

3.5 Keys to a Successful Project

Similar to project failures, there are several factors that can help you deliver successful projects. Here is a list of items that are key to any project to be successful.

3.5.1 Goal (SMART Goals)

This may sound very obvious, but if you don't know what the end state and success looks like, you'll never be able to plan and execute toward that.

It is important to be able to articulate and state the project goal clearly in a few sentences. If you cannot do that, you may not have the right understanding of the goal, or the goal might be ambiguous and chances of successfully achieving that goal is comparatively low.

The goal needs to be SMART—specific, measurable, achievable, realistic, and time bound. If the goal does not have these attributes, you may not be able to measure whether you have achieved the goal.

3.5.2 Stakeholders (Communicate and Manage)

In the beginning of the project, the team needs to work on identifying all the stakeholders. A rhythm needs to be built with the stakeholders for meetings and communication. It is very important to spend time with the project's stakeholders to understand their expectation and to keep them updated on the project.

Stakeholders contribute to the project in multiple ways: they provide their political or commercial endorsement, which will be essential to the project's success. Typical stakeholders of the projects are the customer, marketing, business, etc.

3.5.3 Team (Motivated and Involved)

The project team is the most important element you have in the project available. The team's enthusiasm, passion, and motivation will make or break the project. The project manager needs to work closely with the team members and ensure that they are motivated and operate together as a single unit (team), and not as a collection of individuals.

Ongoing communication within the team is vital! The project manager should plan to invest time in promoting hard work, working together, trust, and ensuring that every member of the team knows what he or she has to contribute to the bigger picture. It might be a good idea to talk about the project expectations, rewards, and the feedback process. The project manager needs to lead by example and create working conditions where people enjoy being part of the project.

3.5.4 Project Planning (First Step in the Project)

Usually the teams are under pressure to deliver, and it is often seen that people jump in and start working without a plan in place to "get the ball rolling." That is the traditional mistake we should avoid making. It is not a good idea to leap before you are ready. Once the team starts working and the project gets moving, it is very difficult to change direction. Also, without a plan, if there are several changes, the team morale might get impacted with them.

So, it is important to spend some time in deciding exactly how the team is going to be organized and how they are going to build the product and complete the project in the most efficient way. The project plan helps the team and management to better understand the project and helps in resource allocation and trade-off decisions.

3.5.5 Set Expectations (Promise Low and Deliver High)

Believe it or not, it is true. People don't like it when a project is late or is under delivered, even if it was on an aggressive timeline or the team worked 16 hours a day to deliver the project. People are happy if the project is delivered early.

I am not trying to say that we should add lots of buffer in the project plan, but to ensure that a realistic expectation is set for the project and that the team can achieve it with regular effort. This also gives some room for the team to do more and delight the management and the customer and, at the same time, have a decent work–life balance. Don't overpromise on results.

Project planning should take into consideration a few items such as vacation, time offs, unexpected risks, etc. This will help your team to deliver happy surprises and not unpleasant ones. By promising low (reasonable goals) and delivering high (delivering more than you promised), you

1. Build confidence in yourself, the project, and the team
2. Generate a positive and receptive atmosphere
3. Buy yourself contingency in the event that something goes wrong
4. Gets the right level of reward and recognition from management

Think about it—if everything goes right, the project will finish early, and everyone will be happy; if something goes wrong, you might still finish on time; if things go really badly, you might still not deliver what you anticipated, but it will still be better than if you overpromised!

3.5.6 Design (Know Before You Code)

Similar to the project plan, it is very common for people to jump into coding without creating the design. It might be very appealing, and the design might appear straightforward and redundant. I have been on projects where the coding started before the design or was done in parallel to the design. All the time it resulted in rework—some code had to be thrown away or a lot of effort went into modifying the code, and in majority of the cases, we had quality issues with the product.

The design phase gets the team to think through all the components, their interaction, and technology aspects. It gives a good platform for every team member to contribute and consider all the potential issues before starting to code. This also avoids a lot of rework, and several quality-related problems can be avoided.

There are several design templates and notations available in the industry. Use the right one for the project.

3.5.7 High Quality (Doing It Right the First Time—Everytime)

This is simple and straightforward to understand but a little difficult to implement, and would be a cultural and mindset change, especially in the software industry. In software, I have seen several people usually focused on the coding and getting the work done, and then expecting the testing team to find the defects. This is not the most effective way to get to develop the product.

The focus of the test team should not be to find defects, but instead, to ensure that there are no defects in the code. This mindset change drives a positive attitude and helps to build the product of the right quality right from the beginning. The test team can then focus on finding more complex issues.

This is not impossible to achieve. I implemented this concept in several projects and was able to get good results. It's a combination of leadership, process, and accountability.

3.5.8 Iterate and Evolve (Start Small and Build on Top of It)

There are multiple ways to develop the product: there is a *big bang approach* that focuses on developing the full product and then testing and subsequently releasing it. There is a good chance of finding major issues during the testing phase, and it might then be too late to fix or the fix might cause lot of code churn and rework.

It is a good practice to develop the product in small chunks, test them, integrate them with other components, and then iterate the cycle. This is also called *iterative development approach.* When the team builds small components at a time, they get adequate opportunity to integrate and fix any issues. At the regular interval, some parts of the product can be evaluated by the customer to see if it is on the right track to meet customer expectations from the project.

3.5.9 Testing (Test Early and Frequently)

Software development projects involves creativity, and while working with several thousands of lines of code, it is very common to make mistakes. You may have all the right processes in place to prevent common mistakes, and everybody has right intentions not to make mistakes, but still, it is human nature to err, and some errors will make it into your final product.

Although everybody has the right intention not to make mistakes, and there are processes in place to prevent common mistakes, it is not possible to prevent all of them. To make your project successful, you should have controls in place so that if any mistakes happen, they can be caught early. At the same time, the development team should not delegate the quality responsibilities to the testing team. The development team should continue its focus on quality and continue to invest in preventing defects.

Testing should start as early as possible. In our projects we should involve the testing team from the requirements phase. This gives a good opportunity for the testing team to understand the project, provide feedback on the requirements, and start creating the test plan, etc. Testing needs to happen on every integration, and the team should also leverage unit testing and peer testing.

3.5.10 Track (Are We on the Right Path to Achieve the Goal?)

You have the project goal set and have spent adequate time and effort in planning, but, without any tracking, you may not get the full benefits. To be effective, you need to know if the project is on track to deliver on the goals. The goal can be to deliver high quality on time, etc. but you cannot wait until the end of the project to see if the goals were achieved. There has to be appropriate KPIs (key performance indicators) that can show the health of the project, if the project is on track or deviated, and the chances of deviation. Based on that the project manager and team can work methodically toward the goal and make appropriate decisions to ensure that the project is on track.

During the planning phase, there is the need to define KPIs and have tracking and reporting mechanisms in place. The project manager and team are expected to understand the process and tools to ensure that schedule and budgets stay on track.

Consistent project tracking and timely reporting to the stakeholders is what separates professionals from amateurs.

3.5.11 Manage Change (Don't Let Change Manage You)

We live in a changing world. Change is a fact of life for most projects, particularly software development projects. It is observed that the major cause of software development project cost and schedule overruns is frequent changes in scope. Several projects do not fail in their goals or directions, but usually their plans are not able to deal with change. Change can be good or bad, and it can be change in scope, processes, expectations, etc., but it is expected and has to be managed.

There are continuous changes in technology, business, marketing, IT, infrastructure, etc., and the project you started 6 months back may need to change due to change in business priorities. As the project moves ahead, there is a strong temptation to deviate from the plan and incorporate a few changes to adopt some additional requirements or expectations.

It is common to see several people (stakeholders, management, etc.) coming up with new and interesting ideas, your team will bolt down all kinds of rat holes, and your original goal will have all the permanence of a snowflake in quicksand. Scope creep or drift is a major source of project failure, and you need to manage or control changes if you want to succeed.

Resistance to change is usually rooted in fear of the unknown as project managers and people in general prefer stability and predictability. This doesn't imply that your plan should be rigid or no other ideas should be incorporated. You need to build a flexible approach in your project plan that absorbs changes as they arise. If you are too flexible, your project will meander like a horse without a rider, and if you are too rigid, your project will shatter like a pane of glass the first time a stakeholder tosses you a new requirement.

You should plan and manage change; don't let change manage you.

3.5.12 Continuous Improvement (Raise the Bar)

You may have heard this: *If you are doing things the way you have always done, you will get the results you have always got.* This is very true—you cannot expect improvement without changing anything. There are multiple models for continuous improvement, I recommend using Six Sigma to measure and improve the process and the product. If you cannot measure anything, you cannot manage, and if you cannot manage, you cannot improve.

The team should always think about how it can improve the efficiency and effectiveness of the work and actively contribute in thought leadership.

3.5.13 Positive Attitude (Keep an Open Mind!)

While working on the project, you will hear several ideas, recommendations, and feedback. It is very important to welcome ideas and suggestions with a positive attitude, essentially keeping an open mind and being flexible.

The desired outcome of the project is the delivery of the final product to the customer/user who is satisfied with the result. If there are ways or means that can be used to achieve this, the project manager should explore all possible things including deviating from any rules or processes.

1. Don't be very rigid on the processes and rules if the circumstances dictate otherwise.
2. Don't get blinded by methodology.
3. Don't avoid any processes just because they are processes.

The focus should be on delivering the project successfully using all the tools and people available to the project. Keep a close watch on the schedule and adjust the plan, expectations, and execution strategy to suit the current conditions. Deliver the product on time, celebrate the project's success, and then move on to the next project.

Chapter 4

Personal Software Process^SM (PSP^SM)

Developing software requires more than just writing a set of instructions and getting them to run on a computer. To be successful, the programs need to be of high quality and should meet customer requirements at an agreed cost and schedule. This relies on the application of sound engineering practices to software development.

The Personal Software Process^SM (PSP^SM) is a personal process primarily focused on developing software. It can easily be used for practically any other defined activity. PSP is a set of standards, processes, steps, and forms/templates to help individuals to characterize, manage, and improve their personal work. This includes planning, quality, measurement, analysis, and the continuous improvement framework.

The Personal Software Process framework was developed by Watts Humphrey at the Software Engineering Institute at Carnegie Mellon University. PSP is a full, end-to-end self-improvement process that helps engineers to plan, manage, and continuously improve the way work is done. It provides structured framework of forms, guidelines, and procedures for developing high-quality software effectively and efficiently. PSP concepts are very straightforward and can be easily applied to pretty much any process, not just software engineering.

PSP can be considered as Six Sigma applied to software engineering and project management.

4.1 Overview of PSP

PSP was designed to show software engineers how to apply advanced software engineering methods combined with quantitative techniques to their daily tasks. It provides detailed framework for estimating, planning, tracking, and continuously improving their work. There are process elements in PSP that help engineers not just to improve what they do but catch mistakes early, and that helps in maturing the overall process to enable them to make fewer mistakes and move closer towards doing things right the first time. It might sound like an impossible goal, but I have implemented this, and I have seen success in several cases.

In a nutshell, PSP is about planning for everything, tracking against the plan, putting quality processes in place to catch mistakes early enough, understanding deviations, and learning from past history and mistakes. To the reader this might sound like common sense; in fact, it is a lot of common sense, with which we do engineering in every field except software.

Some real world examples: If you are traveling from home to office, how long does it take? The answers are usually, it takes anywhere between XX to YY minutes if I start before 8 a.m. How do you think this information is calculated or tracked? It is based on experience, and often the estimate is very close to actual results except during times when there is some unusual circumstances, such as snowfall, accidents, etc.

I once asked my wife how much time it would take to prepare dinner, and she said "I don't know." I asked her to guess. She was not comfortable as she had not done this before. After a lot of hesitation she said 30 minutes. Actually, it took her 65 minutes. I asked her the same question the next day. Again, she was not comfortable telling me the time as her estimates were not correct the previous day. I told her that it is okay to overestimate or underestimate for something new and suggested to her that she look at the brighter side—she now knew how much time it takes to prepare dinner (which she had been doing for last 12 years and but hadn't known home much time it involved). The dinner that night was slightly different from that of the previous day. My wife started thinking about the effort required and the similarities/differences in making various dishes. She said today it was going to take around 70 minutes. It actually took 80 minutes, and she was very happy as her estimates were coming true. We continued this for three more days, and the difference between the actual and estimated time was not more than 5 minutes (approximately 5–7% difference). There was one day when it took three times the time estimated because of a special circumstance (the blender failed). Now, whenever she gives an estimate, it is pretty accurate.

	Estimate	Actual	Deviation
Day 1	30 min	65 min	117%
Day 2	70 min	85 min	21%
Day 3	75 min	65 min	−13%
Day 4	40 min	38 min	−5%
Day 5	50 min	53 min	6%

As you can see in the table, the variation is less than 10% within few days. It is not rocket science or a difficult task; just try it, and you will see results in a few days.

The whole exercise is not just about estimation; it's about predictability. In any software project, the majority of the failures occur not because of the complexity of the system but because of its project management aspect. Think about it—if you are not planning, estimating, or tracking, you will not know where you are in the project, and often you will be late and will only know about it when you are nearing a deadline. This situation gets translated into a firefighting process, you start cutting corners on the product, and hence, you run into more challenges in quality, and then the overall project gets impacted.

4.2 Why PSP

For getting any work done, you need a series of defined steps, which is also called a *process or template*. A process provides a foundation for planning and guides the work. A plan is a set of steps for a specific job, plus other elements such as effort, costs, and dates. When you apply a process to your personal work, it is called a personal process. Usually, you will start with a proven process that was developed by someone else and then fine tune it with your experience to better suit your needs.

In PSP, each software engineer has a defined personal process framework and measurable criteria for accessing, evaluating, and learning from his or her mistakes and historical performance. With the knowledge and experience from historical data, engineers can decide on methods and processes that can best suit their particular tasks and abilities. With the defined processes, the engineers' ability and skills get developed, and they then continue to develop higher-quality programs. Continuous process improvement is enhanced by rapid and explicit feedback. As the technology continues to evolve, the engineers' job becomes more challenging, and the processes may not be useful to them. To prevent this, the processes need to evolve with the engineer.

Software engineers will better understand their work if they define, measure, and track their work.

The key benefits of using personal process are

- Predictability
- Efficiency
- Quality

4.2.1 Predictability

By using a defined personal process, you can achieve consistent results. The results are likely to be similar each time you use the same process. Your work becomes more predictable, and you can better plan it and manage the project effectively.

As you use more and more PSP in your work, you understand the work and effort required very well and can have sound measurements in place. These measurements help you in estimation, planning, scheduling, and tracking, and in turn help you in delivering predictable results in project schedule, cost, effort, and quality. All of these are dependent on hard data.

4.2.2 Efficiency

By having a personal process, you can plan, measure, analyze, and continuously improve your development process. These steps help in optimizing work, reducing variation, reducing rework, and keeping the focus on the big picture—on what needs to be done. As developers gain more expertise with the PSP principles, their ability to develop the software right the first time increases dramatically. Also, with the introduction of personal review, inspection, and unit testing, there is less dependence on the test phase. This improves the overall efficiency of individuals and the team.

4.2.3 Quality

The PSP principles drive processes that can deliver better quality right from the first time. As discussed earlier in the book, a majority of the quality problems can be attributed to poor planning and the level of the individual's development process maturity.

The quality of any software can be determined by the quality of its worst components. The quality of the software modules is dependent on the individual who developed it. The process used to develop the code is a major contributor to the quality levels of software modules. Having a continuous improvement process helps individuals to measure progress in quality on a continuous basis. The key to quality is the individual developer's skill, commitment, and personal process discipline.

4.3 The PSP Process

The PSP's main goal is to enable software engineers to manage their work effectively and efficiently to develop high-quality code on time. The PSP principles are a set of powerful tools that, if followed in the right way, can help you do your work better, cheaper, and faster.

PSP is not a silver bullet; it will not solve all your software engineering challenges. It will not tell you how to write software, but it will suggest where and how one can improve software based on the data provided and entered in PSP.

PSP follows industry standard improvement cycles such as

- CMM® (SEI's Capability Maturity Model)
- PDCA (Deming's Plan Do Check Act)
- DMAIC (Six Sigma—Define, Measure, Analyze, Improve, Control)
- PMBOK® (PMI's Program Management Body of Knowledge)

While CMM/CMMI focuses on organizations (top down), on "what" needs to be done, PSP takes a subset of CMM methods and processes, focusing on "how" to do at an individual level, developing small programs. PSP is a disciplined software engineering approach for software development and for continuously improving the process in delivering high-quality product on time and within budget.

Through a series of cumulative processes, software engineers learn the following:

1. Project Management
   a. Planning
      i. Proxy-based statistical estimation using historical data
      ii. Size, effort/time estimation
      iii. Scheduling
   b. Project tracking
      i. Time recording
      ii. Task completion
      iii. Defect recording
2. Quality Management
   a. Self-review and inspections for high quality
   b. Design templates and notations
   c. Find and fix defects early in cycle
   d. Continuously improve the process with PIP (Process Improvement Plan)

These PSP skills enable software engineers to

- Build high-quality programs
- Plan and find their own defects effectively
- Reduce defects in their products
- Manage time and schedule
- Make realistic commitments they can meet
- Continuously improve their process

PSP can be applied to many parts of the software development process, including

- Requirement definition
- Document writing
- Software module development
- Test case writing
- Test automation
- Test execution
- Systems maintenance
- Enhancement of large software systems

The PSP method will be very effective if it is gradually introduced, one step at a time, and with a very well planned implementation strategy. The project needs should be selected in advance to implement PSP, it should not be an afterthought.

There is no point in preaching quality to someone whose project is already delayed or in trouble. When PSP is introduced in a project, the engineers may not see the value immediately. As the project progresses they will start to realize the benefits of structured process. It is best to introduce PSP in multiple phases to make it effective. The PSP for engineer training also suggests implementation of PSP in multiple phases. These phases are:

- PSP0 (PSP—Phase 0): It is the first step in implementing PSP, the focus is on creating the baseline of performance with the current process—no process change is made at this time.
- PSP1 (PSP—Phase 1): In this phase, the planning concept is introduced and engineers are trained to do estimation and tracking for size, effort, and schedule.
- PSP2 (PSP—Phase 2): Engineers are exposed to quality management concepts, starting from planning to defects and tracking them. They also start using templates and perform reviews and inspections to ensure high quality in an effective way.
- PSP3 (PSP—Phase 3): This is the final stage of PSP where the focus is to get all the individuals together to work on a project using the cyclic development approach.

The following sections will explain these in more detail.

4.3.1 PSP0: The Baseline Process

The first step in any improvement methodology or project is to have a baseline before changes are made. PSP has a similar approach—the engineers are expected to establish a baseline. This step includes basic measurements such as time, size, and defect, along with a reporting template. The baseline will serve as a foundation on which engineers can improve their work over time. It also provides a consistent basis for measuring progress and sets a foundation on which engineers can improve their process and their final product. In the case of software engineers, they can write simple software to establish their baseline for time and size.

In PSP0, engineers use their current processes, development methods, and design. They gather data on their activities such as time spent by phase, size of the product produced, and defects found in the compile and test phases, and analyze the data and report it. This data becomes their personal process baseline data for future reference.

With PSP0, engineers have a foundation for basic personal process improvement, and learn to use a simple framework for doing small tasks, including:

- Measuring data on their personal work
- Learning how to measure the sizes of the products they produce

- Gathering baseline data on their personal processes
- Setting the foundation for process improvement

PSP0 typically focuses on measuring the following data:

- Time spent per phase
- Defects found per phase

At the end of PSP0, the engineers are able to use the following:

- Baseline for the current process
- Time data-recording process and techniques
- Defects data recording
- Coding standards
- Size measurements
- Process improvement proposal process

4.3.2 PSP1: Personal Planning Process

PSP1 focuses on estimation, planning, and tracking for size, effort, and schedule. Based on the process techniques learned in PSP0, engineers start recording size, time, and defects and building relationships among these metrics. This gives them a good understanding of the correlation between size and time, and they can then calculate their productivity. With this information, engineers can plan their work more effectively and make more realistic commitments accordingly. With ongoing tracking, they can manage their work more effectively and take corrective actions to bring it back on track.

PSP1 adds the following new processes to PSP0:

- Size estimation
- Effort estimation
- Test report
- Task planning
- Schedule planning

Plan effectively and delivering as per the plan.

In PSP1, estimation techniques are taught using the PROBE methodology (PROxy Based Estimation). The engineer collects all the historical estimations and actual data and uses PROBE to prepare future estimations.

4.3.3 PSP2: Personal Quality Management Process

PSP2 focuses on planning for defects, quality, and phase yield management. It helps engineers to learn early how to deal realistically with their errors that result into program defects. Engineers should not feel embarrassed with their defects; it is natural for people to make mistakes. People don't make mistakes on purpose; it is just that they are more common in software. Trying hard to avoid mistakes may not help that much after certain time; the key factor is inherent ability and skills.

Engineers learn about quality management in PSP2 and develop skills to be able to plan, track, and manage their defects data. This data is then analyzed further to help them improve their development process. The focus should be on improving the engineers' ability to perform high-quality work, and then quality work will be naturally done without any extra effort. The key to this is understanding what type of mistakes you usually make and taking actions to prevent them.

A perfect programmer will be able to write a perfect program.

Data collected and analyzed from PSP-trained engineers and others shows that PSP-trained engineers tend to write code right the first time (high quality), and their defect density is much lower than that of other engineers (in the order of 1:4).

PSP2 adds the following new processes to PSP1:

■ Design templates
■ Self design review
■ Self code review

If somebody else can find a defect, why can't you yourself find them?

The review techniques are based on self-review concepts in which engineers review their own work, find and fix defects and, only when they feel comfortable, pass it on to the next phase. This helps them find the defects in their work very early in the cycle in the most cost-effective way, and when it is comparatively inexpensive to fix. Engineers can gather the defects data, analyze it, and build a review checklist to prevent these defects in future.

PSP does not give prescriptive guidance around how to make the design. However, it provides the framework and guidance regarding what design templates can be used and how to complete the design, that is, what a good design should look like. PSP suggests a few design completeness criteria, and verification and consistency techniques. These are called *phase completion criteria*.

The phase completion criteria are important because, without them, you cannot perform an effective review of the work done in that phase. The same approach can be applied to several other process phases, including requirements, specification, documentation, design, development, and testing.

4.3.4 PSP3: Cyclic Personal Process

So far we have focused on basic techniques that will improve the engineer's ability and skill to deliver small (up to 2000 lines of code) programs predictably (effort, schedule, and quality). However, in the real world, the program size ranges from

10,000 to a few millions of lines of code. Even if all the engineers do their best and develop high-quality, well-commented programs, it becomes impossible to manage the large volume of code, and as you review the code, you will lose track of the program logic. Engineers will have to spend a lot more time just to understand the program logic and might miss major design or integration issues. Also, testing the whole system in one go might be another challenge, and the risk is that it may not get fully tested, and there may not be adequate time to fix all the reported issues.

PSP3 needs to scale the PSP2 process to deliver the same rigor and benefits to large systems. The strategy here is to subdivide the big system to smaller programs, which can be managed effectively by the PSP2 process. The cyclic process of PSP3 works very well for programs between 2000 and 20,000 lines of code .

Start with a small program and build on it iteratively.

During the development phase, start with the base module and add other modules in each of the iterations in iterative cycles. In each of the iterations, all the programs will be developed using the PSP2 process from design, code, compile, and test. Each iteration is complete only after it is integrated with the program that was completed in the last iteration. Try to focus on completing the design and design review for all the program before coding starts; this will help in preventing issues in future. As you move through all the iterations, the product starts shaping up, and it is well tested for individual modules and integration. The PSP3 process is effective only if each of the iterations build a high-quality program. With this, one does not have to worry about testing all the programs. During testing, you can focus only on testing the current addition to the code base and the integration. However, even if one module is of poor quality, you might not get the full benefits of the personal process. In the increment, development regression issues (new increments causing problems with previously working functions) are very common.

With PSP3 you will be able to build programs in the order of 20,000 lines of code. However, the system you are working on might have multiple people in the team, and the code size might be much larger. As the size of the team and the code grow, different problems arise around habituation, program interaction within modules, within team members, etc. After working on the project for some time, the team members may not be able to detect issues in the programs because they have become used to seeing the programs.

4.3.5 TSP^{SM}: The Team Software Process

The Team Software Process (TSP) focuses on project management (planning, tracking, reporting), team building, quality, processes, and continuous improvement of the project (Figure 4.1). It functions on the philosophy of a team working together toward a common goal, its members helping each other to get the project completed. This also solves the habituation problem by means of reviewing and inspecting each other's code and learning from each other.

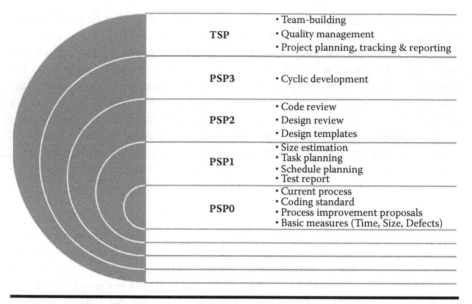

TSP	• Team-building • Quality management • Project planning, tracking & reporting
PSP3	• Cyclic development
PSP2	• Code review • Design review • Design templates
PSP1	• Size estimation • Task planning • Schedule planning • Test report
PSP0	• Current process • Coding standard • Process improvement proposals • Basic measures (Time, Size, Defects)

Figure 4.1   The PSP Process.

The team works together to build the right product, the right way, and in the right time.

4.4 Key Measurements in PSP

PSP is like Six Sigma for software—it has excellent guidance on measurements and metrics along with the processes. These collectively help software development teams to understand their own process and measure and to continuously improve.

The high-level measurements for PSP are

- Size
- Time
- Defects

4.4.1 Size

Size is the measure of volume. PSP principles are focused on planning and tracking the work based on the volume of the work, rather than effort. Traditionally, the majority of the projects uses effort for estimation, planning, tracking, and reporting.

The major problem with using effort (hours or days) in estimation is consistency and repeatability. The estimation process and value will differ from person to person. Because the volume of the work is not known, the estimation data is of very little use for the future. Tracking the project on effort estimation itself poses an additional challenge—if 3 hours are spent on 6- hour task, does it mean we are 50 percent complete. Try the following: Go to 3–5 different people with very specific software requirements and ask them to estimate how much effort (time) it will take to complete coding what they need. You will see variety of responses, and the variation will be huge (anywhere from 50% up to 400%). Even with this, you will observe some people estimating the hours required (e.g., 350 hours), some other people will estimate in terms of schedule (4 weeks from now), and so on. As you can see, with so much variation in estimation, what would you choose? Is it really an estimate or a guesstimate?

Also, with effort and hours used as estimate, there is a problem of tracking. If a work item needs 10 hours, and you have spent 9 hours, does it mean 90% of the work is done? What happens when you spend 15 hours on a task that was planned for 10 hours? The first thought that comes to mind is that the estimation was incorrect or the person took more time, but there might be another reason—the scope might have changed, and 50% more work was added. All these questions are difficult to answer. However, if you have size as a measurement, you can have a slightly better scenario (e.g., 1500 lines of code was planned to be completed in 50 hours, but the scope changed, and the lines of code are now changed to 2100, which will take 70 hours. The actual estimates were 2400 lines of code done in 85 hours).

Different software elements might have different size measures. In several cases, even if the size measures are the same (e.g., lines of code or LOC), they cannot be compared (e.g., 10 lines of SQL code cannot be compared with 10 lines of Visual Basic code). With size estimation, measurements, and the tracking in place, the process becomes mature and is more predictable. Here is a quick outline of the process that needs to be followed for achieving better accuracy in creating estimation, tracking, and using it for future projects.

- While estimating, mention how much code will be used as base, how many new lines of code will be added, modified, deleted, and reused, and how many new reusable codes will be written.
- During project execution, record actual size (e.g., LOC, database elements), itemized by base, added/new, modified, deleted, reused, and new resalable components written.
- Size is necessary to estimate time and quality, and as a "normalizing" measure for tracking and analysis.

4.4.2 Time

In PSP/TSP, time is used to plan/track only available/productive/engineering/Time on Task hours, that is, only time spent on tasks that create a deliverable or enhance it. From now on, we will call it *Time on Task*. The main objective of capturing this information is to determine where the bulk of the time was spent and how the distribution changes as the processes are changed over time or you progress in the project. The time should be recorded in minutes and immediately after the work is performed.

Time-recording log:

Date	Start time	End time	Task details	Phase	Interruption time	Delta time	Comments

Date: The date on which the task was performed.

Start time: The actual time (in a 24-hour format) when the task started (or resumed).

End time: The actual time (in 24-hour format) when the task completed (or paused). If you are working overnight on the same task, close the task at 23:59 and then have another record for the next day starting at 00:01 (this is to avoid any calculation mistakes).

Task details: Give as much detail as possible around the task (module name: task), for example, LoginModule: UI.

Phase: The phase of the task (e.g., design, code, design review, test, etc.).

Interruption time: If while working on the task, you were interrupted (e.g., phone call, chat, coffee break, etc.), log the time (in minutes) here (if the interruption time is going to more than 1 hour (lunch or long meetings); try to pause the task and then start again after the interruption is over.

Delta time: The time difference between end time and start time, after removing the interruption time from it.

Comments: Any other information needed to give more information about this task.

The practical way to calculate this is to exclude any major breaks, such as vacation and training. Then look at the available hours for this project (typically that will be 40 hours per week if the person is 100% allocated to this project; this number needs to be prorated based on the percentage allocation).

$$\text{Productive hours} = \text{Total hours} - (\text{vacation} + \text{meetings} + \text{trainings} + \text{e-mails} + \text{any other recurring items})$$

Time spent on the following activities is *not* to be included in Time on Task.

1. Meetings
2. Trainings

3. E-mails
4. Project status report
5. Vacation
6. Presentation
7. TSP launch/relaunch
8. Post mortem
9. TSP time entry
10. Estimation
11. TSP coaching
12. TSP team meetings
13. People management activities
14. Project management
15. 1:1 Meetings
16. Lunch
17. Breaks
18. Offsites

Time spent on the following should be considered as Time on Task:

1. Requirements
2. High-level design document
3. Detail-level design document
4. Coding
5. User guide
6. Review
7. Inspection
8. Compile
9. Unit testing
10. Test plan
11. Test cases
12. Integration testing
13. System testing
14. Acceptance testing
15. Defect reporting
16. Defect fixing
17. Regression testing

We estimated Time on Task for key people in the team and then tracked it for 2 weeks, and then after several iterations, we were able to fine tune it both from the estimated Time on Task and cutting down on time spent on nontask activities. This, in turn, improved overall throughput from the team.

Here is the table that talks about the "task hours" our teams observed and used in the majority of their projects:

Team member	Hours/week
Architect	8 hours
Lead developer	10 hours
Developer (FTE)	16 hours
Tester (FTE)	20 hours
Developer (contractor)	23 hours
Tester (contractor)	27 hours

Note: This data is based on the offshore development team in Hyderabad, India, who typically have 9 working hours (which includes 1 hour for lunch).

While on the TSP Project, time tracking is very important and critical. If one of the people does not track the time correctly, the whole project's tracking might get impacted. We have usually observed, whenever there is a new person added to the project who has not undergone PSP Training, that the problem comes up very often. Here is the key to effective time tracking.

■ Record time spent directly on development tasks, a.k.a. Time On Task (as opposed to Timecard Time)
■ Task Completion Status ("done" or "not done")

4.4.3 Defects

There are multiple ways people define defects:

■ A defect is a noncompliance of a work product with its specification (i.e., predecessor work product) or its work product standards.
■ Mistakes made and corrected in the current development phase are not defects.
■ Record defect type, injected and removed phases, find and fix time, and description.

Defect-recording log:

Defect number	Date	Defect type	Phase injected	Phase removed	Defect fix time	Related defect	Defect description	Defect cause

Defect number: The defect number, usually a sequence number.

Date: The date on which the defect was found (detected).

Defect type: The type of defect (assignment, functionality, security, etc.).

Phase Injected: The name of the phase where this defect was injected (e.g., if the defect was injected while writing code—"CODE." If the defect was introduced while fixing a code review defect—"CODE REVIEW".

Phase removed: The name of the phase where this defect was removed (e.g., if the defect was found in code review and it was removed—"CODE REVIEW".

Defect fix time: The time it took (in minutes) to fix the defect and perform a quick verification test.

Related defect: If this defect is related to any other defect (if this defect was introduced while fixing some other defect)—give the defect number here.

Defect description: The description of the defect (give as much detail as possible).

Defect cause: The cause of the defect—why this defect occurred (oversight, wrong module, etc.).

4.5 Software Project Planning and Tracking Using PSP

Any activity you do needs to be planned. You plan for a majority of them consciously or unconsciously. A task as simple as driving to work also needs planning—what time to leave, which freeway to take, how to optimize any stops on the way, etc. In PSP, planning is the first step, and emphasis is given on having a plan for every activity. Planning helps in the following ways:

1. With a plan, engineers can effectively manage medium-sized projects.
2. Project planning and tracking is a skill that is not taught in school.
3. Often, planning is more focused on schedule rather than on the volume of work.

Chapter 5

PSP^{SM} Training

You can find a list of all trainings related to Personal Software Process^{SM} or Team Software Process^{SM} (PSP ^{SM}/TSP^{SM}) offered by Software Engineering Institute (SEI) at http://www.sei.cmu.edu/tsp/training.html. A high-level list of PSP- and TSP-related trainings are given in the following sections.

5.1 TSP Executive Strategy Seminar (1 day)

This course is for senior managers and executives to learn key concepts and principles about TSP or PSP and its benefits, from a management perspective. This course provides the foundation that managers need to begin introducing and applying TSP or PSP in their organizations.

Typical class size would be 12–15; ensure that every attendee receives the book *Winning with Software* at least one week before coming to the training.

5.2 Introduction to Personal Process (2 days)

This is a generic training module focused on those members of a software development team who are not software engineers (i.e., test engineers, project managers, etc.). This course gives a good overview of the personal process, with its concepts, terminology, philosophy, and principles. Attendees are guided through a series of lectures and exercises that teach TSP or PSP in detail, and prepare them to be part of a TSP project team and to plan or track their work on the team.

Typical class size would be 12–15; ensure that every attendee receives the book *Introduction to Personal Process* at least one week before coming to the training. Every attendee will need a calculator.

5.3 PSP for Engineers (10 days)

This two-week intense course, composed of planning and quality modules, teaches software development engineers the principles, concepts, and benefits of PSP. Attendees go through assigned self-reading and lectures in the morning, followed by a software development program exercise in the afternoon. The program is focused on exercising the theory that the engineer gets exposed to in the morning, with one process change. The training enables engineers to plan, measure, track, analyze, and report their work; they themselves can look at the data, analyze it, and start seeing the benefits of using PSP in their work during the training itself. Engineers get exposed to using their own process data to improve their personal performance, and they apply PSP methods to other structured tasks. The training covers the following:

PSP0: Establish a baseline for current performance; learn about measurements
PSP1: Estimation, planning, and tracking of size, effort, schedule, etc.
PSP2: Plan for quality, defect, and yield management

Typical class size would be 10 to 12 people; ensure that every attendee receives the book *Discipline of Software Engineering* at least two weeks before the training. For this training, every attendee will need a computer with a development environment installed on it.

5.4 Leading a Development Team (Managing TSP Teams; 3 days)

This three-day course is designed for people who are leading TSP-based software development project teams. It covers the key concepts, terminology, and principles of TSP/PSP process, and enables managers and team leaders to effectively lead and coach TSP development teams.

Typical class size would be 12–15; ensure that every attendee receives the book *Winning with Software* at least one week before coming to the training.

5.5 PSP Instructor Training (5 days)

The PSP instructor training course focuses on building the skills required to effectively teach PSP courses to others, grading them and analyzing data. It also covers details on how to become change agents and put PSP and TSP into practice.

On completing this training, the attendee becomes authorized to use the SEI's PSP course suite and to teach the PSP for Engineers, Introduction to Personal Process, Leading a Development Team, and TSP Executive Strategy Seminar courses to others in their organizations. There is a PSP instructor authorization process; you can get the details on the SEI Web site.

5.6 TSP Coach Training (5 days)

This training is focused on preparing a person for effectively launching and coaching TSP teams. The course covers the key concepts, principles, and methodology of TSP from an operational or procedural and coaching perspective. Through a series of lectures and exercises, attendees are taught the TSP process, preparing them to facilitate its use in actual software teams. The PSP for Engineers training is a prerequisite for this. Please visit the SEI Web site for the TSP coach authorization process and details on necessary license agreements.

Chapter 6

Team Software Process^{SM} (TSP^{SM})

This chapter introduces Team Software Process^{SM} (TSP^{SM}) and its benefits. It highlights some of the key elements of TSP, and how it can benefit project teams with its unique abilities to blend process, engineering, team building, project management, and continuous improvement.

Most software is developed by teams. It is not about one person delivering a software, it is a collective effort of the team, which needs good engineering skills, and they all need to get along very well. With more than one person on the team, challenges grow exponentially—there are more communication channels, individual processes or styles of working, common goals, etc. With TSP, we can institutionalize *just enough process*, which has just enough required elements for the project team to deliver high-quality software on time and within budget.

TSP was developed by Watts Humphrey at the Software Engineering Institute (SEI) to address the specific needs for

- Quickly building self-directed, jelled teams that can deliver the project successfully
- Software engineering project teams that can build high-quality products within budget and schedule
- Having a mature development process that can be leveraged by teams and, at the same time, having personal process for individuals
- Ensuring continuous communication, overall project tracking, and optimized team performance throughout the project life cycle
- Enabling software process improvement mechanism in the project

47

6.1 Overview of the TSP

TSP was developed to extend the Personal Software Process^{SM} (PSP^{SM}) to software development teams. TSP addresses several work problems of software development teams such as commitments, estimation, tracking, control, quality, team work, etc.

TSP is a framework and a methodology with a set of guidelines that help project teams to plan, extract, track, and deliver their projects effectively and efficiently.

6.2 Understanding Team Dynamics

When you start a project, you need to build a team. The team members come from different projects, organizations, etc. During team formation, team members go through several well-known phases—forming, storming, norming, and performing. It is necessary to understand these phases and plan your team-building activity accordingly. Typically, team members have concerns about the goal, charter, team structure, working style, internal problems, conflicts, etc. The TSP launch process has inbuilt activities and guidelines that can help the project manager and the team to effectively bring together all the team members and start working on the project in the most effective way.

6.3 Building Self-Directed Teams

As per definition, when a group of people are linked to a common purpose, it is called a *team*. *Jelled team* is a team that works together smoothly and efficiently. The enjoyment derived by people from working in a jelled team is greater than you would expect. In a jelled team, people work in such a fashion that the whole is greater than the sum of the parts. The output is much higher than that of any unjelled team.

Successful teams are those who deliver successful results and achieve business goals. Although many teams come close to meeting their product and business goals, they often do so at the expense of team members.

6.3.1 Team-Building Strategies

Team building is not something that can be done in a workshop or offsite. Generally, when a group of engineers are assigned to a project and start working, they get little or no guidance on how to proceed. If they are lucky, their manager might provide some guidance based on past experience. In most cases, however, teams have to muddle through a host of issues on their own in the beginning of a project and during project execution.

The following is a list of questions every software project team must address:

- What are the project's goals?
- What are the team roles and who will fill them?

- What are the responsibilities of these roles?
- How will the team make decisions and settle issues?
- What standards and procedures does the team need and how do we establish them?
- What are product quality objectives?
- What are the quality measures, how will we track product quality, and what should we do if it falls short?
- What processes should we use to develop the product?
- What should be our development strategy?
- How should we produce the design?
- How should we integrate and test the product?
- How do we produce our development plan?
- How can we minimize the development schedule?
- What do we do if our plan does not meet management's objectives?
- How do we assess, track, and manage project risks?
- How can we determine project status?
- How do we report status to management and the customer?

Most team members spend a great deal of time and creative energy struggling with these questions. This is unfortunate, because none of these questions is new and there are known and proven answers for each one.

6.3.2 *Building a Jelled Team*

There are several team-building exercises such as workshops, retreats, offsite, games, etc., which people typically adopt to build teams quickly. But you may not be able to get a jelled team out of this. For jelled teams, you need more than just a team-building exercise. Jelled teams are a product or outcome of continuous ongoing processes that enable people with diverse experience, style, belief, etc., to work together toward a common business goal. Traditional team-building activities are not likely to produce long-term team success unless they are embedded into the team process and the project.

TSP facilitates team building through a defined team launch process, measurements and project tracking, and team meetings. The team establishes a common understanding of the work involved to deliver the project and the development approach.

TSP can help in delivering business goals by having an end-to-end process that enables a team to plan together; have personal discipline; have clear roles and responsibilities; and have commitments toward plan, schedule, quality, measurements, tracking, and reporting. TSP enables the team to accelerate process improvement continuously and mature the processes for optimized team performance, throughout the project. All team members understand their abilities; they have personal discipline and can make realistic commitments to each other and to the management in delivering the project.

Chapter 7

TSP^{SM} Launch Process

7.1 Using the TSP Workbook*

The first step in the Team Software Process^{SM} (TSP^{SM}) launch is to set up the TSP workbook. The steps on how to go about using the workbook are described in this section. (Note: The images shown in this book are from Microsoft Office Excel 2007, but they are the same for earlier versions such as Excel 2002 and 2003.) While using the workbook, avoid doing any Copy/Cut/Paste functions of Excel. On some of the forms, Copy/Paste might be usable, (in subsequent chapters, I will mention the places where it is fine to use the Copy/Paste functions), but we have seen major issues in using Cut/Paste functions.

The steps are as follows:

1. Get a fresh copy of the blank TSP workbook Excel file (do not use any existing file).
2. Rename the TSP file with the TSP project name (e.g., TSP_ProjectVersion.xls).
3. Open the TSP_ProjectVersion.xls file.
4. Fill out project details in the TSP workbook ("Project" worksheet; Figure 7.1).
5. Fill out team details in the TSP workbook ("Team" worksheet; Figure 7.2).

---

* The tool can only be distributed to licensed users of TSP. For information on getting started with TSP, contact the SEI Web site: http://www.sei.cmu.edu/TSP.

Using TSP workbook (TSP Tool)—Add project information

Purpose: Enter the TSP project details in the TSP workbook before meeting 1 starts

Person: Team Leader

Worksheet name: Project

How: Enter project details in the project worksheet. This information is used for identifying the project; also when you have multiple TSP projects, it is easier to differentiate between them, and it helps in organization-level consolidation. This Project tab is used extensively throughout the project during project status review and reporting.

Location (column)	Details
Name	Name of the team member (this is a placeholder for individual workbooks and be replaced by the actual name of the team member). Because this is still the team workbook, enter "Team" for the time being. In TSP meeting 6, this name will be automatically replaced with the actual team member name (when you create copies of workbook for team members) (e.g., Team).
Project	Type name of the project—make sure the project name is as used or referred to in the organization. Give adequate details of the project, along with version number, etc. Ensure that the project name is unique across the organization—this will help when you do consolidation of all the TSP projects across the organization (e.g., ExpenseReporting Q2 Release).
Team	Enter name of the team as referred to in the organization (e.g., Technical Automation Team, IT Development Team, etc.).
Start date	Enter the date when the project is expected to start. The project should include the TSP Launch. Ensure that the date is either today's or a past date. (*Note:* The TSP workbook does not work correctly if the date is in the future.) The format of the date should be the same as that of the system. Make sure this date is **Monday**. In TSP project planning and tracking, you will often use the phrase "the week of MM/DD/YY." If the project start date is in the future, you should use the purchase "Today's Date Override" (e.g., 12/31/2007).
Cycle	Not used
Today's date override	This field is used to override today's (system) date. This is useful if your project start date is in the future.
Time and defect log controls	Ensure that "Use Time Log" and "Use Defect Log" fields are checked. Time and defect log worksheet can be toggled to hide or unhide by using this toggle.

Notes:

a. Keep all other data/settings as they are. We will return to this form later.
b. Do not use Copy/Cut/Paste commands.
c. After you are done with entering the project information, the project worksheet should look like Figure 7.1.

Figure 7.1   Project worksheet.

Using TSP workbook (TSP Tool)—Add team member information

Purpose: Enter team member information in the TSP workbook before meeting 1 starts

Person: Team Leader

Worksheet Name: Team

How: Enter details for each and every team member and the team lead. Also list other people who will have some tasks to perform in this project who will be devoting engineering time for the same (up to 20 people maximum).

Location (column)	Details
Name	Name of the team member. Enter full name as used within the organization or team or as shown in the address book (e.g., John Smith).
Initials	Type initials of the team member. It needs to be unique for the current project. If there are two or more people having the same initial, make some changes and come up with unique ones. These initials are used during project task assignments and tracking. You might choose either initials or the e-mail alias of the person (e.g., JS, MJ1, SM2, mukeshj, jblack, etc.).
Phone	Enter contact details for the person. This data is used in case somebody needs to be contacted. It is kept in a common place, and everybody has a copy (e.g., +1-425-999-9999).
E-mail	Give office e-mail address here. This will be used in case somebody needs to be contacted (e.g., myself@myco.com).
Workbook file name	Decide on a file-naming convention you want to use for the project (filename can be based on team members' initials or names). The filenames should be kept unique, and one should be able to identify the person whose file it is (i.e., don't keep file names as 1.xls, 2.xls, etc.). If you anticipate additional team members in the team, you should consider adding a proxy name and filename (e.g., name: Member1, filename: Member1.xls). Once the person is on board, you can change the name and the file name (e.g., JS.xls, mukesh.xls, member1.xls, etc.).

(Continued)

(Continued)

Notes:

a. Avoid using any Cut/Copy/Paste functions; try to enter data in the Excel sheet directly.
b. Current structure supports only 20-member teams.
c. Do not click on any of the buttons yet. They are to be used in meeting 6 after we have adequate data.
d. After you are done with adding team members, the team worksheet should look like Figure 7.2.

7.2 Project Meetings

Typical meetings in a TSP project can be for any one of the following reasons (there are several more types of meetings, but they are outside the scope of our current discussion):

1. One-to-one TSP coaching meeting
2. Project status review meeting
3. Project planning (TSP launch/relaunch, etc.)
4. Technical brainstorming meeting
5. Requirements gathering meeting
6. Design/Code reviews and inspection meetings
7. Issue resolution and decision making meetings
8. Data analysis and reporting
9. Process improvement discussion meeting

Depending on the type of meeting, various levels of preparation are needed. It is important that every meeting has an agenda and a time frame.

7.3 Roles and Responsibilities of TSP Meetings

Roles and responsibilities of TSP meetings are defined to ensure that they are smooth, useful, actionable, short, and more productive. Typical roles in a meeting are

- Meeting owner (organizer or chairperson)
- Facilitator/Timekeeper/Recorder (ensures that meeting agenda is on track)
- Attendees (participants of the meeting)

ID	Name	Initials	Phone	e-mail	Workbook Filename
01	Joe Smith	JS			JS.XLS
02	Mark Jan	MJ			MJ.XLS
03	Sue Handi	SH			SH.XLS
04	Kyo Ki	KK			KK.XLS
05	Li Sung	LS			LS.XLS
06	Satish Kale	SK			SK.XLS
07	FutureMember1	FM			FutureM1.XLS
08					

Figure 7.2 Team worksheet.

Chapter 8

Meeting 1
Establish Product and Business Goals

Meeting duration: About 2 hours for first-time Team Software Process^{SM} (TSP^{SM}) launch, 1–1.5 hours for a subsequent launch.

Meeting Agenda (Discussion Leader)

1. Agenda and meeting process (TSP Coach)
2. Introduction of team members (Team Leader)
3. TSP and Launch process overview (TSP Coach)
4. Product objectives and goals (Marketing)
5. Business need and goals for the product (Management)
6. Questions and answers (Team)
7. Meeting wrap-up and report (Recorder)

8.1 Overview

Depending on the market and the available technologies, the relative importance of each of the quality dimensions may differ. For example, a low number of defects might be the most important factor in a mature market, where competing products are not otherwise differentiated. In another situation, being first to market may take precedence over reliability.

It is an axiom of the personal computer business that the first product to claim a majority market share of a new platform or in a new product may hold that position for a long time. In this case, product definition and schedule may be relatively more important than the number of defects, especially if there is no preexisting installed base. At other times, features might be cut from a product to increase the amount of time available for testing, or to increase the certainty of making a ship date.

Everybody (management, marketing, program managers, developers, testers, and support personnel) needs to decide as a team about making carefully considered trade-offs between the three dimensions of quality, from planning until the product ships to the customer.

TSP Launch meeting 1 ensures that the management and marketing people get to meet the project team and understand the overall TSP launch process. In this meeting, management/marketing personnel communicates to the team the product's objectives/goals, the feature set and business reasons for the product to the team along with management's minimum and ideal goals for the project, and flexibility around the deliverable in terms of quality, schedule, resources, feature set, etc. The team understands the goals, how it fits into the overall organizational business plan, and what a successful outcome will mean to the business. They ask clarification questions to make sure that all the stakeholders are on the same page.

During our TSP adoption phase in Microsoft India, we found this meeting to be very effective, and received good feedback from project teams. With this meeting in place, project teams were able to see/hear from key stakeholders the importance of the project and how it ties into organization's strategic initiatives and business results. This meeting was a good place to hear from management the project constraints, what parts of the project (scope, schedule, budget, etc.) are flexible, etc. In our feedback, we received 100% satisfaction for this meeting. We found that miscommunication-related project issues were reduced drastically, and a good working communication channel was laid between stakeholders and project teams.

It is required that the team be appropriately trained on Personal Software Process^{SM} (PSP^{SM}) before the launch. Experience shows that if we have untrained engineers on the team, the overall effectiveness of the team is impacted, and we cannot get the full value of TSP.

8.2 Logistics

This section gives details about what logistics need to be taken care of for any meeting. It is important to understand the scope of a meeting, its agenda, and expectations, without which it might be difficult to get value out of the meeting:

1. The key TSP meeting roles are as follows:

    Chairperson—Typically, this role is executed by the team leader. He or she takes care of arranging the meeting, agenda, logistics, and leads the meeting.

Recorder—He or she records meeting activities, important discussions (what/ who), planned action items (what/who/when), open discussion items, and follow-up details, and ensures that the meeting discussion notes and actions items are shared with the meeting attendees at the end of the meeting.

Facilitator or Timekeeper—He or she ensures that the meeting stays on agenda and time. The actual time spent on an agenda item is tracked and recorded. He or she also helps the team to follow the meeting agenda and the TSP project launch script.

TSP Coach—He or she ensures that the team understands the TSP, process and scripts, enables team jelling, and guides the team in project planning.

2. All participants should be present and be prepared for the meeting. Each participant should have received the meeting agenda and the TSP launch meeting preparation materials.

3. Send the TSP launch preparation material to the attendees well in advance (by at least 2 weeks).

4. Book/arrange the meeting facility/conference room well in advance to accommodate all the attendees; have a projector or screen, conference call facility, and video teleconference (VTC) if needed.

5. Send the invitation for the meeting at least 2 weeks in advance, specifying meeting agenda, location, time, preparation, etc.

6. Follow up with marketing/management to ensure that they are ready for the meeting. If it is not possible to get them physically, arrange a VTC or conference call.

7. Have a brief meeting with the TSP project team to prepare them for the first TSP launch meeting (meeting 1). This is needed to make sure the team understands what to expect in the meeting, how to ask clarifying questions, and to ensure that management goals and expectations are well understood.

8. Team leader needs to ensure that team members attend these meetings with the right attitude and an open mind.

9. Try to get a conference room with an oval or round table and projector capabilities. If management/marketing are not in the same city, request them to attend this meeting in person; if this is not possible, choose a VTC or conference call option.

10. During the meeting, ensure that it is kept on schedule and focused on the agenda. If the discussion goes in a different direction, try to get it back on track. Any off-topic item should be noted for future discussion.

11. Ensure that all attendees participate actively and get a chance to express their views.

12. Ensure that all agenda items are covered in the meeting or noted for future discussion.

13. Ensure that the meeting facilitator sends out meeting minutes covering topics covered, discussion outputs, action items, follow ups, and open

discussion items. This report needs to be sent out to all the attendees, and a copy needs to be kept with the TSP material.

14. The team leader needs to ensure follow-up on all the action items and open topics.
15. You will need at least two computers for the launch meeting: One for using the TSP tool, and the other for recording the minutes of the meeting.
16. In meeting 6, you might need additional machines when all the team members will be creating their individual plans (people may choose to work in sequence to get their individual plans completed).
17. You might decide to print a few copies of the launch material and keep it handy for people to refer to during the launch.

8.3 Meeting Discussions—Approach and Positive Attitude

Products are often needed much sooner than they can be developed. It is normal for management to expect better, cheaper, and faster products. Management have expectations of goals for the project that may not be possible to achieve. Under such conditions, it is important that team members actively contribute to the TSP launch and the planning process with a positive attitude. Here are some tips for dealing with such a situation:

1. Participate in and contribute to the meeting discussion with an open mind.
2. Make sure everybody understands management's needs and desires regarding the project.
3. Encourage everybody in the team to ask clarification questions.
4. As team leader, you must make it clear to management that the team will devise the best plan they possibly can.
5. If management's needs cannot be fulfilled with the existing plan, the team should explore other alternatives and give management confidence that it will try to rework the plan to meet management's goals.
6. If management does not believe you are trying to meet their needs, they will not likely accept the plan.
7. In asking questions, try to be positive. Ask management what they want and explore how to achieve it. Do not discuss how difficult the job looks or the problems you anticipate.
8. Ask about alternatives, such as added resources or expert assistance.
9. Regardless of how impossible the task may appear, you cannot know what is possible until you produce a plan.

As team leader, you will be in a tricky and difficult position in this meeting because the team might view you as part of management and management would think of you as part of the team. To satisfy the meeting objectives, you should encourage the team to ask questions, instead of asking questions yourself. You can start the discussion by asking the leading questions so that the team members can ask further ones. However, try to get them to speak up. It will make the team members feel better about the meeting and may even bring up some important concerns.

8.3.1 Discuss with a Positive Attitude

Every team member should approach the discussion with a positive attitude. Think from the management's perspective, what you would have done if you were in management's shoes. Nobody wants to set up the team for failure. Management is not setting any arbitrary goals that will lead the team to failure. There are always business reasons and, in some cases, even management is not sure about a reasonable deadline.

The question management has in its mind is, "Will this team really try hard to deliver the project as per expectations?" It is almost impossible for management to know if the team will be able to come up with a plan to meet the requested date, or if they will come back with a relaxed schedule. The team will always try hard to deliver on the shortest possible schedule, and this will be reflected in the project plan. The problem is, how will management know about this? Will they trust the team and their plan?

In the meeting, from the team members' attitude toward goals, management will gain perception regarding the questions on its mind such as: would they start with the thinking that the goals are impossible, or would they approach the project with an open mind to evaluate the alternatives to meet management goals? The opening meeting, the final meeting, the detailed plan, and the team's attitude will create an impression on and influence management, based on which it will decide if the plan can be trusted.

At the end of the meeting, the team does not know if it can or cannot meet management goals, but team members will leave the meeting with a positive attitude, determined to do their best. So, it is very important to prepare the team for the first meeting, to have them demonstrate the right attitude and belief that they can strive to meet management goals. If the team is not able to come up with a plan that meets management's expectations, it will be able to convince management why this is so. A positive attitude is the key for building the credibility of the team and gaining management trust.

8.3.2 Potential Meeting Discussion Questions

Some potential questions for management are the following:

1. Should the team consider releasing the product in versions? What initial product feature set would make the most sense?
2. In balancing cost, schedule, and product function, what is management's suggested trade-off priorities?

3. What was the reasoning behind the project delivery date expected by the management? Are there any specific business reasons?
4. What would it mean if the team is not able to meet the date in delivering the project?
5. As team leader, if you come up with a plan that will deliver the project later than the expected date, should you consider adding human resources or reducing scope?
6. If adding more human resources is an option, is it possible to get the additional people early enough so that they could be trained on PSP and be part of the team from the beginning?
7. To shorten the schedule, should you consider early or overlapping involvement of other groups such as testing or dependent groups?

8.4 Introduction of Team Members

Duration: 5 minutes (Everybody)

The project kickoff meeting needs to start with the introduction of team members. Everybody on the team should know who is who on the project. This is a good place to introduce team members to each other. The introduction should cover the person's name, software engineering discipline, experience on the project or domain, technical expertise, etc. During this time, you can understand the expectations of the team members, marketing, and management about TSP.

8.5 TSP and Presentation of Launch Process Overview

Duration: 30 minutes (TSP Coach)

The TSP coach gives an overview of the launch process to the project team and management/marketing. The presentation covers an overview of the TSP process and details about each TSP launch meeting. The details of the presentation are as follows.

8.5.1 Purpose of TSP Launch

TSP launch should be considered as a project kick-off meeting, and it is important to start the project with a launch. The process of forming teams does not happen overnight; it takes time to get the team members to build relationships and work well with each other. Time spent on TSP launch at the beginning of the project helps the team members understand each other and overcome any team-building issues. All the team members then will have a strong sense of belonging to the team and will be committed to its common goals. The work processes and plans are developed and owned by the team; it is a team's plan, not a project manager's plan. It is important to have the entire team participate in producing this plan during the launch. This realization brings in commitment from each team member.

TSP launch is typically a 3 to 4-day process with all the project team members getting together for the time period. During this time period, the TSP coach guides the project team with the TSP process, building the project plan and enabling team building.

The TSP launch process establishes a common understanding of the project within the team and management. The launch provides a platform for the team to plan the project in an effective manner, and acts as a catalyst in team jelling. Specifically, the launch covers the following:

1. Management's and marketing's goals for the project and product
2. Team's and team members' goals
3. Roles and responsibilities of the team members
4. Development processes to be used by the team
5. Development work to be done by the team
6. Detailed work plan for the individual team member and the team
7. Detailed quality plan to ensure that the product meets the quality bar
8. Analysis and continuous improvement process
9. Risk management
10. Process for reporting project status to management and customers

8.5.2 TSP Launch Meetings 1–9: An Overview

This section provides an overview of every TSP launch meeting and details of what will be covered in each meeting. A launch presentation will cover the following meetings in detail.

Meeting 1: Opening management meeting for establishing business and product goals—The TSP coach explains the TSP launch process and sets the expectations.

The first step in the launch is for management and marketing to explain to the team the importance of this project to the business, describe the product and project goals, constraints, flexibility, success measure, etc., and answer any questions to gain common understanding.

Meeting 2: Establishing team self-direction with team goals and roles—The TSP coach and the team leader guide the team in goal identification and team role selection.

The team leader working with the team, ensures that team's goals address management needs and are SMART and relevant. The team leader then guides and facilitates team role selection.

Meeting 3: Project conceptual design and development strategy—The team reviews the conceptual design for the product and high-level size estimates, and discusses project-building strategies. The prime objectives are to have the team decide how it wants to build the project right the first time and to minimize project risks exposures. The outcome of this meeting is a common understanding of the conceptual design, the team's development strategy, and the process to build the project.

Meeting 4: Building a team's overall top-down project plan—The team collectively builds a top-down plan for the project. A work breakdown structure (WBS) is created, listing all the project components and tasks to be performed. The tasks are sequenced from project start to finish following the team's process and development strategy. Size estimates are done for each component, and using productivity data, time/effort estimates are derived. Tasks are scheduled based on the team's available hours. From this the team gains a good understanding of the possibility of their being able to meet management's goals. If not, they can either start creating alternative proposals or contact management with the issue.

Meeting 5: Developing the quality plan—The team builds the project quality plan for a product and covers the details of how it will achieve its product quality goal. The plan includes specifics on where defects will be injected, what phases will be catching these defects, and the estimated final quality of the product.

Meeting 6: Building a detailed individual plan for each team member—The team members start with the overall team plan and make their individual detailed work plan based on their productivity rate and availability. They sequence their tasks to take care of dependencies and constraints, and balance the workload so that everyone completes his or her tasks at approximately the same time. The team merges the individual work plans into a consolidated team plan, which is used by the team to guide and track its work.

Meeting 7: Conducting risk assessment—The team identifies and analyzes major risks to the project and the plan. Every member of the team contributes his or her views on risks and impact. Each risk is assessed for impact and likelihood and, accordingly, mitigation plans are developed for high- and medium-priority risks. Each risk is assigned to a team member for tracking.

Meeting 8: Preparing launch report presentation for management—The team prepares a presentation that includes major components of the TSP project plan (schedule, risks, size estimates, effort estimate, resources, etc.). If the team's project plan does not meet management's goals and expectations, the team includes alternative plans with more resources, reduced functionality, multiple releases, additional weeks etc.

Meeting 9: Reviewing the project plan with management—The team presents its plan to management and, if necessary, the alternatives to meet business needs. Management considers the team's plan, probes for more information, checks the quality of the team's work, and decides if the plan (or an alternative) is acceptable. Otherwise, it asks the team to examine other alternatives.

8.5.3 TSP Launch Artifacts

During the TSP project launch, a team generates the following project plan artifacts:

What?
  Team goals
  Conceptual design
  Planned products
  Size estimates
How?
  Team development strategy
  Team process
When?
  Task hour plan
  Schedule plan
  Earned value plan
Who?
  Team roles and responsibilities
  Task plan
  Detailed plans
How well?
  Quality plans
What if?
  Risk assessment
  Alternative plans

8.6 Marketing Presentation—Product Objectives and Goals

Duration: 30 minutes (Marketing)

In this meeting, the marketing manager or a representative presents a product overview and its intended usage, and discusses the product, its competition, the timeline for the product's release, etc. This discussion is led by a marketing manager who understands the desired product, market demand, timeline, what the customer and anticipated users intend to do with this product, and the kind of product that management wishes to produce. He or she personally presents these details to the team. The objective of the presentation is to provide all team members with a common understanding of what is expected of the product and the background needed to intelligently balance conflicting user, business, and technical needs.

The following topics are covered in the manager's presentation and subsequent discussion:

1. The intended customer or user for the product
2. Summary of customer/user needs regarding the product and its intended use

3. Major product scenarios
4. The ideal set of functions and features of the desired product
5. The minimum acceptable (critical) set of product functions and features
6. How the work relates to other products and projects
7. Strategic alignment of this project
8. Comparison of user needs with key competitive offerings (when appropriate)
9. Response to the team's questions about the product and customer/user, or management's needs, objectives, and project expectations

After this discussion, the team will be able to appreciate management's and the customer's/user's desires and proceed with development planning. The team will be in a position to make better trade-offs in the business, functional, and technical aspects throughout the project and produce a more desirable product. The team members will also handle unanticipated problems better, capitalize on new opportunities, and seek appropriate guidance when needed. They should make sure that they understand the product objectives, users' and customer's needs, and any items that are especially important to the customer.

8.7 Management Presentation—the Business Need and Goals for the Product

Duration: 30 minutes (Management)

In this meeting, a representative of management presents the business needs of the project, high-level budget, and constraints. He or she meets with the team to describe the organization's goals for the project and provides the background information needed to intelligently balance conflicting user, business, and technical needs. The senior manager who originally decided to launch the project and knows why this project was undertaken is the ideal person to make this presentation, lead the discussion, and answer the team's questions.

Typically, management goals center around the principle *faster, better, cheaper*. Goals usually set the direction for an organization. Management should not focus too much on short-term goals; rather, it should focus on how the project and/or the goals align with the overall strategy and direction of the organization that is, the big picture. The organization's image depends on its ability to deliver what it promises; project predictability is the key. If the project does not meet the "better, cheaper, faster" expectations of customers, securing future projects might be a challenge. If management wants the team to focus on continuous improvement, it needs to be expressed in executive communication and be part of the organization's mission. Only then will the team be able to appreciate management's focus on project delivery excellence.

The management's presentation covers the following topics:

1. What the organization's overall business objectives are
2. Why the business decided to undertake this project
3. What the business wishes to gain from doing this project
4. How the executive would characterize a fully successful result
5. What this project will lead to if fully successful
6. How the executive would characterize a minimally acceptable result
7. What resources are available and planned for this project
8. Specific expectations and constraints for the project, such as
   a. Project scope
   b. Timeline/schedule
   c. Technology
   d. Dependencies or constraints on other systems
   e. Resource availability
   f. Quality expectations
   g. Flexibility and constraints around resources, schedule, and scope
9. Response to the team's questions about the business, its goals, and the project

The team asks the management clarification questions about the goals and what they mean to the team's work. At the conclusion of this meeting, the team will understand management's ideal and minimum goals for the project, reasons for the goals, resources available for the work, constraints on the project, and how management will measure goal attainment, that is, success criteria. As a result of this discussion, the team will be able to appreciate management's stand on the importance of the project, what it means to deliver on the expectations, and how a successful outcome of the project will help the organization as a whole.

8.8 Goal Priorities

It is important for the team to know and understand the priorities of all the stated goals. Management should make sure that these are communicated to the team. If not, the team needs to ask and ensure that everybody is on the same page with regard to the priorities. For example, one of the goals management might state is, "the product needs to use beta technology." However, if beta technology is very unstable, should the team continue with a stable technology or stop the project? What is more important for the project needs to be clear, that is in this case, the team is not able to meet one of more of the goals; how can they decide which one to focus more on compared to others. Another example would be quality versus schedule. For this project, is it more important to hit the date or meet high quality?

Clarification on goal priorities to be required is sought during meeting 1. Once the priorities are understood, the team can work very well in other meetings towards creating a good project plan to meet the goals in the order of their priority.

8.9 Potential Issues and How to Handle Them

Everybody on the team and management want to get the full benefits of using TSP. However, sometimes due to some problems, the anticipated benefits may not accrue. Some of the potential issues that might occur right from the first TSP meeting and what can be done to prevent them or minimize their impacts are discussed in the following sections.

8.9.1 Management Availability for Opening and Closing a TSP Meeting

Management needs to understand and appreciate the importance of the first TSP meeting. This is the meeting in which a project team gets to hear from management the importance of the project, and its goals and objectives. If management does not attend this meeting, it might be perceived by the team that management does not see the project as important, with the result that the team may not have the same level of focus and interest in the project.

Although it may not be possible to have management attend all the opening and closing TSP meetings, it is important to have someone from senior management represent it in the meetings. If no one is available, or there is a last minute no show or cancellation, reschedule the opening TSP launch meeting for some other day or time. It might be inconvenient for some people but is better than having the project in peril. It might be perceived that if management does not believe in TSP, it is more likely to skip these meetings. If management have attended TSP executive seminars or managed TSP teams, they will be more likely to appreciate the importance of TSP and attend the meetings when they are expected to.

In my work, my team launched and coached 84 TSP projects. There were two projects (A and B) in which management was not present at the opening meetings. However, management did send their goals in an e-mail, and we decided to go ahead with the projects. For one project, we could not get the team to focus on the TSP launch meetings. During meeting 9, attended by management, there was extended debate on project goals. Even though the team created an aggressive project plan that met management's expectations, it thought the plan had a relaxed schedule. This impacted team morale; we saw a lack of focus during the project execution, the project was delayed, and there were quality issues.

8.9.2 Team Availability Throughout the Launch

It is very important to have all the team members, the team leader, and the TSP coach available throughout the launch. If somebody misses one or two meetings due to any unavoidable circumstance (e.g., medical emergency), it might be excused, but any other absence should not be allowed. The launch meeting should not start until all the team members are present. In cases where a few people have to attend other meetings or are not available, the launch meeting should be rescheduled to some other day or time. It is a good idea to ask in the TSP launch preparation meeting about the availability of the team members during the whole TSP launch period.

If the management, team leader, or somebody else does not believe in the importance of everyone attending the full launch, the TSP coach should try to explain its importance and make it clear to everybody why full attendance is needed.

8.9.3 Team Member and Management Training

It is sometimes not possible to get all the team members trained in PSP. I have observed that if one or two of the engineers from a team are not trained in PSP, they can go through an introduction to PSP training so that they can participate in the TSP launch, and immediately after the launch, they can complete their PSP engineer training.

In my experience in launching and coaching TSP teams, there was one project in which half of the team (7 out of 14) was not trained. The team size was big enough to raise concern. We assessed the risk and informed management and the team leader about the possible impact of this situation. Due to project pressure, management wanted the team to go ahead with the launch. (*Note:* Management and the team leader did not have any TSP training—neither Executive Seminar nor Managing TSP Teams.) The launch started well, but then we observed that each of the meetings took up a lot more time than planned. A major chunk of the time was spent explaining the process. There were people who opposed some parts of the TSP process and were not convinced that it would help them. They were the people who were not trained. We observed that the overall team morale and launch effectiveness was getting impacted. We spent two long days (12 hours each) and were still in meeting 4. On day 3, I called a brief meeting with management and the team leader and explained the situation. Both still wanted to get through the launch. So I persisted with the launch: it became a 5½-day launch (Monday–Friday and half of Saturday, total 58 hours) and the team had a really bad experience.

In the closing meeting (meeting 9), we could see the overall impact. The team managed to complete the project plan, but the plan did not meet management's project goals or expectations. Management did not agree to the plan, and asked the team to come up with another to meet a deadline of 6 months. The team spent another 4 hours and came up with the plan management wanted (they reduced review and inspection time by more than 75%).

You can see that the launch was completed, but the plan was more to meet the deadline rather than for the work. The TSP plan had estimated a schedule of 7 months (management expectation was 6 months). The project actually got delivered after 9 months (after addressing several issues of quality and rework).

If we have untrained members in the launch, they will not have the right attitude toward TSP and project planning. This will impact the team and build wrong perception about the team and TSP as a whole.

In summary, if there are a few untrained people, consider deferring the launch until you get the majority of the people trained.

8.10 Meeting Wrap-Up

At the end of meeting 1, team members understand management and marketing expectations and are able to make a plan that best meets their needs. This meeting serves as a foundation for the planning and execution of the project. So, having the opportunity to meet management face to face, understand its expectations and ask clarification questions is very helpful to the team.

The meeting facilitator writes up the meeting notes, distributes them to the attendees, and saves them with other TSP launch and project documentations. Meeting notes cover the following:

- List of meeting attendees
- Agenda items and time spent on each item
- Descriptions of decisions made and by whom
- Details of major discussion items
- Documents on pending actions or open issues: what, when, and by whom
- Verification of the meeting report with meeting attendees to ensure that everybody has the same understanding of the discussion and action items
- Documentation of process improvement suggestions made during the meeting

The team takes a break and then moves on to the next meeting: meeting 2.

Chapter 9

Meeting 2
Define Team Goals and Select Team Roles

Meeting duration: About 3 hours for first-time Team Software Process[SM] (TSP[SM]) launch (1–1.5 hours for subsequent launch).

This chapter focuses on defining team goals, the importance of TSP roles, the role selection process, and how this process helps the team in successfully executing the project. It lays down the process of understanding management needs and translating them into team goals.

Meeting Agenda (Discussion Leader)

1. Agenda and meeting process (TSP Coach)
2. Review management's stated goals (Team Leader)
3. Identify management's implied goals (Team Leader)
4. Establish team goals (Team Leader)
5. Overview of TSP roles (TSP Coach)
6. Select team roles (Team Leader)
7. Assign goal tracking responsibility (Team Leader)
8. Meeting wrap-up and report (Recorder)

9.1 Overview

In a project, things fall through the cracks when it is not clear who is doing what, and people are in assumption—the task will be taken care of by someone else. Also, overlapping responsibilities can run into conflicts. Defining the roles, understanding its responsibilities, and agreeing on who will handle it is an essential first step in any project. TSP roles are selected by the team members themselves, based on their expertise, preferences, and interests. For the first-time project, a team leader and TSP coach can give some guidance to help a team in selecting its goals.

TSP Launch meeting 2 ensures that each of the management's stated and implied goals are understood by the team, and responsibilities are allocated for tracking them among the team members. When all team members consistently meet their role responsibilities, follow the defined process, and work to agreed goals and specifications, the team will be most efficient and effective, will not have team issues, and will be able to deliver as a team.

In the initial implementation of TSP there was a lot of confusion. In the feedback this meeting was rated as one of the lowest (30% satisfied), as people didn't know what was expected of each role, even after being given a handout. In the first few launches, we struggled and spent a big chunk of time in explaining roles to people in detail. But, after a few launches—we thought of skipping some aspects and covered them in detail after 2 weeks—launching worked out really well.

The team members had project data, which was more relevant for them when I said—as a quality manager—look at this and see how you can articulate feedback, drive changes and so on. When we conducted a post mortem, people rated this meeting and activity to be very useful for giving the opportunity to learn something new and also be able to manage some aspects of the project along with the team lead. This really helped us build a "self-directed team" that could move from the traditional "do-it-all" project manager approach.

9.2 Reviewing Management and Marketing Stated Goals

During this meeting, the team reviews management and marketing goals with the team leader heading the team discussion. The focus of the discussion is to obtain a common understanding and agreement on the goals for the project and the product. The TSP coach opens the meeting and gives an overview on the importance of agreeing to a set of defined explicit goals. This is good for the individuals, team, team leader, and management. These defined sets of goals can also be used to resolve any issues within the team.

Goals are very important for setting the right direction for the team's focus and effort. They define the success criteria (results) and help in establishing appropriate priorities. Without up-front goals, it is difficult to get the team to focus and almost impossible to measure team success in delivering on expectations.

Goals are usually motivators for individuals and teams. They give a reason for the work being done and help in understanding the big picture. If the project goals are achieved, the team feels satisfied and will not remember how many long hours they put in; they will feel that all their hard work has paid off. That gives a sense of high achievement.

One of the major discussion items is uncovering and defining implied goals. The team explores management's stated goals and evaluates the possible implied (unstated) goals without which the project may not be considered successful. Some examples of implied goals are high performance and usability, interoperability, etc. For getting these implied goals, the teams need to think about end-users, customers, stakeholders, and businesses. Even though some of the implied goals might appear to be obvious, they should still be discussed and documented.

Some examples of goals are

- Responding to customer queries in timely manner
- Building reliable software
- Ensuring the product meets accessibility and usability expectations
- Creating an application that responds to the user action in a reasonable amount of time

After discussion, the team gains a good understanding of the goals and documents them in an appropriate order of priority. The team leader shares these goals with the management to validate understanding and reduce any communications gap.

9.3 Establish Team Goals

If the team does not have a common goal that every team member agrees on, you will only get individuals who are working together and not a team. The purpose of the goal is to motivate every individual in the team and bring them together for the common cause.

The team reviews management goals and their importance for individuals, the team, and the organization. The next logical step for the team is to translate the management goals into team goals, which they can track on a regular basis. That is, if the management goal is to ship high-quality product, the team will have specific goals around quality at multiple execution levels; they cannot wait until the product is shipped. They need to set up measurements that can monitor the trends and give a sense of how the end-result product quality will be.

Make sure the team does not come up with several primary team goals. The number of primary goals needs to be concise (4–5) and should focus on goals that are really important for the team to achieve. The teams can then set a few secondary and tertiary goals. Typically, focus should be on primary goals that will define success. Primary goals fall into the categories of cost, quality, schedule, and scope. The secondary goals are for the team to strive for, also, and tertiary goals are met as or after the other goals are reached.

The discussion, guided by the leader, starts with the management's stated and implied goals and what the team can do to achieve them. The team starts defining goals for project, product, process, and quality. To make goals meaningful and useful for everybody, the team needs to make the goals SMART (Specific, Measureable, Attainable, Realistic, Timely). This ensures that all the goals can be measured in a standard way, and there is no ambiguity.

The measurements should be carefully devised to prevent any misuse. If the measurement involves delivering on a particular date, ensure that it is combined with other goals such as quality and scope. Also, try to avoid productivity-related goals (e.g., if you have a goal of LOC/hour); there are multiple ways people can abuse this and build programs that are very high on LOC count. Some other person might write a optimized complex algorithm in fewer lines; this might be seen as being low on productivity.

Steps for building team goals are to

1. Agree on all the management goals
2. Derive 1–2 team goals from management goals
3. Come up with a measurement for measuring these goals
4. Define the ongoing goal-tracking, managing, and reporting process with timeline and responsibilities
5. Document the goals in the Goals worksheet of the TSP workbook (Figure 9.1)

	A	B	C	D	E	F
			Measures		Tracking	
2	Stakeholders	Goal	Goal	Actual	Who	When
5	Management	Schedule & effort Variance	+/-10%		SP	TSM
6	Management	Post production incidents	0		NB	TSM after drop to test
7	Management	Sev 1 & sev 2 code/ dev defects in UAT	<~5		SK	TSM after drop to test
8	Management	Sev 1 & sev 2 code/ dev defects in Production	0		JS	TSM after drop to test
9	Management	Seamless integration with v3 0	0 defects		JS	TSM after drop to test
10	Team	Support issues w.r.t installation/ deployment	0		NB	TSM after drop to test
11	Team	Build issues and version control issues	0		DG	TSM
12	Team	SIT complete date	14-Dec-04		SC	TSM after drop to test
13	Team	BRD to FS traceability issues when in UAT	0		ER	TSM
14	Team	FS review/ understanding issues when in UAT	0		ER	TSM
15	Team	No UAT dev defects w.r.t external dependency MSApps	0		NB	TSM
16	Team	Yield in reviews and inspections	80%		DG	TSM
17	Team	Sev 1 & sev 2 code/ dev defects in UAT	3		SC	TSM after drop to test
18	Team	Size estimation (dev + test)	+/-20%		SP	TSM
19	Team	Effort variance (dev + test)	+/-20%		SP	TSM
20	Team	Quality Goal --> Code Review/ Inspection Rate	125 LOC/hr		SK	TSM
21						
22	Team	Quality Goal --> TC Review/ Inspection Rate	5TC/hr		SK	TSM

Figure 9.1   Goals worksheet.

Here are detailed steps on adding project goals in the TSP tool:

Using the TSP Workbook (TSP Tool)—**Add Goals**

Purpose: Enter management and team goals information in meeting 2

Person: Team Leader

***Worksheet Name:* Goals**

How: Enter all the Goals information; use separate rows (lines) for each goal

Location (Column)	Details
Stakeholders	Enter name of the stakeholder for the particular goal. This helps clarify how the team got the goal, for example, Management, Marketing, Team Lead, Team, etc.
Goal	The actual text of the goal. Be as specific and detailed as possible, for example, "Deliver Beta 1 before October 23, 2007."
Measures | Goal	Specify the actual measurement for the goal, for example, if the goal is to have 80% of the features completed by Beta 1, then the measure would be 80%.
Measures | Actual	Keep this blank for now. This needs to be filled in after the goal has been achieved or the project is completed, for example, if 75% of features are completed for Beta 1. The actual column will reflect 75%.
Tracking | Who	Typically the goals are tracked by the TSP role managers (explained in the next section). Enter the role manager who is more appropriate to track this goal, for example, if the goal is related to schedule. The planning manager will be more appropriate to track this goal.
Tracking | When	Specify the frequency of tracking this goal. Even if the goal might be based on the project end result, it is required and important to track the goal on a regular basis to ensure that the project is on track in achieving the goal, for example, for schedule, the goal tracking can be done weekly.

Notes:
1. Ensure that all the stated goals of management are captured.
2. All the goals that are developed by the team need to be logged here.
3. Avoid using any Cut/Copy/Paste functions; try to enter the data in the Excel sheet directly.

9.4 Importance of TSP Roles and Responsibilities

Role is defined as expected behavior in a given situation. It gives a set of rights and obligations for the individual who is playing the role. With defined roles and responsibilities, engineers are able to manage the project better and make important decisions based on need. Engineers in the role focus on not just what is told to them but they also execute role responsibility by building the plan and managing and controlling the project. They also engage the right set of people and send major issues to senior management as needed. This is one of the most important aspects of TSP roles; every team member feels responsible for the team's project success and seriously executes the responsibility.

TSP roles provide a framework for the team where everybody can divide the project management responsibilities among themselves. Defined roles ensure that all team members can concentrate on specific aspects of the project: quality, schedule, customer interface, design, etc. With roles, each team member has an opportunity to specialize in one or more project management areas along with the regular engineering work they have been doing. This enables faster team building.

Roles accelerate team building by ensuring that every team member is involved in project management. For this to be fully effective, it is important for each member to know what the responsibilities of each role is. If these roles are not handled by team members, either they will not be handled by anyone or will have to be taken care of by the team leader. Team leaders will already have several other responsibilities. They will not be able to handle all of the roles effectively, and in some cases will not be able to handle them at all. We want the team leader to focus on leadership, motivate team members, and remove roadblocks. Also, it is observed that if the team leader is handling any role, team members may not be very open with the team leader in sharing the bad news and/or ask for help. Conversely, the team leader may not get feedback from the team members.

9.5 TSP Roles* and Responsibilities

The TSP coach does the presentation in this meeting. It is best to select/assign the roles immediately after the project and team goals are established. The TSP coach should ensure that all the team members are present during the role assignment. This gives an opportunity for the TSP coach and the team to understand more details about the project and other team members.

TSP establishes the following nine standard roles:

- ■ Team leader (preselected by management)
- ■ Customer interface manager

---

*See SEI's TSP Launch Material.

- Planning manager
- Quality manager
- Process manager
- Design manager
- Implementation manager
- Test manager
- Support manager

In addition to these standard TSP roles, we have identified the Team member and the Inspection manager as key roles for any TSP project. These roles focus on the project management tasks that need to be done to effectively manage the project and deliver on management expectations. Even though a team member is assigned a particular role, it does not mean that this person has to do all the work for that role. Responsibility extends to providing focus and leadership for that activity; the work can be done by other team members. A role manager ensures that activities get the right amount of focus and attention, and any issues can be uncovered early and handled appropriately.

Depending on your project and the business needs, you may actually require some additional roles and/or may not need one or more standard TSP roles.

Some examples of additional roles are:

- Installation manager
- Performance manager
- Usability manager
- Security manager
- Subcontract manager
- Offshore manager
- Outsource manager
- Vendor manager

During the TSP project launch, the team should discuss the project complexity and unique issues, and identify any additional TSP roles that might be required for the team. When the team finalizes any new roles, the role manager should define these role responsibilities and get them reviewed with the team to ensure transparency and agreement. If there are only a few additional responsibilities, consider adding them to the existing role manager's responsibilities list and communicate them to the team.

It is important to understand a role in detail, including its goals, typical activities, etc. In the next section you will see all the roles and responsibilities, etc. If you are changing any responsibilities for a role, make sure it is documented and communicated back to the team.

9.5.1 TSP Role: Team Leader

Team Leader

Role overview

The team leader is responsible for smooth execution of the project overall, including management of the project and the team.

Goals

The team leader's goals are:

- Goal 1: Lead and motivate every team member to work aggressively on the project and make it successful
- Goal 2: Build and maintain a motivated and effective team
- Goal 3: Keep management informed about project status
- Goal 4: Review project status regularly and take actions to keep it on track

Responsibilities and activities

The team leader is the team's face to the management and management's face to the team. Here are list of responsibilities and some of the typical activities performed by the team leader.

Project Management

- As a project manager, ensures smooth execution of the project
- Manages project resourcing—people, funds, machines, contractors, etc.
- Removes any roadblocks and resolves conflicts
- Builds relationships and partnerships with other teams or departments
- Tracks project schedule status closely and makes appropriate changes to bring it back on track, if needed
- Reports project status to management and the customer
- Manages project risk, evaluation, and tracking
- Leads project issues and tracking problems, and drives resolution
- Leads launch and relaunch meetings
- Builds a rhythm for reporting project status to management on a weekly basis
- Manages job assignments and TSP role allocation to team members
- Ensures assumptions for requirements and design are reviewed, verified, and tracked
- Ensures impact assessment is done for all requirements and design changes
- Participates in the configuration control board
- Reviews any major change in project scope that impacts schedule, cost, or quality, and updates project plan to reflect the changes before implementation
- Helps the team to allocate tasks

Leadership

- Leads the team in the right direction
- Maintains a clear and continuous focus on the team's project goals
- Represents the team to the management
- Represents management to the team
- Motivates, coaches, and supports the team
- Challenges the team members' decisions to ensure that alternatives and other options are considered
- Maintains a sense of urgency and pushes to accelerate tasks where practical
- Ensures that all team members utilize their skills and work productively and effectively toward project success
- Ensures participation from all the team members in TSP
- Motivates team members' for recording their work on a daily basis and encourages them to track their work for slippage
- Ensures adequate focus on quality and for doing things "right the first time, every time"
- Delegates responsibilities for TSP roles to team members
- Manages the team, coaches them, motivates and enables them to do their job
- Avoids taking a TSP role. In some cases, team lead might take customer interface manager role
- Facilitates inter-team and intra-team communication

People Management

- The team leader manages and resolves all team personnel issues
- Coaches, mentors team members on improving their effectiveness
- Has 1:1 meeting with each team member on a regular basis (weekly or every 2 weeks)
- Manages project staffing, recruiting, training, and retention
- Handles any team conflicts and resolves the problems
- Considers team members' interests and abilities in making job and TSP role assignments, and manages work pressure accordingly
- Protects the team from randomization and time-consuming distractions

TSP Coaching

- Leads the weekly TSP project status meetings
- Ensures all team members produce their own plans and tracks progress
- Keeps management and the team informed about project status
- Encourages team members to create individual and team plans that are aggressive but realistic

(Continued)

(Continued)

- Ensures all team members follow disciplined personal practices (PSP℠/TSP℠) and adhere to the agreed team standards and processes
- Encourages team members to record their TSP data in time
- Ensures role managers analyze TSP data and report appropriate metrics
- Encourage team members to continuously improve their work
- Maintains a consistent focus on quality and demonstrates that through communication and action
- Ensures that quality metrics are regularly gathered and analyzed
- Motivates team members to continuously analyze their data, come up with improvement plans to meet project's quality goals
- Leads the team reviews of integration, system test, and user acceptance testing (UAT) production defects
- On weekly basis ensures that all the team members have completed their committed tasks

Weekly TSP Project Status Meeting

- Checks status on weekly planned versus actual activities completed
- Discusses deviations from planned activities and takes action
- If a few team members are very behind on the tasks, understands the reason, gives feedback, and takes action to load-balance the work
- Checks chances on Issues and Risk List
- At each phase gives a postmortem, and at project conclusion, leads the team in producing or updating the project final report
- Reports team status and progress to management and the customer

Skills and abilities

Following are characteristics and skills set that helps the team leader in executing responsibilities:

- Enjoys being leader and naturally assumes a leadership role
- Able to identify issues, analyze them, and make decisions to resolve them effectively
- Doesn't mind taking unpopular actions that may not make everybody happy
- Willing to press and motivate people to accomplish difficult, challenging, but achievable tasks
- Respects people, listens to their views, understands their aspirations and gives tasks accordingly to enhance their skills
- Encourages and helps team members to perform to the best of their abilities, gives them growth opportunities, and represents them to senior management

Reporting

The team leader reports to management in a weekly project status report. This report covers the following details:

- Planned versus actual earned value for the project
- Projected project completion date
- Planned versus actual defects injected per phase
- Process yield and phase yield
- Project highlights and lowlights
- Major risks and issues
- Help needed

Time commitment

These tasks require at least 3 hours per week.

9.5.2 TSP Role: *Customer Interface Manager*

Customer Interface Manager

Role overview

The customer interface manager manages the team's coordination, interaction, and communication with the customer, providing the customer with information and guidance on the project and product progress. The customer can be internal or external.

Goals

The customer interface manager's goals are:

- Goal 1: Lead the team in delivering product as per customer expectations
- Goal 2: Understand the customer's wants and needs
- Goal 3: Build a good working relationship with the customer
- Goal 4: Manage requirements and resolve issues effectively

Responsibilities and activities

The customer interface manager is the team's face to the customer and the customer's face to the team. Here is a list of responsibilities and some of the typical activities performed by the customer interface manager.

Customer Focus

Customer interface managers are the one-point contact person for handling customer queries and communication, and they

- Maintain continuous focus on customer's needs throughout the project
- Define prototypes and review with the customer to help them understand proposed product features

(Continued)

(Continued)

- Conduct usability studies or testing to find any usability issues with the product, giving the report back to the customer and the team for action
- Provide a communication channel between team and customer for handling queries, clarification, etc.
- Communicate with the customer and provide project updates on a regular basis
- Provide customer feedback and visibility to the team

Manage Requirements

As customer interface manager, you establish team standards and procedures for documenting and reviewing the product requirements, and manage changes to it, including

- Leading the team in development, review, verification, and evolution of the product requirements
- Ensuring that all the product requirements assumptions are identified, documented, tracked, and verified with the customer
- Ensuring that the customer agrees with the requirements and requirements changes
- Working with the team to identify requirements issues, track them, manage their resolution, and confirm with the customer and the team
- Managing changes to the requirements, ensuring that every requirement changes goes thru impact analysis, estimation and documentation
- For every requirements change decision, notifying in a timely manner the configuration control board, other partner-teams, and the customer

Project Delivery

The customer interface manager ensures smooth project delivery to the customer, and

- Works with the customer to obtain user acceptance test (UAT) criteria, timeline, and plans; documents the acceptance test plans, reviews and agrees with customer; communicates plans to the team
- Facilitates user acceptance testing and communicates results back to the team
- Guides the team in building customer/user documentation and training plans
- Leads the team in analyzing and resolving product usability issues
- Ensures that all the issues during UAT and product deployment/installation are resolved by the team in a timely way
- Gets a final sign-off from customer after deployment (based on the contract/agreement)

Questions to address

Here are some of the questions the customer interface manager is expected to address:

- Are the team members aware of all the customer-related issues and concerns?
- Are all requirements and changes captured, evaluated, reviewed, approved, documented, communicated, and planned before being implemented?
- Are the right people involved in evaluating, reviewing, and approving the requirements?
- Are customer requests being handled effectively and efficiently?
- Are there any road blocks between team and requirements?
- Is a right balance being struck between requirements, work, and development?
- Are the requirements detailed enough and do they have the right quality to guide development work?
- What changes, improvements should the team be making to improve the project deliverable?
- Are team members aware of the environment in which the system will be deployed and used by the customer/user?

Reporting

The customer interface manager tracks and reports weekly to the team on the status of the requirements, open issues, deployment status, customer feedback, etc.

Skills and abilities

The skills that are helpful for customer interface manager:

- Enjoys working with team members and customers, understands their needs, and can empathize with their concerns
- Can describe technical complex problems in simple non-technical terms
- Interested and passionate in defining and building a superior product
- Knows how to handle situation where bad news is needed to be communicated and/or manage an unhappy customer

Time commitment

This role typically requires a time commitment of 1 hour per week.

9.5.3 TSP Role: Design Manager

Design Manager

Role overview

The design manager leads the design work, sets processes, establishes design standards, and manages design changes.

Goals

The design manager's goals are:

- Goal 1: Lead the team in producing robust design to meet project goals
- Goal 2: Engage the team, utilize team member's skills and ideas in producing the design

(Continued)

(Continued)

- Goal 3: Manage changes to the design; document, and communicate them
- Goal 4: Ensure that the design and its documentation are of high quality
- Goal 5: Track design quality throughout the project and report status

Responsibilities and activities

The design manager is responsible for managing the design process of the project. Here are list of responsibilities and some of the typical activities performed by the design manager:

Leads the Product Design

- Maintains continuous focus on product design throughout the project
- Leads the team in producing, reviewing, and documenting product design from requirements and architecture
- Identifies, analyzes, resolves, documents, and communicates all design issues
- Guides the team in anticipating and focusing on product interoperability, compatibility, integration, and performance issues
- Using techniques like prototypes or experiments, ensures that all the design issues and assumptions are identified, documented, and resolved

Manages Design Changes

- Manages, controls, and communicates the design changes
- Analyzes impact of design changes; leads estimation, approval, documentation and communication of these changes
- Ensures that the configuration control board receives complete and timely data to make design change decisions

Designs Process and Standards

- Establishes design methods, standards, templates, checklist, and guidelines the team can use to produce design materials
- Guides the team with documented process, roles, and responsibilities for design development; reviews inspection and design-change process

Questions to address

Here are some of the questions, the design manager is expected to address:

- Are all the team members aware of the team's design standards and understand how to use them?
- Are the team's design standards and process capable of producing a high-quality robust design?
- Are the team members able to work together to produce high-quality design?
- Has the architecture produced by the team considered future product evolution?
- Does the design conform to the architecture?

- Are architecture and design artifacts appropriately documented, maintained, and controlled?
- Are design dependencies with other teams and systems appropriately identified, managed, and tracked?
- Do team members have the required fluency level with the design methods? If not, what actions are being taken to improve this?
- Are there any other design issues that the team should be aware of?

Reporting

The design manager reports weekly to the team on the status of product design work, design standards, issues, and design quality.

Skills and abilities

The characteristics helpful for a design manager are:

- Enjoys developing design and building new products
- Is very familiar and experienced with design methods and standards
- Is interested in and passionate about producing a robust design
- Appreciates other people's ideas and designs, and works with them

Time Commitment

This role typically requires a time commitment of 2 hours per week during design phase and 1 hour per week after that.

9.5.4 TSP Role: Implementation Manager

Implementation Manager

Role overview

The implementation manager establishes implementation and size standards, and manages the overall implementation process.

Overall goals

The implementation manager's goals are to

- Goal 1: Lead the team in producing superior implementation
- Goal 2: Ensure that implementation fully conforms to the design
- Goal 3: Implement a high-quality product
- Goal 4: Ensure that team members use implementation standards in their work

Responsibilities and activities

Here are list of responsibilities and some of the typical activities performed by Implementation Manager:

Leads the Implementation

- Maintains continuous focus on product implementation throughout the project

(Continued)

(Continued)

- Identifies, resolves, documents, and communicates all implementation issues
- Leads the team in producing, refining, and verifying high-quality product implementation
- Leads the team in measuring and identifying potential issues with performance, integration, and compatibility issues
- Uses prototypes or experiments to validate assumptions used in implementation
- Leads the team in planning for and handling product distribution, installation, and migration problems

Manages Changes to Product Implantation

- Manages, documents, and communicates the implementation change process
- Leads the team in estimating, documenting, and communicating the impact of every change on product implementation
- Ensures that the configuration control board is provided with complete and timely data to make implementation change decisions

Establishes and Manages Implementation Standards

- Establishes implementation standards, procedures, templates, and guidelines that the team can use to produce a high-quality product
- Establishes standards for coding, counting, language, review, checklists, and documentation that will aid the team in product implementation

Questions to address

Here are some of the questions the implementation manager is expected to address:

- Are all of the team members comfortable in implementing the product in the required languages?
- What is the plan to ramp up team members that are not fluent with the required languages?
- Are team members consistently using the implementation standards that have been developed, established, and adopted for this project?
- Are all the team members leveraging existing, shared and/or reused code wherever possible? If not, what actions can be taken to improve this?
- Are team members aware of implementation issues and changes?

Reporting

The implementation manager is expected to do a weekly reporting on the status of product implementation, standards adoption, and issues. These reports include details on plan versus actual LOC coded, reviewed, compiled, inspected and fixed, unit tested, and released to integration.

Skills and abilities

Characteristics of a successful implementation manager:

- Enjoys building products
- Understands very well implementation tools and the environments
- Passionate in producing a high-quality product
- Good familiarity and experience with creating implementation standards

Time commitment

Typically, implementation managers need a time commitment of 2 hours per week during the implementation phase and 1 hour during other phases.

9.5.5 TSP Role: *Planning Manager*

Planning Manager

Role overview

Planning managers lead the team in producing a detailed project plan. They track the project status and report on progress, guiding the team with estimating, planning, tracking, and risk management.

Goals

The planning manager's goals are:

- Goal 1: Help the team successfully run a well-planned and tracked project
- Goal 2: Produce a complete, precise, and accurate project plan
- Goal 3: Help the team members with their individual planning and tracking
- Goal 4: Regularly track and report accurately the team's status against the plan every week

Responsibilities and activities

The planning manager is responsible for overall planning and tracking of the project. Here are some of the responsibilities and typical activities performed by the planning manager.

Leads Project Planning

- Documents and communicates estimation and planning process to be used by the team
- Guides the team with work breakdown structure (WBS) and detailed size estimation for each of the work module
- Assists the team members in generating their individual plans
- Ensures that team members take into consideration their vacation plans, project dependency, and end date when sequencing activities
- Leads launch meeting during planning session

(Continued)

(Continued)

- Generates individual worksheets, gets them filled out by each team member, and consolidates them to create overall team plan
- Helps the team maintain a balanced plan at all times
- Maintains all team and individual workbooks

Project Tracking and Reporting

- Checks that all team members have submitted the required data for weekly TSP project status team meeting; urges late team members to promptly provide the required project data
- Tracks that all committed tasks have been completed by every team member
- Ensures that every team member work according to their documented plan
- Checks that all the time and defects logs are up to date for each team member
- For all the completed tasks, checks that team members updated the task list with the completion date and size data
- Checks on the status of incomplete tasks, discusses with team members about the status
- Checks and validates any changes to schedule; makes risks, and issues list
- Supports the team leader in tracking project issues and risks
- Tracks team progress against the plan and reports and reviews project status weekly with the team and team leader
- Ensures that plans are revised at every team launch and relaunch or whenever the project schedule or resources change substantially

Questions to address

Here are some of the questions the planning manager is expected to address:

- Is every team member's plan sufficiently detailed?
- Do the individual plans accurately represent the work they are currently doing? If not, what is the action recommended?
- Are all the team member's workloads reasonably well-balanced? If not, what improvement actions are recommended?
- Are project dependencies within the team members and with other teams known and tracked?
- Are there any other planning issues that the team should be aware of?
- If the project is not on track, are corrective actions taken to bring it back on track?

Reporting

The planning manager's duties also include:

- Producing a consolidated report of team project status against the plan and distributing it before the weekly team meeting

- Based on the current project velocity, task completion rate and current schedule, informing the team and team leader about likely milestones and project completion dates
- Helping the team leader to create weekly project status reports for management and customer
- Maintaining all the TSP data to produce the schedule, resource, size, and productivity sections of the project report during the phase and project postmortems

Skills and abilities

Here are some of the skills and abilities that are most helpful for planning managers:

- Experience in project management—planning and tracking
- Able to motivate without authority every team member on estimating, planning, following, and tracking a project plan while doing the work
- Able to produce a plan for the work and enjoy following and tracking it
- Able to measure and analyze process data, report status, and make recommendations for improvement

Time commitments

The planning manager usually needs around 3 hours of commitment per week.

9.5.6 TSP Role: Process Manager

Process Manager

Role overview

The process manager leads the process and procedure definition work for the team, owning and maintaining the team processes and driving continuous improvement.

Goals

The process manager's goals are:

- Goal 1: Ensure all the team members have defined processes for all the key activities and that they use the processes promptly
- Goal 2: Ensure that team process data are promptly reported and analyzed
- Goal 3: Assist the team in identifying and resolving process problems and continuously improving the process

Responsibilities and activities

The process manager's responsibilities and some of the typical activities performed are:

Process Support

- Maintains a continued focus on team processes throughout the project

(Continued)

(Continued)

- Leads the team discussion during TSP project launch in defining the development strategy and process for the team
- Assist team members in defining and using processes they need for their major development, management, and team activities
- Ensures that all the team members are familiar with defined processes and are trained to use them
- Ensures that every team member always follows a defined and documented process for all activities

Process Tracking

- Ensures all team members report their process data weekly in a timely way
- Identifies where the team or any team member has problems following the process and assists them
- Alerts the team whenever process problems are encountered, suggests actions, and helps the team to resolve the problems
- Follows up with team members who do not provide process data on time, escalates issues to team leader if needed

Process Analysis and Improvements

- Analyzes the team's process data, makes recommendations to improve
- Manages the elicitation, gathering, recording, tracking, and handling of the team's process improvement proposals (PIPs)
- Assists team member's improvement efforts

Questions to address

Here are some of the questions the process manager is expected to address:

- Are there defined processes for the team to use for its principal activities? If not, what are the action items for getting this done?
- Do processes reflect the way work is done currently? If not, are PIPs being submitted to correct the processes?
- Are the engineers properly recording their data?
- Do they record the data as they do the work or after the fact?
- Are the team members following the defined processes that they have?
- Are team members aware of the defined process improvement proposal (PIP)?

Reporting

The process manager reports weekly to the team on the following:

- Current status of all team-related process development and analysis activities
- Informs the team and team leader about any process-related issues that need their attention
- Maintains the TSP data to produce the process section of the project report during the phase and project postmortems

Skills and abilities

The skills that are most helpful to the process manager are:

- Interested in processes and process measurements
- Able to define, use, measure, analyze processes, and recommend changes

Time commitment

Typically, this role needs a time commitment of 1 hour per week.

9.5.7 TSP Role: Quality Manager

Quality Manager

Role overview

The quality manager works with the team and drives the overall quality of the project deliverables.

Goals

The quality manager's goals are:

- Goal 1: Lead the team in producing, following, and tracking a quality plan
- Goal 2: Analyze quality data and provide timely feedback to the team for potential quality problems
- Goal 3: Effectively moderate team inspections or arrange a moderator

Responsibilities and activities

The quality manager is responsible for handling the following activities:

Quality Plan Development and Tracking

- Maintains a continued focus on product and process quality throughout the project
- Leads the team in developing the quality plan during the TSP launch
- Encourages and guides team members in following and tracking the quality plan
- Ensures that a qualified effective moderator is available to lead team inspections or acts as inspection moderator
- Regularly tracks quality measures for product and process quality
- Follows up with team members who do not provide quality data on time; refers to team leader if needed
- Analyzes team and team members' quality data and recommends changes for improving the quality of the personal product output
- Provides visibility to the analysis; reports to all the team members
- Alerts the team whenever the defined process is not being followed; recommends how to correct problems

(Continued)

(Continued)

- The quality manager monitors the overall quality of the product, determines when and where there are quality problems, and recommends corrective actions, such as:
  - Additional reinspection for some of the modules
  - Rewriting some of the modules
  - Repeating self-review

Questions to address

We can expect the quality manager to answer the following questions:

- Are the team members reporting complete data and of adequate quality to be able to conduct analysis? If not, what action can be taken to improve this?
- Are the team members using their data to assess and improve the quality of their work?
- Are all the team members allocating adequate time for personal reviews and inspection during planning phase?
- Does the team members' data indicate that the work is of high quality? If not, what remedial actions can be taken?
- Are the team members conducting team personal reviews and inspections of the requirements, design, and implementation products, and are these inspections being participated in and executed appropriately?
- Is component and module quality being reviewed according to the team's quality guidelines before integration and system testing?
- Is additional support required from management or the team leader in assuring quality work?
- Are there any other quality issues that the team should be aware of?

Reporting

The quality manager gives the following on a weekly basis to the team and team leader:

- Quality measures and product quality status
- A detailed report on defects, phase yield, ratio, and defect detection rate
- TSP data on quality and component sections of the project report during the phase and project postmortems

Skills and abilities

The characteristics most helpful to quality managers are the following:

- Concern and seriousness about software quality
- Expertise in measuring, analyzing, and improving software quality
- Some experience with standard inspection methods
- Willingness and ability to constructively review and comment on other people's work without upsetting them

Time commitment

The quality manager role typically consumes 3 hours per week.

9.5.8 TSP Role: Support Manager

Support Manager

Role overview

The support manager is responsible overall for supporting the tools used by the project team, configuration management, change management, and issue tracking systems.

Goals

The support manager's goals are:

- Goal 1: Help the team in selecting and using appropriate tools
- Goal 2: Manage the team's configuration management and change control functions
- Goal 3: Promote reuse within the team

Responsibilities and activities

The support manager's responsibilities and typical activities are:

Tools and Support

- Ensure appropriate tools are available for the team to use for the project and have the necessary knowledge/training to use them
- Ensure appropriate support is available for the tools used by the team
- Manage and track the performance and effectiveness of tools and the support system
- Lead the team in identifying, recommending, developing, or obtaining special support tools for the team to improve team performance
- Ensure that all the team's risks and issues are documented and tracked in issue-tracking system

Configuration Management

- Obtains and manages the team's configuration management system
- Secures and maintains a master copy of all controlled items and versions
- Makes only approved changes to the controlled version of the configuration items
- Allows only authorized changes to the baselined products

Change Management

- Sets up and leads the configuration control board (CCB)
- Ensures all changes to the controlled products are reviewed by CCB for impact and benefit

Reuse

- Works with the team on defining the reuse goal and tracking it throughout the project

(Continued)

(Continued)

- Works as the team's reuse advocate
- Coaches the team members on how to identify reuse opportunities
- Creates and maintains list of potentially reusable components

Questions to address

We can expect the quality manager to answer the following questions:

- Do all the team members have appropriate tools and necessary support for their work? If not, what additional tools do you recommend?
- Are all team members trained and comfortable in using the development tools? If not, what can they do to come up to speed with the tools?
- Does the team have the tools and necessary support for the configuration management process? If not, what are the recommended actions?
- Is the change control board set up and working as per the expectations?
- Are all changes to baselined products reviewed by CCB and managed appropriately through the configuration control system?
- Are all the products of the project that needs to be baselined appropriately baselined?
- Are there any other support issues that the team should be aware of?

Reporting

The support manager tracks and reports weekly to the team on the following:

- Status of all tools and support
- Reuse status and opportunities
- Changes to the baselined product items

Skills and abilities

The skills and abilities that are most helpful to support managers are the following:

- Interest in using tools and methods
- Ability to assist the team with tools support
- Experience in and familiarity with support tools and systems

Time commitment

Typically, this role needs 1 hour of time commitment per week.

9.5.9 TSP Role: Test Manager

Test Manager

Role overview

The test manager leads the team with test planning and successful test execution of the project, ensuring that the system is thoroughly tested before it moves to the next phase.

Goals

The test manager's goals are:

- Goal 1: Lead the team in creating test plans based on the requirements and system design
- Goal 2: Manage and lead the testing group with test planning, measurement, tracking, and reporting
- Goal 3: Ensure that the overall product is thoroughly tested end-to-end and performs all important functions as per requirements and specifications
- Goal 4: Ensure that the testing group is represented in all the meetings
- Goal 5: Ensure that testing issues are considered in every phase
- Goal 6: Establish an agreement on acceptance test criteria with customer interface manager during requirements phase

Responsibilities and activities

Testing is the final quality gate for the product. The test manager ensures that the all the major functionality of the product is tested thoroughly before it move to the next phase. Here is a list of responsibilities and some of the typical activities performed by the test manager:

Test Planning and Focus

- Leads the team in creating system test plans during the design phase and integration; tests plans during the implementation phase
- Reviews test plans and ensures that they are complete and effective
- Builds a communication channel between development and testing group for continuous communication and focus on quality
- Ensures that the plans are appropriately updated to reflect the changes and current state of the product
- Maintains a continuous focus on testing throughout the entire development cycle of the project
- Ensures that the test team have adequate time for test planning and execution during the project

Test Execution

- The test manager guides the team members with planning and executing all the test activities of the project
- Works with the team in establishing test standards for all the test phases
- Ensures test defects are documented and tracked to resolution and closure
- Reviews and reports all major defects found in integration and system testing

Test Analysis

- Collects and analyzes data from every test phase to identify defect-prone modules

(Continued)

(Continued)

- Captures defect data, creates and maintains a defect density map of all modules and the overall system for every test phase
- Works with the quality manager to identify and recommend areas that are low on quality and which might need additional inspection or retesting

Typical questions to address

We can expect the test manager to answer the following questions:

- Are the test plans produced during the appropriate phases?
- Are the test plans reviewed for completeness, thoroughness, and effectiveness in appropriate phases (system test plans reviewed in requirements phase, the integration plans reviewed during the design phase, and the unit test plans reviewed during implementation phase)?
- Are engineers comfortable in producing appropriate test plans? If not, what can be done to bring them up to speed?
- Are appropriate test tools available for the test team?
- Are the team members proficient in using the test tools? If not, what is done to improve this situation?
- Does the test team have adequate domain knowledge of the application?
- Are there any other test issues that the team should be aware of?

Reporting

The test manager tracks and reports weekly to the team on the following:

- Status of the team's test planning, development, and execution work
- Defect metrics (opened, resolved, priority, mean-time-to-fix, etc.)
- Test schedule information

Skills and abilities

The skills and abilities that are most helpful to the test manager are the following:

- Passionate about understanding how things work
- Enjoys taking things apart
- Intrigued by puzzles
- Gets excited in finding defects by using several innovative approaches

Time commitment

The test manager role typically needs 2 hours of time commitment during the test phase and 1 hour at other times.

9.5.10 TSP Role: Team Member

Team Member

Role overview

All team members actively contribute to the project in design, implementation, and testing work, and support other team members as needed. When each and every member of the team consistently meets role expectations and responsibilities, follows the team process, and works toward agreed goals, the team will be most efficient, effective, and successful.

Overall goals

The team members' goals are:

- Goal 1: Be team players, work with the team to deliver successful project
- Goal 2: Meeting their team and team member's commitments
- Goal 3: Execute on role expectations and engineering responsibilities
- Goal 4: Plan, manage, continuously improve, and report their personal work on time
- Goal 5: Contribute in developing and following team process and personal process

Responsibilities and typical activities

All team members are responsible for meeting their responsibilities as a team member and delivering successful projects. Typical activities that are expected from the team members are:

Personal Process Discipline

For the team to become more effective and efficient, all the team members need to follow personal disciplines. Here are some of the highlights for these:

- Cooperate with all the team members to maintain an effective and productive team working environment
- Always document and follow disciplined software engineering practices in planning and doing the work
- Understand customer needs, expectations, and application environment, and use this information to build a superior product to delight the customer
- Identify the need, arrange for and get the necessary education and training needed to do superior work, and produce high-quality products on time
- Record information on each and every defect found by yourself or any team member
- Use defects information to continuously improve the process, prevent defects wherever possible, and remove defects as early in the process as possible
- Analyze personal data, establish personal improvement goals, and work towards these

(Continued)

(Continued)

Personal Work Management

All team members are expected to manage their work using PSP in a professional manner as follows:

- Plan their work, create detailed individual plans, and commit to project schedule and deliverables
- Track, manage, and report their personal time on the project
- Track their personal performance on the project—time, size, defects, and schedule
- Record all the necessary data (defect, size, time, etc.) in the TSP tool and report it on time for the team members to analyze and report project status
- Ensure continuous communication on project status and deviation (if any) to the team members and management
- Leverage historical data for project estimation and for negotiating project schedule if the schedule expectations from management are unreasonably aggressive
- Work with the team to ensure that management understands their views on the project scope, schedule, and the data to support these views
- Work aggressively and leverage the right resources to meet their commitments with quality products

Team Responsibility

- Effective teamwork requires that every team member
- Work closely with the team members to maintain an effective and productive team environment
- Proactively participate in avoiding and resolving team problems
- Work objectively with the team members to settle issues in the best interest of the team and the project goals
- Call on the team for any help needed
- Support and help other team members actively whenever they need any help
- Handle one or more team roles responsibly and perform as per the expectations
- Actively participate in team activities and make sure the views and ideas are communicated and understood
- Listen, respect, and understand other team members' views and ideas

Reporting

All the team members are expected to record their work data every day, as and when they perform the work. As per the weekly schedule set by the team lead or planning manager, the completed TSP workbooks need to be checked-in by the agreed time period. In the project status meeting, any roadblock, issues, project status deviation, quality problems and any other issues should be reported.

Typical questions to address

The team leader and other role managers might ask questions to the team members during the project status review meetings. Here are some of the typical questions:

- Are you on track as per the project schedule?
- Are you blocked?
- How is the quality of the product so far?
- What are the personal process improvements you are working on?
- Any vacation plans?
- Are there any issues or risks that you think might impact the project's success?

Experience/skills

- Are all team members proficient in the development environment and the language?
- Are all team members trained on PSP?

Along with technical skills and discipline, the most important skill needed is positive attitude and openness to try new things and continuously improve.

Time Commitment

It is observed that each team member needs to spend around 1 hour per week for logging time and another 1 hour analyzing data with quality manager to identify improvement opportunities.

9.5.11 TSP Role: Inspection Manager

Inspection Manager

Role overview

Inspection is an integral and important part of the TSP process. Inspection meetings are most effective and efficient if they are run as per the inspection script and roles.

Overall goals

The goals of any inspection meeting are:

- Goal 1: Provide a platform for team members to provide feedback to other team members on work and products, uncover sophisticated design issues, and report defects
- Goal 2: Get an understanding of other team members' work
- Goal 3: Ensure that the quality of every module is high

(Continued)

(Continued)

Responsibilities and activities

Inspection activities have a few roles that are to be followed to make sure inspections are effective and efficient. The main purpose of inspections is to focus on sophisticated design and architectural issues, not on finding simple defects. It is often seen that a few simple defects can distract reviewers and might miss major issues. Here are list of responsibilities and some of the typical activities performed by people in the key inspection meeting roles:

Moderator

This role is usually filled in by the quality manager of the team or somebody appointed by him or her.

- Performs the inspection moderator's tasks
- Ensures all the team members understand the inspection process
- Chairs the inspection meetings
- Leads the inspection process across the team
- Ensures that all the participants actively participate in the inspection meetings and provide feedback on the work products
- Gets the inspection meeting arranged with the appropriate participants and meeting room
- Ensures that the work product is ready for inspection and all the entry conditions are met, or decides to postpone the inspection meeting until they are ready
- Encourages all the participants to contribute and evaluate the product both for completeness and correctness
- Ensures that the meeting focuses on identifying issues or defects and not on fixing the defects
- After the inspection, ensures that all the identified defects were fixed in the product, and reviewed and inspected (if necessary)
- Analyzes the numbers of defects reported against the plan, estimates remaining defects, and/or recommends the team to spend more time or calls for reinspection after the defects are fixed
- Gathers the inspection preparation data and ensures that the meeting recorder enters them in inspection forms
- Reports the inspection results and data back to the team
- Files the inspection forms in the TSP project notebook after the inspection meeting is complete

Producer

Producer is the person who has developed the product and is getting it inspected by the team.

- Supplies the product and details to the reviewers well in advance
- Provides product overview, background information, and other details, and answers questions
- Walks through the product with the reviewers and explains, if necessary
- Actively seeks feedback and listens to it instead of arguing or defending his or her approach
- Makes sure to thoroughly understand all the issues raised by the team, asks clarification questions, and reiterates the issue to avoid any miscommunication
- Fixes all the identified issues and defects in the product and reports back to the team for validation and verification
- Organizes follow up reinspections, if needed
- Validates all the defect fixes to ensure they completely and accurately resolve the issue, and do not cause any other problems
- Updates the TSP workbook to reflect all the defects data and time spent, and updates the size information

Recorder

- Records the inspection meeting details, action items, etc.
- Logs all the defects data in legible format, ensures that all the defect descriptions are agreed by all the involved reviewers and the producers
- Supplies inspection data to the moderator

Facilitator/Timekeeper

- Ensures that all the meeting logistics are taken care of
- Keeps track of the meeting time
- Ensures the meeting is on the agenda, and adequate time is spent on all the agenda items

Reviewers

- The team members prepare for and participate in the inspection process
- The reviewer reviews the team member's product in detail, and highlights (or notes) issues, questions, or defects
- Records preparation time and defect data on TSP worksheet
- Ensures that every issue raised or question asked is answered adequately to participant's satisfaction, and appropriate action is taken whenever necessary

Metrics

The product inspection includes number of people involved, time spent by each, and defects found.

Reporting

The moderator reports the inspection results and data on to TSP workbook, covering these issues.

(Continued)

(Continued)

Typical questions to address

- Did all the expected reviewers inspect the product?
- Were all the defects logged and understood by the producer?
- Did all the sections of the product get inspected?
- Are there any action items from the inspection meeting? Is somebody accountable for follow-up?

Experience/skills

It is advisable for people to undergo some formal training on reviews and inspections. Have somebody with the architect having senior development experience to be able to challenge the design and find out major issues rather than just focusing on finding defects.

Time commitment

There is no separate time commitment for this. Everybody contributing to the inspection process will have a task and have time allocated for it.

9.6 Role Manager Commitments

Everybody who takes on role manager positions has to commit adequate time to handling the responsibilities. The amount of time needed is based on the role. Typically, the planning manager and quality manager need more time compared to other roles.

If the organization has a software engineering process group^{SM} (SEPG^{SM}) or similar groups for process, quality, and support, they can take on some of the role manager's tasks. The role manager should work with them and give as much of the task to them as possible. This will free up some of the role manager's time, which can be used for other activities. While a number of the role manager's tasks can be delegated, it is important to keep the key roles within the team, specifically with the planning manager, quality manager, and the design manager. When one or more managers are not available, other members of the team can fill in for them. Usually an outside person won't be able to offer much help, especially for the planning, quality, and design managers roles.

Apart from the time commitment, it is required to have individual commitments from the role managers. We can then observe that we are able to make the roles very effective in driving change and continuous improvement. People need to understand that this is not a voluntary job; there need to be a commitment and goals regarding what the role manager will drive and achieve for the team.

For first-time projects, the role manager should take help and coaching from the TSP coach in examining the team's data, and understanding and analyzing them (especially the planning manager and quality manager). This will help the role managers to better understand the expectations of the role and how to be effective. The role manager will then be able to provide effective feedback to fellow team members in following the process and continuously improving. The quality manager will be responsible for reviewing individual data and providing feedback.

The team leader should focus on motivating the team members to follow the process. The process manager should help the team members in understanding it and ensuring that the process is followed by the team and is effective.

9.7 Selecting TSP Roles

TSP roles are a very important part of the project, and all of the team roles must be handled efficiently and effectively or the team might run into problems during the project execution. The team lead and the TSP coach work together to ensure that all the team roles are assigned to members willing to do it, have the required expertise/capability to fulfill role responsibilities, and actually execute on the role expectations.

9.7.1 Role Category

Each role has its unique importance; the roles can be classified into four major categories:

1. Project management
   - Team leader
   - Planning manager
   - Support manager
2. Process and quality management
   - Quality manager
   - Process manager
3. Product development
   - Design manager
   - Customer interface manager
   - Implementation manager
4. Quality control
   - Test manager
   - Inspection roles

For the teams that are doing TSP for the first time, the details and expectations around the TSP roles will not be obvious to them. The TSP coach needs to ensure that all the team members understand the role expectations and take that into consideration while selecting the roles.

The role managers are not expected to do everything that is implied by each role. Each role manager needs to maintain the focus for the activities that are covered by that role and work with the team members to ensure that things are taken care of.

9.7.2 Guidelines for Selecting TSP Roles

Here are some of the tips concerning role manager selection and the assignment process:

- The approach should be "role selection" as opposed to "role assignment."
- Make team role assignments during launch and relaunch.
- The team leader is typically designated by management before the project starts.
- The team leader should involve all the team members in selecting and agreeing on their roles.
- The team leader might prefer some particular engineer to take on certain compatible role(s) that will help in making the project successful. The team leader should talk to that person before the meeting and discuss this. Then, during the meeting, the person can put his/her name down for a particular role.
- During the role selection and assignment process, we should ensure that each team member gets a chance to select roles and agree on the roles that are ultimately assigned.
- It is very common to see that each team member will prefer particular roles over other roles. This all depends on their expertise, experience, and interest. In that case, the team leader can facilitate the discussion around role selection.
- It is advisable that the person who takes on the planning manager role should not take any other role, as the planning manager role requires a substantial amounts of work.
- The person taking on the quality manager role should understand the needs of the role and should be capable of performing the role properly. As this role needs significant amount of time, it is advisable that the person should not take on any other role. If the team is short, the process manager role can be taken along with the quality manager role.
- For smaller teams, you might assign multiple roles to a single person (e.g., customer interface, design, implementation, and test manager responsibilities). Depending on the project phase, more focus might be needed on one area compared to other areas, in which case it would be best to assign it to another person.
- The process manager roles can be combined with quality manager or support manager roles and can be handled by a single person.
- Every team member should be comfortable in taking their role by asking themselves if they can act and execute as if they were running the project in all respects relating to it.

9.7.3 Role Selection Process

If there are eight or more people in the team, the role selection and assignment becomes straightforward. Each of the team members can be primary role manager on the standard roles and a few newly added roles. All the team members can take backup role manager responsibility. For smaller teams, it is advisable to follow the process.

The backup role is equally important for the team. In case the main person is not available, the work should not stop, and the backup person can fill the position and keep the team moving on with the project. Also, this is a good way to ramp-up new people on the project. The person in the backup role is expected to work closely with the primary role person, helping with some work from time to time.

There are multiple ways to run the roles selection meetings. One of the role selection processes is to ask each team member to decide on a first, second, and third role choice, write them down on a paper, and keep them handy. If there are more than eight people in the team, then give only two choices—first and second preference. The team lead creates a table in Excel or on a white board or flip chart with the roles on the top and the team members' names down the left side.

Role selection metrics								
Name	Planning manager	Customer interface manager	Design manager	Implementation manager	Quality manager	Process manager	Support manager	Test manager
Pravin								
Wilfred								
Bianka								
Janet								
Ankur								
Mike								
Mark								
Jim								
Vivek								

Steps:

1. Please refer to the role selection guidelines from the previous subsection.
2. Enter each team member's first, second, and third choice on the table (label 1, 2, and 3, respectively).
3. If any role has only one person, assign the role to that person.

4. If any role has two people, try the following:
   a. If both persons have given the same preference to the role, skip this and move to the next step. Otherwise, continue.
   b. Assign the role to the person who has selected it as the first preference. (If there is no first preference, go with the person who had it as second preference.)
   c. For the remaining persons, assign the backup role.
5. For any roles that have three or more people:
   a. If there is only one person with a first preference (if there is no first preference, go with the person who had it as second preference), assign the role.
   b. For the remaining two people, if there is one person with second preference and another with third preference, assign the backup role to the person with second preference.
6. With these steps, hopefully some of the roles and some people might be covered (at least for the primary role assignment). Hide the roles and the people for now, until all the primary role assignments are completed.
7. Repeat steps 3–5 until you are not able to assign any more roles.
8. Go through each role to see if the team agrees on how the role should be assigned. Usually, it is seen that the team agrees on one person to whom this role can be assigned.
9. If the team cannot reach consensus, the team leader can facilitate further discussion to gain consensus and assign one person as primary and a second as backup for the role.
10. For roles that no one has selected, ask the team who wants to take on the primary role responsibility (preference is given to people who do not have any primary role or to the person who has the least number of roles).
11. Once all the roles have a primary assignment, take each of the team members and assign backup roles based on preference (you might use the same steps as outlined above).
12. Ensure that every team member has at least one primary and one backup team role. In case the team size is large and it is not possible to have one role for each person, see if you can add an additional role for the team and allocate it accordingly. It is good to have everybody assigned.
13. At the end, check to ensure that people are appropriately given role assignments, and everybody agrees as a team on these.

9.8 Entering Role Details on TSP Sheet

Record the names of the team members on the TSP roles worksheet for primary and backup roles. Here is the detail process of how to do it:

Using TSP Workbook (TSP Tool)—**Add Roles information**

Purpose: Enter project roles assignment information from meeting 2 (Figure 9.2)

Person: Team leader

Worksheet Name: **Roles**

How: Enter initials of the person who will be role manager in that particular phase. Use the first line for the primary role manager and second line for secondary (backup) role manager.

Location	Details
Primary role	In the appropriate phase column, on the first line for the role manager, enter primary role manager's initial. This same person or a different person can be the role manager for other phase(s). Accordingly, update this across all the phases. For team leader, first line, click on drop-down under requirements phase and select the team leader's initial.
Backup (secondary) role	In the particular phase column, in the second line for the role manager, enter secondary/backup role manager's initials. This person or a different person can be the role manager for other phase(s). Accordingly, update this across all the phases.
Additional roles	If any additional roles are identified by the team, add those in the space provided below the test manager role. Ensure that you leave one blank line after each role to enter initials of the backup role, for example: Security Manager.
Roles entry for each phase	Repeat the steps until all the phases and all the roles are covered.

Notes:

a. You can do Copy/Paste on this worksheet. Avoid using Cut function.
b. You can choose to use the drop-down or enter the information directly (ensure that the initials are correctly entered).
c. The team can have different role managers for different phases or can choose to have the same role managers throughout the project.
d. Use Copy/Paste if you want to copy the role manager names to the other phases.
e. Use only the team member initials.
f. After you are done entering the role details, the Roles worksheet should look like Figure 9.2.

Team Member Roles	Requirements	Design	Implementation	Integration and Test
Team Leader	SP	SP	SP	SP
	ER	ER	ER	ER
Customer Interface Manager	ER	ER	ER	ER
	SP	SP	SP	SP
Design Manager	JS	JS	JS	JS
	ER	ER	ER	ER
Implementation Manager	JS	JS	JS	JS
	NB	NB	NB	NB
Planning Manager	SC	SC	SC	SC
	SK	SK	SK	SK
Process Manager	DG	DG	DG	DG
	SC	SC	SC	SC
Quality Manager	SK	SK	SK	SK
	JS	JS	JS	JS
Support Manager	NB	NB	NB	NB
	SK	SK	SK	SK
Test Manager	SK	SK	SK	SK
	SC	SC	SC	SC
Training Manager	DG	DG	DG	DG
	NB	NB	NB	NB
Security Manager	DG	DG	DG	DG
	JS	JS	JS	JS

Figure 9.2   Roles assignment.

9.9 Goal Tracking

If you have a goal, you should track it. Tracking is the only way the team can find out if it is on the right path to meet the end goal of the project. If not, they can make any course correction. It is not a simple task to come up with a goal tracking mechanism. A majority of the discussion is about the end goal, but there should be some way to find out if the team is on track. We cannot wait until the project is delivered to see if we have met the goal. The challenging part is to devise that mechanism to identify and monitor key process indicators for success, for example, if the end goal is the high-quality product. A SMART (specific, measurable, attainable, result-oriented, timebound) goal can have less than a 0.7 defect/KLOC (1000 lines of code) in system testing. We cannot wait until system testing to see if we have achieved this; instead, we should have measures at the right phase to calculate if we are on track.

The next step is to assign responsibility for tracking the goal to a team member. The responsibilities are assigned, depending on the goal and the team roles (e.g., defects-related metrics should be tracked by the test manager or quality manager). The project schedule should be tracked by the planning manager.

As part of this responsibility, the goal tracker is expected to report progress against the goal on a regular basis in weekly team meetings, discuss issues, take action, make recommendations and monitor progress. Even though the responsibility of tracking a goal is assigned to a particular person, team members need to ensure that they are on track with the goal. If a team member is deviating from the goal, this should be discussed in the team meeting. The frequency of tracking and reporting is decided based on the particular goal, (e.g., progress against schedule should be checked weekly, and so on).

9.10 Meeting Wrap-Up

Discussion leader: Recorder
Duration: 10 minutes
The TSP coach goes through the exit criteria for meeting 2 and ensures that all the necessary activities are done by the team.

The meeting recorder summarizes the meeting and performs the following actions:

- Reads the list of action items; confirms the person responsible and the timeline for task completion; ensures that all the team members are on the same page.
- Documents the list of attendees and absentees.
- Documents the time spent on each of the agenda items.
- Documents details around major discussion items.
- Lists all the major decisions made and the name of the person responsible.
- Reads out the meeting report to the team members and confirms its correctness, completeness, and the action item assignment (if any).
- Ensures with the team that there are no other action items.
- Documents the meeting notes and hands it over to the planning manager to file it with the other TSP project notebook.
- Reviews the list of roles and assignments with the team to ensure everybody is on the same page.

Chapter 10

Meeting 3
Produce Development Strategy

Meeting duration: About 4 hours for first time Team Software Process^SM (TSP^SM) launch (3 hours for subsequent launch).

This meeting is the start of the project planning process. This chapter focuses on getting the team together to develop and review the conceptual design, and produce the development strategy, development process, and support plan to be able to successfully complete the project.

Meeting Agenda (Discussion Leader)

1. Agenda and meeting process (TSP Coach)
2. Produce and review the product conceptual design (Design Manager)
3. Devise the development strategy (Team Leader)
4. High-level list of products to be produced (Design Manager)
5. Define the development process (Process Manager)
6. Produce the process plan (Process Manager)
7. Produce the support plan (Support Manager)
8. Define the Change Control Board (CCB) membership (Support Manager)
9. Define role tasks and weekly status (TSP Coach)
10. Meeting wrap-up and report (Recorder)

10.1 Overview

Once we know what to build, the next important matter is how to build. Usually people do project planning by arranging features/milestones/drops appropriately. Often, this is not done with the team. To know what it is building, the team needs to start with the conceptual design and have a development strategy on how it can build the design effectively, and then plan for milestones/drops based on that. This ensures that the team has a clear understanding of the development strategy/plan that is tailored/catered toward the product based on the conceptual design. Also, this is the place where the team identifies if it needs any additional process/tools to execute the project effectively.

The TSP launch meeting 3 ensures that the team produces the product conceptual design, the development strategy, development process, and support plan. The team notes down the prioritized list of all the components, elements, or features along with their gross sizes. This helps the team in shipping the right product at the right time.

Development strategy is something that people thought was not important; all were in agreement that we can use the same development strategy and process that we did last time. However, when we started asking questions and had the process manager drive the meeting, many matters became clear, and we got good participation from everybody and their contribution in delineating the development strategy and process.

10.2 Produce Conceptual Design

Discussion leader: Design Manager
Time: 45 minutes
The TSP coach starts the meeting and discussion by explaining the importance of conceptual design and how it will be used by the team to devise the development strategy and project plan. Conceptual design should not be confused with the actual design the team will produce during the project. So, when the team asked to produce the conceptual design, it should be in a position to complete it within 20–30 minutes. The team might run into few issues while producing the conceptual design; it might be too detailed or too vague (or abstract). Either of these issues will impact the overall planning.

During the launch preparation, it is advisable to communicate this and have one or two people develop a draft conceptual design. This saves time during launch and also allows people to provide feedback on the design.

The conceptual design should represent the product that is to be built; a high-level architecture would represent it. This gives a good overview of what the team is building, and how it interacts within and with other systems. Here are some of the major components of the conceptual design:

- Databases
- Dependencies
- Interfaces with other internal/external systems
- Interaction between components
- Reporting
- User interfaces
- Network—Internet/Intranet

The team reviews the conceptual design, asks clarifying questions, and provides feedback. The design manager updates the design, and a final agreement is reached. This conceptual design is then used in subsequent planning meetings.

To produce an effective strategy, the team needs to have some idea of how big the total product will be. The team looks at the conceptual design, adds gross size estimates for each of the major components, and evaluates how it can be divided into small parts that can be managed by one or two team members. (The team might choose to do a detailed size estimate here instead of TSP in launch meeting 4.)

10.3 Team's Development Strategy

Discussion leader: Team Leader
Duration: 45 minutes
The team leader leads the team in establishing the project development strategy. There are multiple options for the development strategy: waterfall, iterative, versions, cycles, etc. The overall approach is to find out how the product can be divided into multiple parts that can be developed in series, parallel, or iteratively and put together to produce the final product. While producing the product development strategy, the team considers the following:

- The conceptual design
- Major components, elements, or features
- The gross size of each component
- How the product should be developed
- Major dependencies
- High-risk features/components
- Multiple versions
- Iterative development
- Waterfall development
- Development cycles
- Should the team develop prototypes?
- Content of each of the development cycles
- What should be the milestones?
- Should we go for a "big bang" approach?

If the system is large, the team should avoid using the big bang approach where the full system is built and put together to see if it works. It is always a good idea to build the system in multiple versions or in cycles to ensure that there is a feedback loop that helps in doing course correction. However, this approach usually takes much longer, and it is more difficult to find integration and system defects (which are usually related to architecture). Defects found late in the cycle consume a lot of time in fixing, and it can potentially destabilize the product. In the case of other development models, it will take comparatively less time to find and fix these defects.

If the version or cycle approach is considered, the team needs to come up with strategy on what features or components go in which version such that the high-risk portions and dependency are completed as soon as possible. This also gives the system adequate time and opportunity to be tested while the team builds on top of the system. If it is a product enhancement project, the team should look at the history of how other enhancements were made and what were the problems encountered; that will help them to fine tune the development strategy for this project.

While there are many things to be considered for producing the product development strategy, it may not be possible to continue with the project planning until all the team members agree on a strategy.

The final result of this discussion is a list of product components or elements, gross size estimates, and development strategy. This list needs to be documented and filed with other TSP documentations of the project.

There was one project on which the team didn't spend enough time to think through the product development strategy and jumped in the next meeting. It had to do much rework in meeting 6, and ultimately the team ended up starting all over from meeting 3. Without a development strategy in place, it is not possible to align the development of the modules and other aspects of project planning.

10.4 List of Products to Produce

Discussion leader: Team Leader
Duration: 30 minutes
The team leader leads the team in defining and recording the work products to be produced for the current project cycle and all subsequent cycles.

The work done in the previous meetings around conceptual design, gross size estimate, and development strategy will be used in this meeting to come up with a comprehensive list of all the products that the team is planning to produce for the final product/system. Even if some of the subproduct elements might not be so important for some people, it is a good idea to list all of them because it will take time to produce them, the responsibility needs to be assigned to the appropriate team member to manage, and the team wouldn't want to lose sight of that.

Once the team starts producing the comprehensive list, it will pretty much cover all of the items. Here are some of the examples of the products to be produced:

■ Requirements documents
■ User specification documents
■ Design documents
■ Prototypes
■ Database design
■ External interfaces
■ User guide, installation manuals, etc.
■ Test plan, test cases, test data, scripts, and programs
■ Product elements or modules

The TSP tool may not have all the options available for testing team tasks. You will have to use size measures such as "Text Page" or something similar to be able to use testing as an assembly and subassembly.

It is highly recommended that all the people involved in the project should have their tasks in the TSP sheet. In one of our projects, we tried to keep testing tasks out of the TSP tool because the TSP tool did not have any option for the testing tasks. We thought that would be the right thing to do, but as the project moved ahead, we realized that we were taking more time in consolidating project status from two different places. Also, the testing teams felt they were alienated. We started facing several issues while doing project management, and we saw that quality was also impacted. From that time, we made sure that all the disciplines were covered in the TSP.

When listing product elements or modules, try to provide an adequate level of detail. This helps in planning and makes the modules easier to understand when the team refers to them in the future. To meet the requirements of high-level design phases, a high-level component might be sufficient, but for the implementation phase the team will need details of the components in terms of modules or objects. The team uses the SUMS worksheet to record details about product elements and components.

10.4.1 The SUMS Worksheet

The SUMS worksheet provides a way for the TSP tool to build a structure for product elements/components and use it for estimation and tracking actual data for

■ Size
■ Time
■ Defects

All of the following details are recorded on the SUMS worksheet. Here are specific steps on using the SUMS worksheet.

Using TSP Workbook (TSP Tool)—**Add Product Details in SUMS**

Purpose: Enter product details in the SUMS sheet in meeting 3

Person: Team Leader

Worksheet Name: **SUMS**

How: Enter each of the products that are identified in the SUMS sheet. This is the master sheet, and it will be used by all the automatic calculations in the TSP workbook.

Location	Details
ID	Autogenerated as soon as you start entering data in each line. Don't modify this value.
Assembly, subassembly, or part name	Assembly, subassembly, and part names are nothing but components of the product. These need to be arranged in a tree format so that multiple parts get rolled up into subassemblies, and subassemblies get rolled up into subassemblies and eventually into assemblies. It is advisable to have the top-level assembly as "Requirements," "Development," "Testing," "Documentation," etc. This helps us to organize the product assemblies and also in data rollups, tracking, and reporting. Subassemblies will be the next level of assemblies. For meeting 3, the team can focus on the top-level assemblies and may go down one level for subassemblies. It might be tempting to come up with a comprehensive list of subassemblies. Save those ideas until meeting 4. The rule of thumb is that the number of top-level assemblies be not more than 7, for example: Development • Front end • Back end
Assembly or part	Enter "A" if it is assembly or subassembly. For parts, enter "P" (only used if individuals add any additional assemblies—not used much). For the majority of the time, you should use subassemblies for any product components. In this book we will use subassemblies as the components (unless specified otherwise).
Parent assembly name	Enter the name of the parent assembly. For the top-level assemblies, enter "SYSTEM" as the parent assemblies. (This is a reserved word and needs to be entered in all capital letters; otherwise it will not work.) For example: SYSTEM • Development • Front end

Location	Details
Owner	Enter the alias of the team member who will work on this assembly. It should be only one person. If you have more than one person working on this, consider dividing the subassembly/parts into multiple items to ensure that it can be assigned to a single individual. If it is not possible to divide the assembly, enter the initials of the person who will be doing the majority of the work, e.g., MJ.
Size Measure	Select the size measure for your subassemblies. Here is the list of size measures available in the tool. • **REQ Pages** (used typically for requirements documents and high-level specifications) • **HLD Pages** (used primarily for architecture or high-level system design document) • **DLD Pages** (used for detail-level design, technical spec, pseudocode, algorithms, database design, model, etc.) • **LOC** (Lines of code—used for coding tasks, database-stored procedures, queries, etc.) • **Text Pages** (used for documentation, user guide, help, test plan, test cases, test execution, or any other task that cannot be covered by any other size measure) Try to use the size measure that is very close to what you are using. (If the list does not cover your particular size measure, use Text Pages.) The size measure for all the subassemblies within the tree needs to be the same as that of the top-level assembly. If you want to have a few components that are of a different size, you will need to move to a different parent assembly or create a new parent assembly to handle that particular size measure. For example: LOC.

Notes:

a. The macros need to be enabled before using the worksheet.
b. This worksheet is based on several macros. Do not use Copy/Cut/Paste/Delete/Insert. If you need to add an assembly/subassembly in between, right-click on the cell and click on "Insert Part." Similarly, use "Delete Part."
c. There is data validation built into the tool. So, if you try to move away from any cell without entering data, you will get errors. If you get errors, just specify something in the cell, and you can modify that later.
d. Sometimes it may appear impossible to get rid of errors, in which case try deleting the whole line using "Delete Part."
e. Navigation between the cells can be simple by using TAB instead of ENTER.
f. For all the items in SUMS that have LOC as the size measure, all the tasks are auto-generated whenever the task generation option is selected (usually in meeting 4).
g. There is no direct size measure available for testing related tasks (test case/test execution/etc.). If you want to use testing tasks in the TSP sheet, you might use "Text Pages" for size measure.

Example:

ID	Assembly, subassembly, or part name	(A)ssembly or (P)art	Parent assembly name	Owner	Size measure	Planned Size						
						Base	Deleted	Modified	Added	Reused	New and changed	Total
1	Requirements	A	SYSTEM	MJ	REQ pages							
2	Architecture	A	SYSTEM	RJ	HLD pages							
3	Development	A	SYSTEM	VJ	LOC							
4	Testing	A	SYSTEM	SJ	Text pages							
5	Documentation	A	SYSTEM	MJ	Text pages							
6	Main req doc	A	Requirements	MJ	REQ pages							
7	HLD frontend	A	Architecture	RJ	HLD pages							
8	HLD back end	A	Architecture	RJ	HLD pages							
9	Frontend code	A	Development	VJ	LOC							
10	Back end code	A	Development	VJ	LOC							
11	Administration	A	Development	VJ	LOC							
12	Backup/ recovery	A	Development	VJ	LOC							
13	User account	A	Testing	SJ	Text pages							
14	Transactions	A	Testing	SJ	Text pages							
15	User manual	A	Documentation	MJ	Text pages							
16	Online help	A	Documentation	MJ	Text pages							

Example of a SUMS Sheet

10.5 Development Process Definition

Discussion leader: Process Manager
Duration: 30 minutes
Process definition is one of the initial steps before making the project plan. The project plan is incomplete without the details of the process the team is going to follow. The process definition enables the team to have a common process to get the work done in the most efficient and effective way. If project planning continues without process definition, the team will be more focused on resources and schedule—how fast we can deliver. If they are not able to meet management expectations, the team becomes conscious about it, and concerned that they may be unable to deliver in time, as a result of which process definition will take a back seat and will never be visited or considered.

While creating the process definition, the team looks at the products to be produced and thinks about how they should do the work, what the issues are that they are likely to encounter, etc. They also incorporate experiences with previous projects and use them in the process definition. When the process definition is done up front in the process, the team gets to decide how to do the work before creating the project plan. This helps simplify the estimation process, and the team members can create better estimates and project plans.

It is highly likely that the organization might have a standard process (especially if it is one that has adopted ISO 9000 or CMM/CMMi standards/models). If standard processes are available, the team should review them to ensure that they cover all the activities and to see if the team can use them to produce the final product. You might observe that the organizational processes might be at a high level and the team might need more prescriptive guidance or details to be able to use them. If some changes are needed to the organizational processes, follow the guidelines to request the deviation.

The process manager leads the team in creating the process definition, which covers the following:

- Definitions of all the major processes the team will be using from project start to release and support.
- The sequence of phases for the project (e.g., should the team compile before review? How many people should there be for inspection? In which phase test are plans created?).
- Key activities performed in each phase.
- Steps required to produce the products during each phase.
- Steps to verify the product quality.
- List of items that are needed to be baselined at each phase.
- Criteria for baselining the products at each phase.

Here is an example of the development process:

- Requirements
  - Requirements (for the project)
  - Requirements review (team)
- High-level design
  - High-level design (HLD) (for the project)
  - HLD review (team)
- Detail design
  - Detail level design (DLD) (appropriate team members—for each component)
  - DLD review (self—for each component)
  - Design rework—fix bugs (self—for each component)
  - DLD inspection (appropriate team members)
  - Design rework—fix bugs (self—for each component)
  - Unit test case writing (self—for each component)
- Code
  - Code (appropriate team members—for each component)
  - Code review (self—for each component)
  - Code rework—fix bugs (self—for each component)
  - Compile (self—for each component)
  - Code inspection (appropriate team members—for each component)
  - Code rework—fix bugs (self—for each component)
  - Unit testing (self—for each component)
  - Code rework—fix bugs (self—for each component)
- Integration
  - Integration (appropriate team members)
  - Code rework—fix bugs (self—for each component)
  - Integration testing (test team members)
  - Code rework—fix bugs (self—for each component)
- System testing
  - System testing (test team members)
  - Code rework—fix bugs (self—for each component)

During the launch, ensure that the team is not influenced heavily by the team leader, TSP coach, or a particular person. It needs to be made certain that the process definition should be a collective team exercise, and open discussion should be encouraged.

It is very critical for all the members of the team to understand the importance of the process for the work they are doing on the project. This can be made possible only if all of the team members actively participate in producing the process definitions.

10.6 Process Plan

Discussion leader: Process Manager
Duration: 30 minutes
The development process definition meeting gives the team a good understanding of why processes are important and what processes are needed for the successful execution of the project.

Examples of process items to develop are

- Engineering processes
    - Design standards
    - Coding standards
    - Size-counting standards
    - Naming standards
    - Message standards
    - User interface standards
    - Configuration management standards
    - Review process
    - Inspection process
    - Code check-in process
    - Release process
    - Templates

- Team processes and procedures
    - Team communication process
    - Disaster recovery and business continuity
    - Issue resolution process
    - Escalation process
    - Decision making
    - Approving standards
    - Change management process
    - Time reporting
    - Project status reporting

While creating the process plans, check with other groups in the organization if they already have some processes that can be leveraged. Explore options where some other software engineering process groups (SEPG) might be able to help with creating some standard processes. This will save some time, and the team can focus on the engineering activities.

At the end of this meeting, the team would have a list of a few action items on developing processes or modifying some existing ones and who will do them. Along with the list of processes, the team estimates hours and the phases by which the processes need to be ready.

10.7 Support Plan

Discussion leader: Support Manager

Duration: 30 minutes

Based on the process and tools the team adopts for development, there is a need to have a support plan in place to cater to the team's support needs.

The support manager leads the team with discussion around the following:

- Does the team have the right set of tools for development?
- Is the development environment adequate for the projects' complexity and needs?
- Is the team comfortable in using the tools?
- Is there any training that needs to be arranged?
- Are the required facilities available?
- Are systems, servers, disk space, and connectivity adequate?
- Backup and recovery?
- Does the team need one or more of the following tools?

    - Requirements tools
    - Design tools
    - Editors
    - Compilers
    - Test case tools
    - Testing automation tools
    - Performance, stress, and load testing tools
    - Case tools
    - Defect management
    - Configuration management
    - Risk and issues tracking
    - Size (LOC) counting
    - Microsoft Office Excel and Word
    - Data analysis

Although it might appear trivial to ask these questions, it might take significant amounts of time and effort to acquire these tools, get them installed, and team member ramp-up time. It is useful to think over these questions ahead of time so that the support manager can make sure that the tools are available when the team needs them.

These activities listed could take significant amounts of time. The support manager should explore other options available in the organization for handling tools and support needs. As far as the team members are concerned, they will contact the support manager for all their tools and support needs, and in turn, the support manager ensures that they are taken care of in time.

At the end of this meeting, the support manager would document the list of tools to be used by the team, support needs, action items, and timeline. This would become the support plan.

10.8 Change Control Board

Discussion leader: Support Manager
Duration: 10 minutes
The support manager leads the team in discussing the Change Control Board (CCB) membership. It is important to obtain CCB membership and finalize the procedure up front in the project. This ensures that the process is in place and any changes go through the right channel for approval before they are adopted and implemented.

Change control is not just for engineering items; it should be adopted for standards, processes, the development environment, and team plans. At the beginning of the project, all these items should be baselined and retained; new items should be baselined as soon as people start using them. Once the team development environment is finalized, it should be baselined, and any changes to it need to go through the CCB.

The typical CCB membership includes (but are not limited to) the following:

- Support Manager (chair)
- Design Manager
- Customer Interface Manager

At the start of the project, there will be very little activities for CCB. But as the project moves ahead, the activities grow, and CCB becomes the gatekeeper of any change.

10.9 Define Role Tasks and Weekly Status

Discussion leader: TSP Coach
Duration: 15 minutes
The TSP coach leads the team in explaining the weekly reporting for each role. It is essentially the overview of procedures mentioned in the earlier section of each TSP role. This ensures that all the team members are aware of their roles' expectations and weekly reporting and can plan for the activities accordingly.

For new TSP teams, we have found that explaining the role tasks becomes easier with some data to play with. So, usually, we try to run fast in this meeting and then spend some time coaching the team members during the weekly project status review meeting.

10.10 Meeting Wrap-Up

Discussion leader: Recorder
Duration: 10 minutes
The TSP coach goes through the exit criteria for meeting 3 and ensures that all the necessary activities are performed by the team.

The meeting recorder summarizes the meeting and performs the following actions:

- Reads the list of action items, indicating the person responsible and the timeline for task completion. Ensures that all the team members are on the same page.
- Documents the list of attendees and absentees.
- Documents the time spent on each of the agenda items.
- Documents details of major discussion items.
- Lists all the major decisions made and the name of the people involved.
- Reads out the meeting report to the team members and confirms its correctness, completeness, and action item assignment (if any).
- Ensures with the team that there are no other action items.
- Documents the meeting notes and hands them over to the planning manager to file with the other TSP project notes.

Chapter 11

Meeting 4
Building Overall Team Plan

Meeting duration: A normal meeting lasts about 6–12 hours depending on project size and Team Software Process[SM] (TSP[SM]) experience. For teams that have good experience in using TSP, it takes around 4–6 hours.

After finalizing the team's development strategy and process definition in TSP launch meeting 3, the team starts working on creating the top-down project plan. This chapter focuses on this aspect. Meeting 4 is a very important and time-consuming meeting in the TSP project planning phase. It usually takes lot of time and, if not done correctly, might take several days for the team get it right. The major outcome of this meeting is the top-down project plan, resource requirements, and project schedule, and it also serves as a basis for creating a quality plan in the next meeting.

Meeting Agenda (Discussion Leader)

1. Meeting agenda and overview (TSP Coach)
2. Work breakdown structure (Design Manager)
3. Size estimation for all project products (Design Manager)
4. Overall resource requirement (Planning Manager)
5. Creation of project tasks list (Team Leader)
6. Weekly team's availability (Planning Manager)
7. Generation and review of overall team project plan (Planning Manager)
8. Meeting wrap-up and report (Recorder)

11.1 Overview

The only time we will have a 100% estimation accuracy is after we ship; however, to plan the project, we need to begin to estimate at the start of the project. We can use any method for estimation, but its true value lies in learning and historical data. How often do we look at historical data for estimation? Do we estimate everything that is needed? For effective project planning, we need to estimate the size, effort, and bugs—yes, we should estimate bugs, too. Usually, estimation in traditional project planning is done at the "effort" level only, that is, if I have to build this feature, I will take 2 days. However, with the change of mindset, we should start estimating the size of the component in terms of lines of code (LOC) or final product. This helps us improve the estimation accuracy over time and, at the same time, the effort required becomes a function of component size and not just a gut feeling. For the first project, the size estimation accuracy may be ±50%, but as the team matures, accuracy tends to be within ±10%.

$$\text{Effort} = \text{Size/Productivity}$$
$$\text{Productivity} = \text{F (technology, feature complexity)}$$

11.1.1 Available Hours in a Week and Task Hours

Usually people work 40 hours per week. However, are these people 100% productive during the 40 hours? Think about it. Project meetings, organizational activities, e-mails, training, etc., are nonengineering activities that an employee performs in the organization. Planning for all the 40 hours will do no good. The engineer will end up spending 60+ hours to meet the deliverables planned for 40 hours. So, to be realistic, do the exercise of identifying nonengineering activities and planning hours for the same. I have seen around 27–30 available task hours for an engineer and around 15–20 for a lead.

TSP launch meeting 4 ensures that the team estimates everything—requirements for documenting pages, designing classes size, program LOC, test cases, etc. The team looks at historical data for size information and estimation accuracy for similar technology/feature. After size estimation is done, productivity data is looked into for considering technology and complexity. The team then looks at its availability (vacation, holidays, trainings, other projects, etc.) and updates the schedule sheet. Then the overall plan is generated, which gives a good overview of how many task hours are needed to complete the project. It ensures that the team has adequate resources and will be able to commit to a date and meet the project delivery date.

This meeting was the one we used to take more than 10 hours to complete. When we analyzed this, we found that we are not doing a good job with the meeting's conceptual design. We started improving that, and with some practice, we were able to complete the meeting consistently in less than 4 hours.

11.2 Work Breakdown Structure (WBS)

Discussion leader: Design Manager
Duration: 30 minutes
The first step in task planning is to assess the completeness and correctness of the available requirements documentation. The team might observe that the requirements are not enough to start the work and that significant amount of effort is needed to get them in usable state. The team brainstorms up front to find out the amount of work to be done initially. This should be done before top-down planning starts so that they get enough time and can make the necessary adjustments.

The design manager leads the team to create the WBS from the conceptual design. It is done in such a way that the modules are small enough to be given to a single team member and, at the same time, not too small to have thousands of items in the list. The interdependencies of the modules are given adequate attention, and effort is spent on grouping likewise items together and building them in a hierarchy. The team works together to create WBS—discussion and participation from each individual is encouraged. WBS can be recorded in any excel file to make it easier to use and share across the team. This is the top-down plan for the team, and the team takes this further for the task-planning process.

11.3 Size Estimation for All Parts of the Final Product

Discussion leader: Design Manager
Duration: 30 minutes
The design manager leads the team in reviewing the conceptual design and coming up with size estimates for each of the major products and parts to be produced for the project. During this meeting, ensure that all team members get a chance to participate in the renew, and give them the option to speak or ask questions.

The team uses the list of products created in meeting 3 to start making size estimates. Usually, I have seen teams doing a good job in providing adequate details in the conceptual design; this would make the size estimation process fairly simple and straightforward.

11.3.1 Team Estimation

There are several estimation techniques available for use. Each has its own benefits and limitations; there is no silver bullet or one right estimation method. Based on experience, project complexity, etc., the team can prefer one method over another. I looked at multiple estimation techniques and created a custom estimation technique, based on parameters such as historical data, individual experience, and consensus. We have used this technique in several projects to estimate size, effort, and many kinds of tasks and observed that our actual task performance is pretty close to the estimates (−10% to +20% variation).

The main benefit of this estimation methodology is that it takes into consideration views of multiple individuals, and team members get to ask questions and express their perspective which help in getting many of the assumptions clarified. The chances of estimation getting wrong are pretty low because this is not about a single person's opinion.

Here are the steps involved in this estimation process.

1. **Team selection**. The team leader selects 3–5 team members and a moderator, and gives them a set of WBS tasks to estimate. The purpose of selecting few team members is to ensure that the work is divided equally. In small projects, you may have all the team members estimating for the full projects. It is necessary that the person assigned to the task be part of the estimation team. If there is nobody available to take on the moderator role, the TSP coach can act as the moderator. The estimation team needs to have the right set of people based on the different groups, experience, exposure, ability, and skills. If the project size is small, the team may decide to work on the estimation of multiple tasks together.

2. **Kickoff meeting**. The moderator leads the discussion and helps the team understand the overall estimation processes, ground rules, timeline, and expectations. The team then works together to brainstorm assumptions, estimation issues, risks, high-level requirements, review WBS, and decide on the units of estimation. WBS is updated if required. Every member of the estimation team is given an estimation form that has a list of tasks from WBS. The moderator discusses with the team the timeline for submitting their estimates to him or her and the date and time for the next meeting. This meeting is the important starting point for all future iterations of the estimation process.

3. **Individual estimation**. After the estimation kickoff meeting, each member of the estimation team creates his or her initial size estimate for each task from the WBS list. Members use their experience or engineering judgment to come up with estimates. Remember that it should still be an estimate, not guesstimate. We should make sure that the estimates are not discussed among team members during this time. If they are, there is a risk of people becoming biased and getting tempted to change their estimates. Also, while estimating, they can uncover any missing assumptions and suggest and document changes to WBS. At the end of this activity, the team members submit their estimations anonymously to the moderator.

4. **Estimation consolidation**. The moderator leads the team with a series of iterative steps to consolidate the estimates and gain consensus between team members. The estimations are listed against the WBS task item in the tabular format in an Excel file or on the white board. All the estimators see the range of the estimates for each of the tasks and check if the range span is within 25% of the average (reasonable consensus).

For example,

- Four people's estimates—200, 230, 250, 200.
- The range is 200–250.
- Range span is 50 (250–200).
- Average is 220.
- 25% of average is 55.
- Is the range span less than 25% of the average—Yes.
- So, the team can take the estimate for the task as 220 and move on to review the estimates for other tasks.

5. **Wide range of estimation**. If the estimates' range is wide and the range span is not within 25% of the average, the moderator asks the team members to talk about the assumptions and issues related to the task. The discussion happens without actually revealing specific numbers. The focus is on the task on hand and ensuring that everybody understands the complexity of the task and work involved. If you see any serious disagreement on any estimate, ensure that the team takes the time to discuss that in detail, and try to build a common understanding of the work involved and related issues.

During this discussion, it is required that nobody talk about the actual estimation—people should not challenge or find fault with the estimates. As long as the discussion is about the task, it is productive and moving in the right direction.

6. **Estimation iteration**. After the discussion, team members are asked to go back and redo their estimates. Some people might increase their estimates, and others might reduce them. Again, the same process is followed as mentioned in the earlier step "Individual Estimation." The iteration cycle is continued until nobody wants to change his or her estimates or three cycles have been completed.

I have observed that, within two iteration cycles, a reasonable consensus is reached among the team members, although it is not uncommon to have situations where a reasonable consensus cannot be reached.

7. **Resolving the estimation issue**. There have been three situations where, even after three cycles, the estimation range was very wide, and the team could not reach a consensus. In the beginning we used the team leader as a tiebreaker, but, over time, we found that it may not be the right approach. We often observed that the team leader, to be on the safer side, usually chooses the highest estimation. We wanted to come up with a better way to handle these situations, a more scientific and realistic way to get the correct estimation.

We developed a process that approaches such a variance situation in a slightly different way, enabling it to move ahead.

The estimation resolution approach works as follows:

a. Ask the person who has made the highest estimate to explain his or her assumptions behind that particular task.

b. Ask the person who has made the lowest estimate to explain his or her assumptions behind that particular task.

c. Encourage the team to have a discussion around those and ask the team members to comment or challenge the assumptions.

d. After the discussion, encourage the team members to revisit their estimates and make any changes one last time.

e. If, after the changes, reasonable consensus can be reached on the estimates, take the average and move on.

f. If a reasonable consensus cannot be reached, remove the outlier estimate (either the highest or the lowest) and see if a reasonable consensus is reached.

g. If, even after removing the outlier, a reasonable consensus is not possible, ask the person who will work on the task to select one he or she is most comfortable with and go ahead with that estimate.

These steps may have to be gone through to ensure that all the tasks have completed their estimation activities.

8. **Estimation completion**. At the end of the meeting, the planning manager collects the estimates from all the team members and compiles the final task WBS list, estimates, and assumptions. The team leader reviews the final list of WBS and estimates with the team members. After this point, the final WBS list and estimates are ready to be used by the team members as the basis for planning the software project.

There is another approach that can be used for estimation, which is a slight variation of this technique, that is, to use range instead of the actual lines of code. This technique groups the size into ranges "small," "very small," "medium," "large," and "very large." The process is similar to using code, but instead of estimating the size in numbers, it is estimated in range. There is an up-front investment in effort to get the data and create a table. This table can then be updated after each project is completed. When doing an estimation for any future project, this table would be very helpful.

11.3.2 Updating SUMS in TSP Workbook

Discussion leader: Planning Manager
Duration: 30 minutes
The planning manager opens the TSP workbook and records WBS and the size of each part in the TSP SUMS worksheet. From now on we will refer to WBS items in SUMS as components.

Using TSP Workbook (TSP Tool)—**Update SUMS with WBS**

Purpose: Extend the SUMS sheet from meeting 3, add WBS items in SUMS sheet in meeting 4

Person: Planning Manager

Worksheet Name: **SUMS**

How: Look at WBS and enter each item in the SUMS sheet. The top-level hierarchy in SUMS that was created in meeting 3 will remain as it is. This is the master sheet and will be used by all the automatic calculations in the TSP workbook.

Location	Details
ID	Auto-generated as soon as you start entering data

Assembly, Subassembly, or Part Name	Each item from WBS is considered as subassembly and should be entered one on each line. Select the appropriate subassembly as parent. All the items from WBS will be part of the subassemblies created in meeting 3. Avoid creating very deep tree. Try and keep the list of assemblies and subassemblies to less than 50. This helps us to organize the product assemblies in manageable chunks and also for data rollups, tracking, and reporting. While writing the names of the list item, consider including the requirements number or design number. This will help in requirements tracing and at any moment of time in the project. This also helps us to get a quick summary of whether all the requirements are taken care of in development. For example, use (R ##), where "R" denotes requirement, and ## is used for the requirements number. For the testing phase, you can use "use case-" or "scenarios"-based assembly, and then track it accordingly. For example, Development
	 • Front end
	   • (R1) Login page
	   • (R3) Main page
	   • (R6) Settings
	 • Back end
	   • (R4) Database
	   • (R12) Queries
	 • Testing
	   • User account
	   • (U1) New account

Assembly or part	Enter "A" if it is assembly or subassembly. For Parts, enter "P" (not used) For the majority of the time you should use subassemblies for any product components. In this book we will use subassemblies as the components (unless specified otherwise).

(Continued)

(Continued)

Location	Details
Parent assembly name	Enter the name of the parent assembly or subassembly. In this case, the majority of them will be the subassemblies that were created in meeting 3. Try using existing assemblies and subassemblies instead of creating more subassemblies. For example, • Front end • Back end
Owner	Enter the alias of the team member who will work on this assembly. He or she should be the only person working. If you have more than one working on the assembly, consider dividing the subassembly or parts into multiple items to ensure that it can be assigned to a single individual. If it is not possible to divide the assembly, enter the initials of the person who will be doing the majority of the work. The name of the owner needs to be in initials as mentioned in the "Team" worksheet. If you are not sure about the name of the person, keep it blank and update it later. It is very important to have this done correctly. During consolidation, the data is taken from the owner's worksheet (as listed in the master worksheet), for example, MJ.
Size measure	Select the size measure for your subassemblies. Here is the list of size measures available in the tool. • **REQ Pages** (used typically for requirements documents and high-level specifications) • **HLD Pages** (used primarily for architecture or high-level system design documents) • **DLD Pages** (used for Detail-Level Design, technical spec, pseudo-code, algorithms, database design, model, etc.) • **LOC** (Lines of Code—used for coding tasks, database-stored procedures, queries, etc. • **Text Pages** (used for documentation, user guide, help, test plan, test cases, test execution, or any other task that cannot be covered by any other size measure) The size measure for all the subassemblies within the tree need to be the same as that of the top-level assembly. If you want to have few components that are of different size, you will need to move to a different parent assembly or create a new parent assembly to handle that particular size measure, for example, LOC.
Planned size (Base)	The base should only be used for existing programs that are leveraged for this project and developed outside it. If the program or document is developed in this project, do not include it in the base. Enter the size of the existing (base) program or documents used in the project to enhance or make changes to it. If you leverage any program as it is without making any change, use the "reuse" column, for example, 300 LOC base program size.

Location	Details
Planned size (Deleted)	Enter the size (LOC or Pages) that you are planning to delete from the existing (base) programs or documents. This is used in conjunction with the base size measure. You cannot have something "deleted" without having any base size. The number in the deleted column should always be less than base size, for example, 100 LOC deleted.
Planned size (Modified)	Enter the size (LOC or Pages) that you are planning to modify or change from the existing (base) program or documents. This is used in conjunction with the base size measure. You cannot have "modified" without having any base size. The number in the modified column should be less than the Base—deleted, for example, 500 LOC modified.
Planned size (Added)	Enter the size (LOC or Pages) that you are planning to add. This column is used for both enhancement and new development. Any new LOC or pages that are added need to be entered here for the subassembly, for example, 1000 LOC added.
Planned size (Reused)	If you are planning to use any code, programs, or documents as they are without modifying or deleting anything from them, enter that size (LOC or pages) here. As the team matures with the Personal Software Process[SM] (PSP[SM]) and TSP processes, this number should increase. People should start focusing on reusing more percentage of software from previous release. The major benefit of reusing software is savings in development and testing time, and it prevents much of defects in the product, for example, 200 LOC reused.
Planned size (New and Changed)	This is an autocomputed column. As you enter the size data in the other columns, this column gets updated. This data is mostly used for further calculations in TSP. Please note that this column will only calculate new and changed size, and is computed as follows: Size (New and Changed) = Added + Modified 200 LOC new and changed
Planned size (Total)	This is an autocomputed column. As you enter size data in the other columns, this column gets updated. It gives the final size total of the assembly or subassembly, that is, the ultimate size measure of the final product. This column is computed as follows: Size (total) = base – deleted + added + reused 500 LOC total

Notes:

a. As you enter the size data in the TSP sheet, the sizes gets rolled up to their respective assemblies in the SUMS.

(Continued)

(Continued)

b. Do not modify size data of a nonleaf assembly or nonleaf subassembly.

c. When the team members work on the project, they will update the respective "actual size" portion of the spreadsheet, and the data gets rolled up appropriately for the parent assembly, and people can compare their plan versus actual data.

d. This worksheet is based on several macros—Do not use COPY/CUT/PASTE/DELETE/INSERT. If you need to add an assembly/subassembly in between, right-click on the cell and click on "Insert Part." Similarly use "Delete Part."

e. There is data validation built into the tool. So, if you try to move away from any cell without entering data, you will get errors. If you get errors, just specify something in the cell, to be modified later.

f. Sometimes it may appear impossible to get rid of errors, in which case try deleting the whole line using Delete Part.

g. Navigation between the cells can be made simple by using TAB instead of ENTER.

h. Be sure to save the TSP workbook and take a backup copy frequently (every 30 minutes).

i. Example of SUMS with details of WBS and size information entered (Figure 11.1):

TSP Size Summary - Form SUMS

Name Team
Team Dev Team
Date 1/6/2008

Cycle

Planned Size

ID	Assembly, Sub-Assembly, or Part Name	(A)ssembly or (P)art	Parent Assembly Name	Owner	Size Measure	Base	Deleted	Modified	Added	Reused	New and Changed	Total
1	Req	A	SYSTEM	SP	Req Pages	0	0	0	80	0	80	80
2	HLD	A	SYSTEM	SP	HLD Pages	0	0	0	52	0	52	52
3	DLD	A	SYSTEM	SP	DLD Lines	0	0	0	0	0	0	0
4	Text	A	SYSTEM	SP	Text Pages	0	0	0	213	0	213	213
5	Code	A	SYSTEM	SP	LOC	0	0	0	3262	0	3262	3262
6	FS v3.1	A	Req	SP	Req Pages	0	0	0	80	0	80	80
7	TS v3.1 developed	A	HLD	JS	HLD Pages	0	0	0	20	0	20	20
8	TS v3.1 to be developed	A	HLD	ER	HLD Pages	0	0	0	32	0	32	32
9	v3.1 Drop1	A	Code	SP	LOC	0	0	0	1724	0	1724	1724
10	v3.1 Drop2	A	Code	SP	LOC	0	0	0	83	0	83	83
11	v3.1 Drop3	A	Code	SP	LOC	0	0	0	1455	0	1455	1455
12	SAN Summary	A	v3.1 Drop1	JS	LOC	0	0	0	527	0	527	527
13	SAN Details	A	v3.1 Drop1	NB	LOC	0	0	0	595	0	595	595
14	SAN Export	A	v3.1 Drop1	DG	LOC	0	0	0	282	0	282	282
15	MSApps CR	A	v3.1 Drop1	NB	LOC	0	0	0	120	0	120	120
16	VS (SMS) Batch Job	A	v3.1 Drop1	DG	LOC	0	0	0	200	0	200	200
17	SAN Assoc	A	v3.1 Drop2	JS	LOC	0	0	0	63	0	63	63
18	SAN Report	A	v3.1 Drop2	DG	LOC	0	0	0	10	0	10	10
19	MSApps CR Report	A	v3.1 Drop2	NB	LOC	0	0	0	10	0	10	10
20	Bug Fix for PS ID 1494	A	v3.1 Drop3	JS	LOC	0	0	0	40	0	40	40
21	VS (Non-SMS) - Server + Alia	A	v3.1 Drop3	JS	LOC	0	0	0	645	0	645	645
22	VS (Non-SMS) - Server Statu:	A	v3.1 Drop3	NB	LOC	0	0	0	570	0	570	570
23	VS Admin page change	A	v3.1 Drop3	ER	LOC	0	0	0	200	0	200	200
24	MTP v3.1	A	Text	SC	Text Pages	0	0	0	45	0	45	45
25	Test Cases v3.1 Drop1	A	Text	SC	Text Pages	0	0	0	70	0	70	70
26	Test Cases v3.1 Drop2	A	Text	SC	Text Pages	0	0	0	65	0	65	65
27	Test Cases v3.1 Drop3	A	Text	SC	Text Pages	0	0	0	17	0	17	17
28	Ops Guide v3.1	A	Text	NB	Text Pages	0	0	0	5	0	5	5
29	Release Notes v3.1 Drop1	A	Text	ER	Text Pages	0	0	0	5	0	5	5
30	Release Notes v3.1 Drop2	A	Text	ER	Text Pages	0	0	0	2	0	2	2
31	Release Notes v3.1 Drop3	A	Text	ER	Text Pages	0	0	0	2	0	2	2
32	Release Notes v3.1 Drop4	A	Text	ER	Text Pages	0	0	0	2	0	2	2

Figure 11.1   SUMS worksheet with WBS and size data.

ID	Assembly, subassembly, or part name	(A)ssembly or (P)art	Parent assembly name	Owner	Size measure	Planned Size						
						Base	Deleted	Modified	Added	Reused	New and changed	Total
1	Requirements	A	SYSTEM	MJ	REQ pages							
2	Architecture	A	SYSTEM	RJ	HLD pages							
3	Development	A	SYSTEM	VD	LOC							
4	Testing	A	SYSTEM	SJ	Text pages							
5	Documentation	A	SYSTEM	MJ	Text pages							
6	Main Req Doc	A	Requirements	MJ	REQ pages				15			
7	HLD Front end	A	Architecture	RJ	HLD pages							
8	HLD Back end	A	Architecture	RJ	HLD pages							
9	Front end code	A	Development	VD	LOC				300			
10	Back end code	A	Development	VD	LOC				250			
11	Administration	A	Development	VD	LOC				200			
12	Backup/recovery	A	Development	VD	LOC				400			
13	User account	A	Testing	SJ	Text pages				40			
14	Transactions	A	Testing	SJ	Text pages				70			
15	User manual	A	Documentation	MJ	Text pages				60			
16	Online help	A	Documentation	MJ	Text pages				100			
17	(R 1) Login page	A	Front-end Code	VD	LOC				400			
18	(R 4) Main page	A	Front-end Code	VD	LOC				300			
19	(R 7) Run report	A	Back-end Code	VD	LOC				700			
20	(R 9) Send e-mail	A	Back-end Code	VD	LOC				300			

Example of a SUMS with sample assemblies and subasssemblies

11.4 Determine Overall Project Resources Requirements

Discussion leader: Planning Manager
Duration: 10 minutes

After the size is determined, the next step is to understand the product and product characteristics and prepare a very high-level schedule and resource estimate for the project. Usually, the resources of the project are predetermined, and the schedule is given as one of the goals. During the TSP launch, at the beginning of meeting 4, the team can determine how many hours the project is going to need and, based on the resources available, when the team can deliver the project.

The entire team is required to work together to create the overall estimate for the full project, that is, plan for next 3 months and decide on the resource allocation accordingly. Engineers can use the overall plan as a reference guide and fine tune their personal plan in meeting 6.

The productivity rate is calculated from the number of lines of code that can be developed in 1 hour's time. While calculating this, all the phases need to be considered end to end—from design to unit test. The phases are

- Detailed design
- DLD review
- Unit test cases and review
- DLD inspection
- Code
- Code review
- Compile
- Code inspection
- Unit test
- Code fixes between phases, including design and unit testing phase

In other words, how many lines of quality code can be written in 1 hour (from design phase till it is handed off to integration testing)?

Historical data is referred to for the productivity rate (LOC/hour or Pages/hour) for the team and for each individual. Often, productivity rates vary across project, programming language, platform, technology, individual experience, etc. For the top-down project plan, you can choose to take the productivity rate from a similar project and use that to get an overall estimate, and then, in meeting 6, each individual can choose his or her own historical productivity data for planning. In case the historical productivity data is not available, the team should consider using data from some other project. If that information is not available or not useful, the team can go ahead with an engineering judgment.

Once the productivity rate is determined, you can get the overall hours required to get the project work done, and based on that and the resources available for the project, you can determine a high-level schedule for the project.

Task Hours needed for project = LOC/Productivity
Weeks = Task hours needed for project/(average task hours per week per person
    * # of people)

For example, if the LOC is 4000, and productivity is around 5 LOC/hour,

Task hours needed for project = 4000/5
800 task hours needed for project
If there are 8 people on the team with average 15 task hours per week,
Weeks = 800/(15 * 8) = 6.66 weeks needed

After this step is done, the team will have a rough estimate of the schedule weeks. Typically add another 20% to the schedule (this is required to take care of the variation in productivity, dependency, etc.). After this is done, you have the correct information about the approximate schedule. This information is very much needed to see if the team is deviating with a high margin from the management goal or are on track. It also helps the team to come up with alternative options for scope, resources, schedule, etc.

It is recommended that the team leader should talk to management about the approximate schedule and explore with them options about alternatives. This will help the team in making course correction for the project plan.

11.5   Create List of Tasks

Discussion leader: Team Leader
Duration: 90 minutes for first-time TSP teams, and 60 minutes for experienced teams
Ensure that the SUMS is final before you jump on to create the task lists. If you happen to miss any item in SUMS or need to change anything, you will have to create the tasks manually.

The team manager, along with the planning and process manager, leads the team in creating the detailed task lists and plan. The team needs to cover all the phases required to get the task done in adequate detail. The task list creation activity involves estimating time for each phase of all the items from the top-down list of product elements (components). The focus is to create the detailed plan for about 3 months. If the project duration is expected to be around 4 months, then you should consider creating the detailed plan for the full duration. If the project duration is more than that, you can choose to have the detailed plan for half of the duration and have a high-level plan for the rest. The detailed plan for the rest of the duration can be completed and adjusted in another TSP planning meeting (relaunch) just before the detailed plan is completed.

11.5.1 Development Phase Percentage Time Allocation

The team should use the development strategy and processes as discussed and decided in meeting 3 for creating the tasks for every top-down list items listed in SUMS. The first step is finalizing the sequence of the phase and percentage allocation of the time for each of the development phases. Typical phases are high-level design, detailed design, and coding. Other phases and steps needed are review, inspection, compile, and testing. All these phases are required to ensure that adequate time is allocated to each of them to make a quality plan. It is important to have this aspect thoroughly reviewed before continuing the task planning activities. Once the team decides and moves ahead it will be very difficult and time consuming to have it retrofixed.

The time it takes to create the task list is highly dependent on the number of components in SUMS. In the beginning, for our first few projects, we had close to 150 components in SUMS, and we had to spend nearly 12 hours to get the task list completed. Then we decided to keep the list small and manageable, and at the same time, detailed enough to keep it realistic.

During our initial TSP projects, we rushed through the development phase and moved to the next one, consequently, we had to spend significant effort to fix it later. Over several TSP projects, we collected data, analyzed it, and learned what percentage allocation was just about right depending on the types of projects. Project teams used this information as a guidance to planning their task time.

The following is the summary of the development phase sequence and recommended percentage allocation of time/effort across the different phases for each of the product elements.

Phase	%
Detailed design	20
DLD review	10
Unit test cases and review	3
DLD inspection	10
Code	20
Code review	10
Compile	2
Code inspection	10
Unit test	15

For complex projects in which more time and effort are required for research and analysis, we increase the time allocated to the design phase and adjust the other phases accordingly. Again, these are general guidelines and reference tables; teams and individuals should use their own historical data for coming up with the percentage time allocated for each phase.

There are a few things that people need to take care of while allocating percentages to the phases. To perform quality assurance and control activities, there need to be adequate focus and time allocation. Here are some guidelines:

1. Allocate at least the same amount of time for the design task as planned for the coding task.
2. Design review should be allocated at least 50% of the time that is allocated to design.
3. Design inspection time should be the same as design review time.
4. Code review should be allocated at least 50% of the time allocated to coding.
5. Code inspection time should be identical to code review time.

These guidelines should be taken into account while allocating appropriate percentages.

11.5.2 Generate Task List

Once the development phase structure and time allocation have been decided, the team starts working on generating the task list based on them. Ensure that your SUMS has all the components needed for the project. Once you create the task list and edit it, it will not be possible to generate another task list and preserve the previous one; then it will have to be done manually.

The details of generating the task list are as follows:

Using TSP Workbook (TSP Tool)—**Generate Tasks**

Purpose: From the list of components in SUMS use **generate task list** in meeting 4 to automatically generate tasks for each component for each phase.

Person: Planning Manager

Worksheet Name: **TASK**

How: Go to the "Task" worksheet and click on the GENERATE TASK LIST button (Figure 11.2).

You will get a dialog box saying "Generating a task list will delete existing tasks."

*   If you are doing this for the first time and do not have any tasks listed on the "Tasks" worksheet, or you already have some tasks but don't care if they gets deleted, go ahead and click OK (Figure 11.3).
*   If you have any tasks that you *need* in the Task list, press CANCEL, and you should never use the GENERATE TASK LIST button again.

Once you press OK, this will create several tasks—a task for each of the components and each of the development phases. So, if you have 40 components and 11 development phases, you will have 440 tasks.

Notes:
*   The current version of the TSP tool only creates tasks for assemblies/subassemblies from SUMS that have LOC as their size measure.

(Continued)

(Continued)

- The phase it generates may not be exactly the same as what you have determined in the earlier step, but once all these tasks are generated, you can modify the phases.
- Details about all the phases that are included in autogenerated task lists are given in the worksheet named "phases."
- Ensure that the macros are enabled.
- If you are not able to click on the GENERATE TASK LIST button, you might be using a reused TSP workbook. Try using a new TSP workbook.
- If you need to manually create tasks, please refer to the table later in this section.

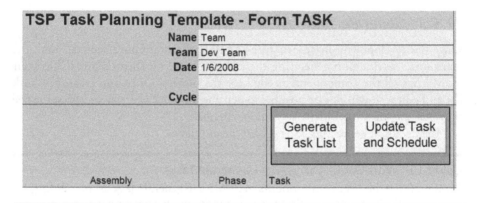

Figure 11.2   Generate Task List button on the "Task" worksheet.

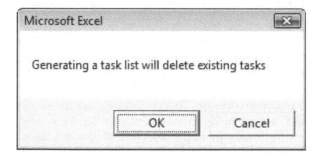

Figure 11.3   Generate task list confirmation dialog box.

Here are the tasks that are generated for the project:

Phase	Task Name
MGMT	SYSTEM Management and Miscellaneous
STRAT	SYSTEM Launch and Strategy
PLAN	SYSTEM Planning
REQ	SYSTEM Requirements
STP	SYSTEM System Test Plan
REQINSP	SYSTEM REQ Inspection
HLD	SYSTEM High-Level Design
ITP	SYSTEM Integration Test Plan
HLDINSP	SYSTEM HLD Inspection
<Phases for each components>	<Tasks for each components per phase>
...	...
IT	SYSTEM Build and Integration Test
ST	SYSTEM System Test
DOC	SYSTEM Documentation
PM	SYSTEM Postmortem

Here are the tasks that are generated for each of the components with the standard (default) TSP phases (Figure 11.4):

Phase	Task Name
DLD	<Component Name> Detailed Design
DLDR	<Component Name> DLD Review
TD	<Component Name> Test Development
DLDINSP	<Component Name> DLD Inspection
CODE	<Component Name> Code
CR	<Component Name> Code Review
COMPILE	<Component Name> Compile
CODEINSP	<Component Name> Code Inspection
UT	<Component Name> Unit Test

If you need to create the tasks manually (either if you add any new assembly in SUMS after the task list generated or you need to add any additional phase for all the existing components), you can follow these steps to generate tasks at any moment of time in the project planning phase.

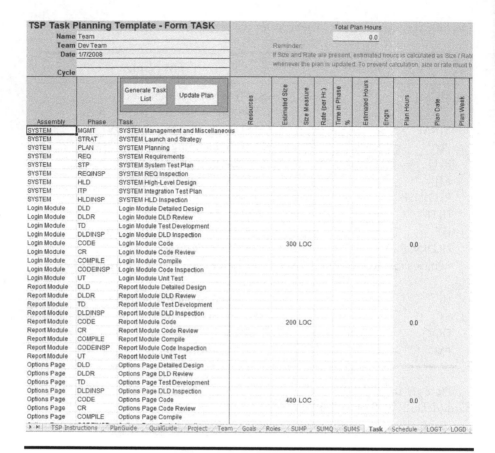

Figure 11.4   Generated task list.

Here are the details around generating the task list manually:

Using TSP Workbook (TSP Tool)—**Add Task**

Purpose: Manually adding tasks in the "Task" sheet (Figure 11.5).

Person: Planning Manager

Worksheet Name: TASK

How: Go to the "Task" worksheet and click on the empty row at the end. If you want to enter any task in between, right-click on any task and insert a blank row. Go through the following steps to enter task information:

Step 1: Right-click on the assembly column and select the assembly/subassembly that you want to create the new task for. (The task can only be created for leaf-assemblies.)

Step 2: Right-click on the phase column and select the phase for this task. (If you are creating a development task, you might want to follow all the development phases as outlined earlier in this section.)

Step 3: Press TAB and you should see that the task name is automatically created based on the assembly name and the phase. You can modify the task name if you want, or keep it as it is.

Step 4: Enter size estimate for this task (it is a numeric field if it is a development-related task (design, code, compile, review, inspect, etc.).

Step 5: Enter size measure for this task (e.g., LOC, Req Pages, HLD Pages, etc.).

Step 6: Repeat steps 1–5 for all the new tasks that are required to be added.

Step 7: Once you have done with adding all the tasks, click on UPDATE PLAN button on the "Task" sheet. This will update all the worksheets with the new information.

Step 8: After you are done with this, refer to the next section on how to update the task list with additional information.

Note:

- Do not do CUT/PASTE in cells. If you want to move any tasks around, select those tasks, click COPY, paste at the target location, come back to the original tasks, and then select them and delete rows.

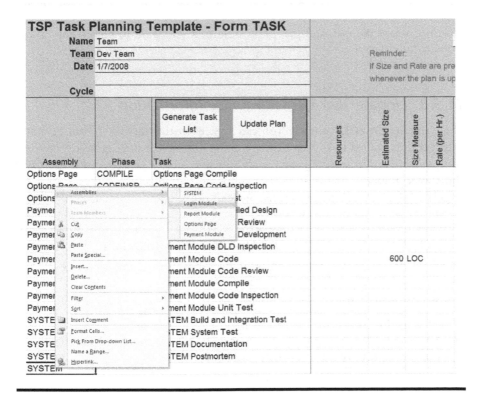

Figure 11.5 Adding a new task on the task list.

Similarly, there might be a need to manually delete some tasks (if you delete any SUMS entries OR you need to remove any phase for the tasks that are created, etc.), you can follow these steps to delete any existing tasks at any moment of time in the project planning phase.

Here are the details about deleting the unwanted tasks manually:

Using TSP Workbook (TSP Tool)—**Delete Task**

Purpose: Manually deleting tasks from the task sheet.

Person: Planning Manager

***Worksheet Name:* TASK**

How: Go to the "Task" worksheet and follow the steps:

Step 1: Right-click on the task and click DELETE …

Step 2: When prompted with a "delete" dialog box, select "Entire row."

Step 3: Repeat steps 1 and 2 for all the tasks that are required to be deleted.

Step 4: Once you have done with deleting the tasks, click on UPDATE PLAN button on the "Task" sheet.

Note:

• Do not select the task and just press delete. If you want to delete any tasks, delete full rows.

11.5.3 *Update Task List with Phase Information*

Once you get the task list ready, you can now enter the missing information and then get the detailed tasks list. This is a manual, time-consuming task. However, you probably do not need all the people in the room for getting this done. Over time, we learned this and wrote a few macros to accomplish the task.

Here is how to update the task list with all the relevant information:

Using TSP Workbook (TSP Tool)—**Update Tasks with Details**

Purpose: Update the task list with information such as resources, size, size measure, rate (per hour), time in phase %, etc.

Person: Planning Manager

***Worksheet Name:* Task**

How: After you have created tasks, Go to the "Task" worksheet and start typing information in the columns as follows.

Location	Details	Example
Task	If you want to add additional information to the task name, you can modify it. Also, if you are planning to break a task into multiple tasks (same component, same phase), you can enter a row with the same assembly name and same phase and make a change in the task name by adding part A, part B, or any other distinction.	
Resources	Right-click on the cell and select the team member from the list who will be working on this particular task. Typically, for all the tasks (except inspection), there should be only one person in the resource column. Inspection task will always have multiple people working on the same task. For tasks that have multiple people, the first resource name in the cell should be that of the main person, followed by other resource names/initials. (E.g., the first person is the author, and subsequent person is the one who will be doing the inspection.) Try to keep the same resource for each phase of the component. While doing these allocations, all the team members need to be involved, and preference should be given to those who have relevant experience, expertise, and interest. While allocating resources for the components and inspection tasks, make sure that they are not overallocated.	
Estimated size	The autogenerated task list will populate the estimated size for the CODE phase. For all practical purposes, this size estimate can be used to compute the time requirements for other phases. So, go ahead and enter the size information for all the phases (use the estimated size value for the component, and use that for the phases). Even for design, review, inspection, compile, and test development, and unit testing tasks, you should use the same estimated size and size measure. As a rule of thumb, the effort to develop design is roughly proportional to the coding effort, and similarly, the effort required for review, inspection, and testing will be roughly proportional to the coding effort, and so on. Keeping the estimated size and size measure the same for all the phases helps in applying the same productivity numbers across the component, and the effort gets distributed to each phase based on the percentage time allocation to the phases. For tasks that are nondevelopmental (e.g., requirements gathering, system test plan, etc.), go ahead and enter the size data based on the component (usually the size data is entered in SUMS, but the autogenerated task list will not copy over the size information).	

(Continued)

(Continued)

Location	Details	Example
Rate (per hour)	Enter the productivity numbers here. As mentioned earlier, in meeting 4, you can use the team's average productivity numbers here and in the individual planning, the engineers can modify it. How many lines of quality code can be written in 1 hour (from the design phase until it is handed off to integration testing)? This includes all the phases such as design, design review, test development, design inspection, code, code review, compile, code inspection, and unit testing. When entering this data, enter it for each task for the same component. You can enter it once and then Copy/Paste in all the cells. The next column (Time in phase %) will take care of effort/time allocation across the phases. For other phases (requirements, test planning, testing, etc.) use other appropriate productivity numbers, for example, Requirements Pages/Hour, Test Plan (text pages)/Hour, Test Cases (Text pages)/Hour.	
Time in phase %	This is the place where you can allocate the percentage of time for each of the phases. As recommended earlier in the section, you can use the same percentage allocation for all the development components. If there are different types of components, you can have a different percentage allocation for the phases. *Note:* While entering this data, DO NOT USE % size. If you want to enter 10% type 10. <table><tr><td>*Phase*</td><td>%</td></tr><tr><td>Detailed Design</td><td>20</td></tr><tr><td>DLD Review</td><td>10</td></tr><tr><td>Unit Test cases and review</td><td>3</td></tr><tr><td>DLD Inspection</td><td>10</td></tr><tr><td>Code</td><td>20</td></tr><tr><td>Code Review</td><td>10</td></tr><tr><td>Compile</td><td>2</td></tr><tr><td>Code Inspection</td><td>10</td></tr><tr><td>Unit Test</td><td>15</td></tr></table> You can do Copy/Paste here. Select all the "% time in phase" for a particular component and then Copy/Paste wherever you need it. If this cell is left blank, the TSP tool will assume 100% time allocation.	

Estimated hours	Based on the data you entered in earlier steps, this column will have autocalculated data around number of hours needed to complete each of the tasks (though manual entry is allowed). *Note:* If you do not see any data in "estimated hours," it might be due to Copy/Paste. You might have to edit each cell (any column, rate per hour, time in phase or size measure) and press Enter (e.g., you can also use the function key F2 and press <Enter>). This will run the macros and update one row at a time. To update all the rows, go to TSP Tool Menu option and click on Update (as shown in Figure 11.6). This will update all the calculations for the project. The formula used for calculating estimated hours is as follows: Hours = (estimated size/rate) * (time in phase/100) There might be some tasks for which you may want to directly enter the number of hours (this is strictly not recommended). Tasks in the areas of launch, planning, management, etc., are the ones that may not have the size estimate.
Engineers	Enter the number of engineers who are going to work on the particular task. If there is only one engineer working on the task (e.g., code, code review, compile, UT, etc.), type 1 here. If there is more than 1 person working on a task (e.g., inspection tasks may involve 2 or more people), that is, (1 author and 1 inspector), you can type 1.5 engineers (inspector will spend 1 engineer worth of time, and author will spend 0.5 for explaining the document and making fixes and changes.
Plan hours	This is an autocalculated field, and data cannot be manually entered or modified. Based on the number of engineer value, the plan hours are calculated to see how many total hours are needed for the particular task. The formula used for calculating this is as follows: Plan hours = (Estimated hours) * (Engrs.)
Plan date	This is an autocalculated field. It contains the date (Monday of the week) when the task is expected to get completed. This will get updated only after resource availability is determined. We will come back to this after resource availability is determined.
Plan week	This is an autocalculated field. It contains the week number (from the start of the project) when the task is expected to get completed. This field will get updated only after resource availability is determined. We will come back to this after resource availability is determined.

Note:

• If there is some data that is supposed to get autoupdated/autocalculated and is not working, most likely you may have macros disabled, or it might be due to Copy/Paste. To fix this, first enable the macros and then go to TSP menu and click Update to redo all the calculation in the spreadsheet (Figure 11.6).

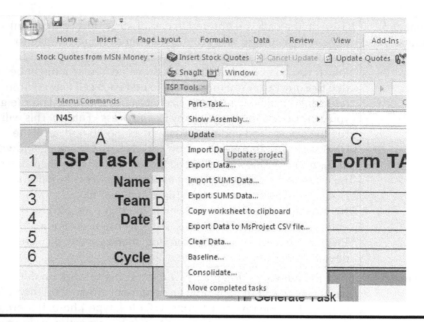

Figure 11.6 Update project from TSP tool menu.

11.5.4 Review the Updated Task List

After you are done with updating the task list, you need to review it to ensure that the task list is accurately created and has the right level of details (Figure 11.7).

- Each of the tasks should be less than 10 hours per team member.
- No task should be less than 0.2 hour (any task less than 10 minutes does not make sense).
- Go through the list and ensure that all the planned activities are recorded in the task sheet.
- If there are more tasks that need to be added, follow the steps as mentioned earlier for adding tasks.
- This is the final chance to see if all the project work is accounted for.
- *Do not* include any meetings/e-mails/training/vacations as tasks (effort and time spent on this would be taken care of when you have determined the task hours for the team).

11.6 Weekly Availability of Team Members

Discussion leader: Planning Manager
Duration: 30 minutes
The planning manager leads the team in determining the weekly available task hours for the team to work on the project. This is often straightforward if the

TSP Task Planning Template - Form TASK											

Name Team
Team Dev Team
Date 1/7/2008

Cycle

Total Plan Hours: 414.4

Reminder:
If Size and Rate are present, estimated hours is calculated whenever the plan is updated. To prevent calculation, size c

Assembly	Phase	Task	Resources	Estimated Size	Size Measure	Rate (per Hr.)	Time in Phase %	Estimated Hours	Engrs	Plan Hours
SYSTEM	MGMT	SYSTEM Management and Miscellaneous	MJ					20.0	1.0	20.0
SYSTEM	STRAT	SYSTEM Launch and Strategy	MJ					32.0	4.0	128.0
SYSTEM	PLAN	SYSTEM Planning	MJ					20.0	1.0	20.0
SYSTEM	REQ	SYSTEM Requirements	MJ	20	Req F	2.0		10.0	1.0	10.0
SYSTEM	STP	SYSTEM System Test Plan	VM	35	Text F	4.0		8.8	1.0	8.8
SYSTEM	REQINSP	SYSTEM REQ Inspection	MJ, SR, VM	20	Req F	4.0		5.0	3.0	15.0
SYSTEM	HLD	SYSTEM High-Level Design	SR	50	HLD F	3.0		16.7	1.0	16.7
SYSTEM	ITP	SYSTEM Integration Test Plan	VM	75	Text F	5.0		15.0	1.0	15.0
SYSTEM	HLDINSP	SYSTEM HLD Inspection	SR, RJ, VM	50	HLD F	6.0		8.3	3.0	25.0
Login Module	DLD	Login Module Detailed Design	RJ	300	LOC	10.0	20.0	6.0	1.0	6.0
Login Module	DLDR	Login Module DLD Review	RJ	300	LOC	10.0	10.0	3.0	1.0	3.0
Login Module	TD	Login Module Test Development	RJ	300	LOC	10.0	3.0	0.9	1.0	0.9
Login Module	DLDINSP	Login Module DLD Inspection	RJ,SR	300	LOC	10.0	10.0	3.0	2.0	6.0
Login Module	CODE	Login Module Code	RJ	300	LOC	10.0	20.0	6.0	1.0	6.0
Login Module	CR	Login Module Code Review	RJ	300	LOC	10.0	10.0	3.0	1.0	3.0
Login Module	COMPILE	Login Module Compile	RJ	300	LOC	10.0	2.0	0.6	1.0	0.6
Login Module	CODEINSP	Login Module Code Inspection	RJ,SR	300	LOC	10.0	10.0	3.0	2.0	6.0
Login Module	UT	Login Module Unit Test	RJ	300	LOC	10.0	15.0	4.5	1.0	4.5
Report Module	DLD	Report Module Detailed Design	RJ	200	LOC	10.0	20.0	4.0	1.0	4.0
Report Module	DLDR	Report Module DLD Review	RJ	200	LOC	10.0	10.0	2.0	1.0	2.0
Report Module	TD	Report Module Test Development	RJ	200	LOC	10.0	3.0	0.6	1.0	0.6
Report Module	DLDINSP	Report Module DLD Inspection	RJ,SR	200	LOC	10.0	10.0	2.0	1.0	2.0
Report Module	CODE	Report Module Code	RJ	200	LOC	10.0	20.0	4.0	1.0	4.0
Report Module	CR	Report Module Code Review	RJ	200	LOC	10.0	10.0	2.0	1.0	2.0
Report Module	COMPILE	Report Module Compile	RJ	200	LOC	10.0	2.0	0.4	1.0	0.4

TSP Instructions PlanGuide QualGuide Project Team Goals Rules SUMP SUMQ SUMS Task Schedule LOGT LOGD Week IRTL IRWe

Figure 11.7   Updated task list.

team members have done some homework (as suggested in the TSP prelaunch activities).

The first step here is to have all the team members estimate for each week how many task hours they will have available for the project. While coming up with this number, they should consider the following:

■ Everyday activities (need to be factored in for task hours)
  – Meetings
  – E-mails
  – Other project assignments
  – Other organizational commitments
■ One-off activities (need to be factored in for those particular weeks)
  – Vacations
  – Holidays
  – Training
  – Organizational events
  – Business travel
  – Ramp-up time

TSP Schedule Planning Template - Form SCHEDULE

Name	Team
Team	Dev Team
Date	12/31/2007

	Total Task Plan Hours	886.4
	Total Schedule Plan Hours	834.0 Warning: add schedule hours
	Difference	52.4

Cycle

Date	Week	Plan Hours	Cumulative Plan Hours	Actual Hours	Cumulative Actual Hours	Planned Value	Cumulative PV	Earned Value	Cumulative EV	Predicted Hours	Cumulative Predicted Hours
12/31/2007	1	90.0									
1/7/2008	2	78.0									
1/14/2008	3	68.0									
1/21/2008	4	72.0									
1/28/2008	5	104.0									
2/4/2008	6	84.0									
2/11/2008	7	116.0									
2/18/2008	8	66.0									
2/25/2008	9	62.0									
3/3/2008	10	94.0									

Figure 11.8   Inadequate task hours.

These need to be estimated for all the project weeks (e.g., if the project duration is expected to be for 4 months, this estimation should be done for 5 months). In case the project is longer than 4 months, and your current detailed plan is only for 3–4 months, then this exercise should be done only for the duration of the detailed plan.

Often I get questioned about what is the right number of task hours everybody should target for? There is no single answer. There are several factors that impact the number of task hours for each individual, and it varies across the type of industry, geographical location, organization culture, team dynamics, experience level, discipline (development, test, etc.), and so on. As a rule of thumb, every team member should target to achieve at least 50% of the total time as task hours (e.g., 20 task hours or more every week).

In the beginning, usually teams are able to achieve only low task hours per week (Figure 11.8). You may want to take that into consideration, and over time they are able to ramp up and achieve more task hours. It is advisable that team members refer to their historical data (wherever available) related to task hours achieved, plan the task hours accordingly, and improvise over time (Figure 11.9).

If the project is for external customers and the management is planning to commit to a date based on the outcome of the TSP Plan, you may want to start with a conservative task hours estimate for each individual and increase that over time. Although it is important to have the project timeline on an aggressive schedule, in the beginning, make sure that it is reasonable, and then collect data and fine tune the plan.

Some of our TSP teams started with 30 task hours; they were not sure what the right number was. So, instead of starting with a conservative estimate, the team

mentation

TSP Schedule Planning Template - Form SCHEDULE

		Name	Team						
		Team	Dev Team			Total Task Plan Hours	886.4		
		Date	12/31/2007			Total Schedule Plan Hours	928.0		
						Difference	-41.6		
		Cycle							

Date	Week	Plan Hours	Cumulative Plan Hours	Actual Hours	Cumulative Actual Hours	Planned Value	Cumulative PV	Earned Value
12/31/2007	1	90.0						
1/7/2008	2	78.0						
1/14/2008	3	68.0						
1/21/2008	4	72.0						
1/28/2008	5	104.0						
2/4/2008	6	84.0						
2/11/2008	7	116.0						
2/18/2008	8	66.0						
2/25/2008	9	62.0						
3/3/2008	10	94.0						
3/10/2008	11	94.0						

Figure 11.9   Adequate task hours.

created a very aggressive plan with 30 task hours for all the engineers on the team. Management had given a schedule goal, and the team thought of meeting that goal by putting in more task hours every week. After 3 weeks, we observed that they were hardly able to average 21.5 task hours per week per engineer. It was the beginning of the project, and the team was already feeling burned out. It was a difficult situation to be in for everybody, and there was a risk of quality problems, along with schedule and team morale.

Management had already committed the delivery date to the external customer. We had a discussion with management and explained the situation. We finally had to add 2 weeks to the schedule and one additional resource to bring the situation back on track.

The lesson learned here that is it is fine to have a reasonable/conservative estimate in the beginning and the team should strive to achieve more. This helps in boosting morale and keeps the project on track and, most importantly, the chances of delivering the project successfully will be very high. If team members are on an aggressive timeline, even if they miss the delivery date by just two days, they may not be considered successful, even though they may have spent several hours working in office.

All the team members need to enter this information in the form.

	Week of	Ria	Raj	Akshay	Minal	Krisha	Aman	Total
Week 1	7-Jan-08	20	0	20	20	12	18	90
Week 2	14-Jan-08	20	0	20	12	18	20	78
Week 3	21-Jan-08	12	8	20	18	20	0	68
Week 4	28-Jan-08	0	12	20	12	12	12	72
Week 5	4-Feb-08	16	18	0	20	0	18	104
Week 6	11-Feb-08	20	12	20	20	20	12	84
Week 7	18-Feb-08	20	0	12	20	12	20	116
Week 8	25-Feb-08	20	18	20	20	20	18	66
Week 9	3-Mar-08	18	12	20	4	0	12	62
Week 10	10-Mar-08	20	12	0	12	0	18	94
Week 11	17-Mar-08	18	4	20	20	12	20	90
Total		164	96	152	158	114	150	834

Once the weekly available hours are estimated, the team can get a good understanding of resource availability for all the team members and move on to the next step of planning.

The planning manager takes this information and enters it in the TSP tool to generate the overall high-level top-down plan.

Here are the detailed steps to enter this information in the TSP tool.

Using TSP Workbook (TSP Tool)—**Update Team Schedule**

Purpose: Update the schedule tab with the team's task hour available for each week.

Person: Planning Manager

Worksheet Name: Schedule

How: After the team determines its weekly availability, the information needs to be entered in the TSP tool. Go to the "Schedule" worksheet and type the team's available hours in the "planned hours" column (Figure 11.10).

Location	Details	Example
Date	This is an autocomputed column that will display the date—the first day of the week. It needs to be read as "week of <date>." You cannot enter/change/delete this directly from the date column. When this starts showing date, check to make sure it is Monday, for example, 12/31/2007.	
Week	This is an autocomputed column that will display the week number—project week. You cannot enter/change or delete this directly from the week column.	

Planned hours	From the table where you captured the weekly team's task hours, get the total hours for each week and then enter it on the planned hours first row. As soon as you enter the hours in the first row, the dates and weeks automatically start appearing. Enter all the data you have about the team's availability for the weeks in this column. After entering the weeks' data, see what is displayed in the center top portion of the worksheet. If you see a red-color text "warning: add schedule hours" (as shown in Figure 11.14), you will have to add more weeks until you see a negative value in difference (as shown in Figure 11.15).
Cumulative planned hours	This is an autogenerated column that gets populated or updated after you update the plan by clicking Update Plan on the task sheet. This column shows total (cumulative) planned hours week over week.
Actual hours	This is an autocomputed column, and it should be kept blank for now. This column gets its values from the LOGT sheet after people start recording their time.
Planned value	This is an autogenerated column that gets populated after clicking Update Plan on the task sheet. This column shows the planned earned value (% work) planned for each week. The total is always 100%.
Cumulative planned value	Once you click on the update plan on the task sheet, this column gets populated. It shows the cumulative earned value (% completion) week after week.

At the end of this, it might appear that the project planning is done and the schedule is finalized; however, it is not. The current schedule and the overall top-down plan is the rough plan and assume that anybody can do anybody's work. It does not take into consideration dependency, the critical path of the project, team member's expertise, unchangeable tasks, etc.

11.7 Generate Overall Team Plan and Review with the Team

Discussion leader: Planning Manager
Duration: 30 minutes
The planning manager leads the team in generating and reviewing the overall plan with the team. After the team's weekly availability numbers are entered in the "Schedule" worksheet, the planning manager generates the overall team plan.

TSP Schedule Planning Template - Form SCHEDULE

Name	Team
Team	Dev Team
Date	12/31/2007

Total Task Plan Hours	886.4
Total Schedule Plan Hours	924.0
Difference	-37.6

Cycle

Date	Week	Plan Hours	Cumulative Plan Hours	Actual Hours	Cumulative Actual Hours	Planned Value	Cumulative PV	Earned Value
1/7/2008	1	90.0						
1/14/2008	2	78.0						
1/21/2008	3	68.0						
1/28/2008	4	72.0						
2/4/2008	5	104.0						
2/11/2008	6	84.0						
2/18/2008	7	116.0						
2/25/2008	8	66.0						
3/3/2008	9	62.0						
3/10/2008	10	94.0						
3/17/2008	11	90.0						

H ◄ ► H TSP Instructions PlanGuide QualGuide Project Team Goals Roles SUMP SUMQ SUMS Task **Schedule** LOGT LOGD Week IRTL

Figure 11.10   Schedule worksheet.

Here are the detail steps to generate the team plan.

Using TSP Workbook (TSP Tool)—**Generate Overall Team Plan**

Purpose: Generate overall top-down team plan (Figure 11.11).
Person: Planning Manager
Worksheet Name: **TASK**
How: Go to the "Task" worksheet and click on Update Plan button.

Notes:
• Macros need to be enabled.
• You might get the following error message if the start date is in the future (Figure 11.12). To fix this, go to the project worksheet and change either the project start date (should be less than or equal to today's date), or use the "today's override date" option (Figure 11.13).
• If all the options and data are correctly set, the plan will be updated, and when you see some dates in the "plan date" column (of the "Task" sheet), it means that the overall plan is generated (Figure 11.14).

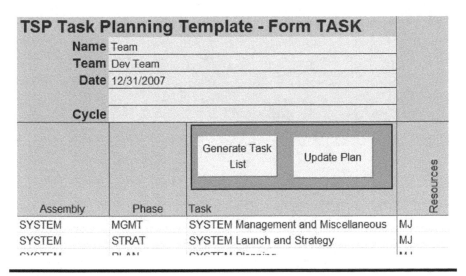

Figure 11.11   Generate overall team plan (Update Plan button).

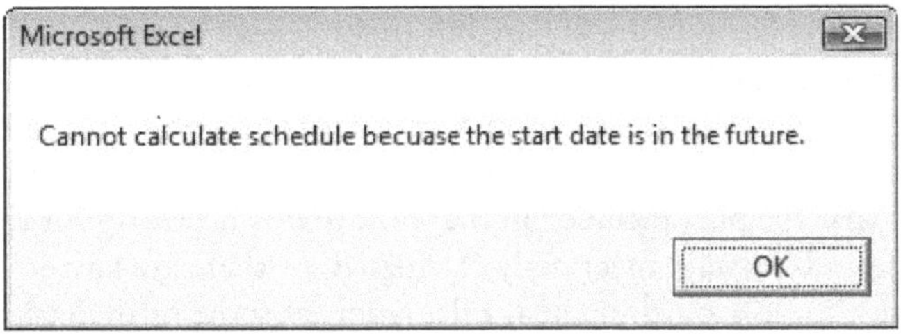

> **Microsoft Excel** ✕
>
> Cannot calculate schedule becuase the start date is in the future.
>
> OK

Figure 11.12   Future start date error.

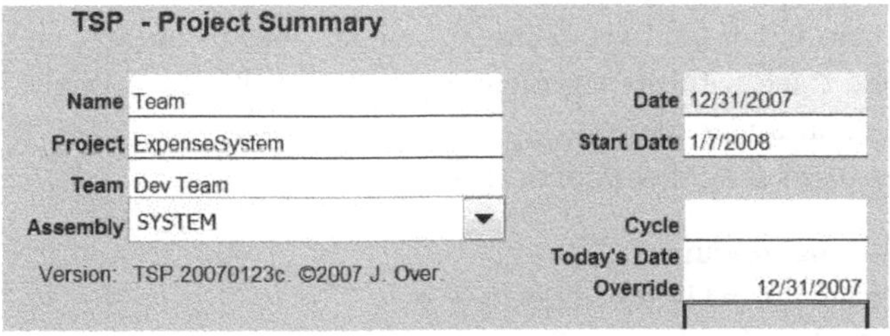

TSP - Project Summary

Name	Team	**Date**	12/31/2007
Project	ExpenseSystem	**Start Date**	1/7/2008
Team	Dev Team		
Assembly	SYSTEM ▼	**Cycle**	
Version: TSP.20070123c. ©2007 J. Over.		**Today's Date Override**	12/31/2007

Figure 11.13   Fixing future start date problem.

TSP Task Planning Template - Form TASK

Name: Team
Team: Dev Team
Date: 12/31/2007

Cycle

Total Plan Hours: 886.4

Reminder:
If Size and Rate are present, estimated hours is calculated as Size / Rate whenever the plan is updated. To prevent calculation, size or rate must be blank.

Assembly	Phase	Task	Resources	Estimated Size	Size Measure	Rate (per Hr.)	Time in Phase %	Estimated Hours	Engrs	Plan Hours	Plan Date	Plan Week
SYSTEM	MGMT	SYSTEM Management and Miscellaneous	MJ					20.0	1.0	20.0	12/31/2007	1
SYSTEM	STRAT	SYSTEM Launch and Strategy	MJ					28.0	4.0	112.0	1/7/2008	2
SYSTEM	PLAN	SYSTEM Planning	MJ					20.0	1.0	20.0	1/7/2008	2
SYSTEM	REQ	SYSTEM Requirements	MJ	20	Req F	2.0		10.0	1.0	10.0	1/7/2008	2
SYSTEM	STP	SYSTEM System Test Plan	VM	35	Text F	4.0		8.8	1.0	8.8	1/14/2008	3
SYSTEM	REQINSP	SYSTEM REQ Inspection	MJ, SR, VM	20	Req F	4.0		5.0	3.0	15.0	1/14/2008	3
SYSTEM	HLD	SYSTEM High-Level Design	SR	50	HLD I	3.0		16.7	1.0	16.7	1/14/2008	3
SYSTEM	ITP	SYSTEM Integration Test Plan	VM	75	Text F	5.0		15.0	1.0	15.0	1/14/2008	3
SYSTEM	HLDINSP	SYSTEM HLD Inspection	SR, RJ, VM	50	HLD I	6.0		8.3	3.0	25.0	1/21/2008	4
Login Module	DLD	Login Module Detailed Design	RJ	300	LOC	10.0	20.0	6.0	1.0	6.0	1/21/2008	4
Login Module	DLDR	Login Module DLD Review	RJ	300	LOC	10.0	10.0	3.0	1.0	3.0	1/21/2008	4
Login Module	TD	Login Module Test Development	RJ	300	LOC	10.0	3.0	0.9	1.0	0.9	1/21/2008	4
Login Module	DLDINSP	Login Module DLD Inspection	RJ,SR	300	LOC	10.0	10.0	3.0	2.0	6.0	1/21/2008	4
Login Module	CODE	Login Module Code	RJ	300	LOC	10.0	20.0	6.0	1.0	6.0	1/21/2008	4
Login Module	CR	Login Module Code Review	RJ	300	LOC	10.0	10.0	3.0	1.0	3.0	1/21/2008	4
Login Module	COMPILE	Login Module Compile	RJ	300	LOC	10.0	2.0	0.6	1.0	0.6	1/21/2008	4
Login Module	CODEINSP	Login Module Code Inspection	RJ,SR	300	LOC	10.0	10.0	3.0	2.0	6.0	1/21/2008	4
Login Module	UT	Login Module Unit Test	RJ	300	LOC	10.0	15.0	4.5	1.0	4.5	1/21/2008	4
Report Module	DLD	Report Module Detailed Design	RJ	200	LOC	10.0	20.0	4.0	1.0	4.0	1/21/2008	4
Report Module	DLDR	Report Module DLD Review	RJ	200	LOC	10.0	10.0	2.0	1.0	2.0	1/21/2008	4
Report Module	TD	Report Module Test Development	RJ	200	LOC	10.0	3.0	0.6	1.0	0.6	1/21/2008	4
Report Module	DLDINSP	Report Module DLD Inspection	RJ,SR	200	LOC	10.0	10.0	2.0	1.0	2.0	1/21/2008	4

TSP Instructions · PlanGuide · QualGuide · Project · Team · Goals · Roles · SUMP · SUMQ · SUMS · Task · Schedule · LOGT · LOGD · Week · IRTL · IRWeek · DefectTypes · QProfPart

Figure 11.14   Task worksheet (after updating the plan).

After this step, the team plan will have information such as size, total hours, high-level schedule, project's earned value over time, etc. (Figure 11.15).

The team leader leads the team in analyzing and reviewing the overall team plan. The team ensures that the tasks, dates, timeline, size, and effort estimates are realistic and that the plan includes all the work that is necessary for the project. If any item is found missing, incorrectly calculated, or there are any errors, it would be a good idea to do a quick manual calculation of some of the tasks and ensure that time was allocated appropriately and is adequate to complete that task. Other items to review are team and management goals, if this plan is as per the development strategy, etc.

If there is any change required in the plan, this is the time to get it done, and the planning manager can recreate the overall plan. After this, the team leader should review the project plan against management goals to see if they are being met. Even though the plan is not final yet, it might be good idea to quickly check and see if the team is on track with management expectations. If not, it might have to start thinking about alternate plans.

Alternate plans should consider the following:

- Additional resource
- Additional time in schedule
- Reduced project scope
- Multiple versions
- Leveraging other teams/tools for some work

TSP Schedule Planning Template - Form SCHEDULE

	Name	Team								
	Team	Dev Team				Total Task Plan Hours			886.4	
	Date	12/31/2007				Total Schedule Plan Hours			924.0	
							Difference		-37.6	
	Cycle									

Date	Week	Plan Hours	Cumulative Plan Hours	Actual Hours	Cumulative Actual Hours	Planned Value	Cumulative PV	Earned Value
12/31/2007	1	90.0	90.0		0.0	3.0	3.0	0.0
1/7/2008	2	78.0	168.0			21.6	24.6	
1/14/2008	3	68.0	236.0			8.4	33.0	
1/21/2008	4	72.0	308.0			13.5	46.5	
1/28/2008	5	104.0	412.0			14.0	60.5	
2/4/2008	6	84.0	496.0			6.1	66.6	
2/11/2008	7	116.0	612.0			22.8	89.4	
2/18/2008	8	66.0	678.0			10.6	100.0	
2/25/2008	9	62.0	740.0			0.0	100.0	
3/3/2008	10	94.0	834.0			0.0	100.0	
3/10/2008	11	90.0	924.0			0.0	100.0	

Figure 11.15   Schedule worksheet (after updating the plan).

Although it is not always possible to speed up project delivery by adding more people, because there is ramp-up and training required for the new person on the team, it may slow down the project. However, if the project is well planned, it might be possible to take an additional resource and accelerate the schedule up to a certain limit.

It might be useful for the planning manager to create a Gantt chart to visually demonstrate the overall project schedule. People are usually more comfortable with the Gantt chart, and it can be used if the team leader is meeting with management before project planning is completed.

11.8 Meeting Wrap-Up

Discussion Leader: Recorder
Duration: 10 minutes
The TSP Coach goes through the exit criteria for meeting 4 and ensures that all the necessary activities are performed by the team.

The meeting recorder summarizes the meeting and performs the following actions:

■ Reads the list of action items, indicating the person responsible and the timeline for task completion. Ensures that all the team members are on the same page.

- Documents the list of attendees and absentees.
- Documents the time spent on each of the agenda items.
- Documents details of major discussion items.
- Lists all the major decisions made and the name of the people involved.
- Reads out the meeting report to the team members and confirms its correctness, completeness, and action item assignment (if any).
- Ensures with the team that there are no other action items.
- Documents the meeting notes and hands it over to the planning manager to file with the other TSP project notes.

This brings to end meeting 4. Make sure that you take a backup of all the documents and the TSP tool.

Chapter 12

Meeting 5
Develop the Quality Plan

Meeting duration: About 1–2 hours depending on project size and Team Software Process^{SM} (TSP^{SM}) experience. For teams that have good experience in using TSP, it takes around 1 hour.

The quality manager leads the team in creating the quality plan for the project. After creating the top-down overall team plan, the next step is to develop the quality plan.

Meeting Agenda (Discussion Leader)

1. Meeting agenda and overview (TSP Coach)
2. Review quality goals (Quality Manager)
3. Estimate defects injected (Quality Manager)
4. Estimate defects removed (Quality Manager)
5. Produce the quality plan (Quality Manager)
6. Meeting wrap-up and report (Recorder)

12.1 Overview

How often do we plan for bugs? We usually have a gut feeling that we will have around 100 bugs during a development cycle for this release, but we end up having 2000, and in the next release—the same story. Maybe there is some guesstimate, but no documentation of a goal or plan, and then the actuals are way off.

Having disciplined methods of estimating the defects injection rate and detection yield will help the team to create the right quality plan for the project. If you are spending 1 hour writing code or requirements, design, etc., you will inject a particular number of bugs (i.e., bugs injected per hour of coding). Then we look at bug detection yield. How good is the design review process to find bugs present in the design at that moment in time? 50%? 70%? What about unit testing? Can you find 80% of the bugs remaining in the code while doing a unit test? To start with, the team can use the industry data as a reference and modify them, based on their scenario. Over time, once they collect enough data, they will be in a position to plan effectively, and their estimate will be more in line with the actual.

TSP Launch meeting 5 ensures that the team plans for defects injection and detection, based on their historical data or the industry data. With this they are in a position to predict how many defects probably will be slipped to acceptance for test and production, and validate that against the goals. This brings in accountability and, over time, maturity of the process, which eventually will result in shipping a high-quality product on time.

Initially, it was very hard for people to imagine a plan for defects. The concept of defect/hour was very new to them. I saw a variety of people estimating both conservatively and aggressively. Over time, we were able to estimate more accurately and track against it.

12.2 Review Quality Goals

The first step in quality planning is to review by the team the management's and team's goals related to quality, and to talk about how to achieve them. The team, along with the guidance from the quality manager and TSP coach, plans for defects—where they will be injected and detected based on their historical data. It is possible that some of the teams may not have any historical data around defects injection and detection, in which case they can use the guidelines as provided in the next sections.

This is the time when the quality manager should briefly explain about the quality guidelines. If the organization has its own, they should use that; if not, use the one listed in the quality guidelines (in the TSP tool open worksheet called "QualGuide").

The overall motto of the teams should be how to write high-quality code right the first time, and prevent defects or find them early—as soon as they are injected. If all the team members follow the TSP process, measure their performance, and continuously improve, you will get a high-quality output.

12.3 Estimate Defects Injected

The quality manager guides the team in understanding the defects injection concept and planning for a defect injection rate across the phases.

The concept of defect injection here is slightly different from what people are used to. There are several ways to estimate defects in each of the phases. In TSP, we use defect injection rates. The defect injected is based on "defects injected per planned hour for that phase." The logic behind this is that if an engineer is working on coding, the more time spent on that the higher the likelihood of injecting more defects. Also, since this is based on planned hours and not LOC, it takes care of the complexity factor. (If the product is more complex, you will need more hours to develop it and chances of defects are also high in complex product.)

During Personal Software Process[SM] (PSP[SM]) training, each engineer goes through rigorous practice with programming exercises, which helps them to reduce their overall defects. As the engineers working on the project and practicing these skills, they are able to reduce the defect injection rate further. On over 75 TSP projects, we observed that variation of the actual defect injection rate across several projects is negligible. While looking at the same data among engineers, we found three major groups of people:

1. PSP trained and experienced TSP (overall very low defect injection rate)
2. PSP trained (defect injection rate slightly better than the quality guidelines)
3. Not trained on PSP (defect injection rate significantly higher than the quality guidelines)

As we collected data we started maintaining a database containing all the data and then made it available for people during their planning. As we added more data, the guidelines become more accurate and people were comfortable using them.

Here are the high-level quality guidelines, we used for the defect injection rate.

Phase	Rate	Details
Planning	0	
Requirements	0.50	Only major defects
System Test Plan	0	
REQ Inspection	0	
High-Level Design	0.50	Only major defects
Integration Test Plan	0	
HLD Inspection	0	
Detailed Design	1	Only design defects
DLD Review	0	

(Continued)

(Continued)

Phase	Rate	Details
Test Development	0	
DLD Inspection	0	
Code	2	All defects
Code Review	0	
Compile	0.1	All defects
Code Inspection	0	
Unit Test	0.1	All defects
Build and Integration Test	0	
System Test	0	

Defects injected = (Defect injection rate) * (Time in phase)

For example, if the coding defect injection rate is 2 per hour and the engineer is spending 4.5 hours, the number of defects injected for this engineer in the coding phase will be 9. Another example: 0.50 in rate column means for every 1 hour of requirements work, there will 0.50 defects injected in the system. Similarly, 2 in coding means, for every 1 hour of coding there will be 2 defects injected. (See Figure 12.1.)

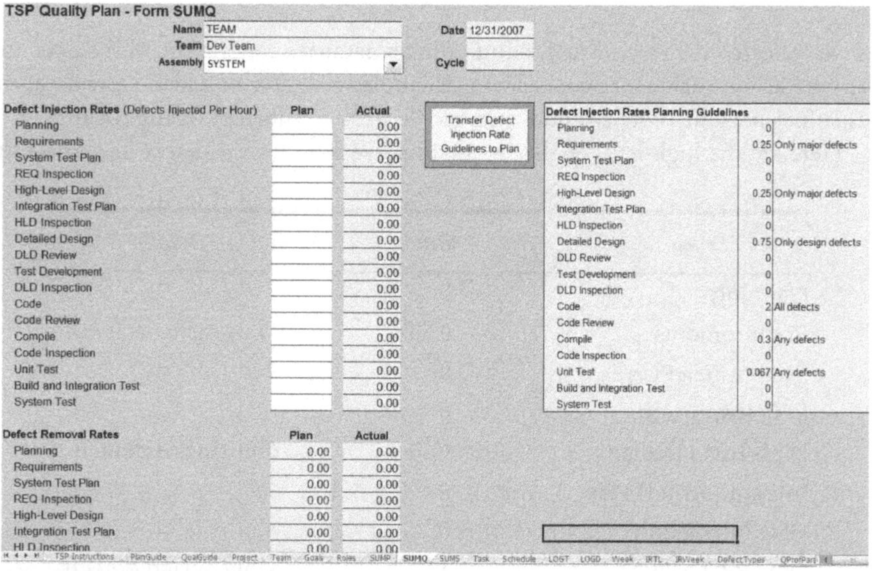

Figure 12.1 SUMQ worksheet for defect injection rate (blank).

Here are detailed steps on how to enter these numbers in the TSP tool.

Using the TSP Workbook (TSP Tool)—**Enter Defect Injection Rate in SUMQ**

Purpose: Update the SUMQ sheet with the defect injection rate information.

Person: Quality manager

Worksheet Name: SUMQ

How: While creating the quality plan for the project, the team reviews the quality goals, and quality guidelines, and then enters a defect injection rate for each of the phases. Click on the SUMQ worksheet and start entering information in defect injection rates (Figure 12.2).

Location	Details
Assembly	In the top left section of the page you will observe a drop down for Assembly. Ensure that the selection is on SYSTEM.
Defect injection rates	Go to the bottom of the sheet, and go to the second section from bottom. The name of the section is Defect Injection Rates (defects injected per hour).
Plan	In the plan column, start entering information for the defect injection rate in each of the phases.
	There are phases where you typically may not inject defects. For the first project, I would advise to take the quality guidelines and use it as it is. Over time, once you have adequate data this information can be fine tuned. If you choose to use the data from the quality guidelines, click on the Transfer Defect Injection Rate Guidelines to Plan. This will copy over all the recommended defect injection rate numbers to the appropriate cells. Once this is done, you can review each item with the team and ensure that the team understands it and agrees with the rates.

After this is done, go through the SUMQ and SUMP to see how the plan is shaping up. With the details from overall plan and now the quality plan, the plan becomes clearer. The team members review the defects information and ensure that the defect count for each phase is a reasonable number (not too high or not too low).

TSP Quality Plan - Form SUMQ

Name TEAM   Date 12/31/2007
Team Dev Team
Assembly SYSTEM ▼   Cycle

Defect Injection Rates (Defects Injected Per Hour)	Plan	Actual	
Planning	0	0.00	Transfer Defect Injection Rate Guidelines to Plan
Requirements	0.5	0.00	
System Test Plan	0	0.00	
REQ Inspection	0	0.00	
High-Level Design	0.5	0.00	
Integration Test Plan	0	0.00	
HLD Inspection	0	0.00	
Detailed Design	1	0.00	
DLD Review	0	0.00	
Test Development	0	0.00	
DLD Inspection	0	0.00	
Code	2	0.00	
Code Review	0	0.00	
Compile	0.1	0.00	
Code Inspection	0	0.00	
Unit Test	0.1	0.00	
Build and Integration Test	0	0.00	
System Test	0	0.00	

Defect Removal Rates	Plan	Actual
Planning	0.00	0.00
Requirements	0.00	0.00
System Test Plan	0.00	0.00
REQ Inspection	0.00	0.00
High-Level Design	0.00	0.00
Integration Test Plan	0.00	0.00
HLD Inspection	0.00	0.00

TSP Instructions PlanGuide QualGuide Project Team Goals Roles SUMP **SUMQ** SUMS Task Schedule

Figure 12.2 SUMQ worksheet defect injection rate.

12.4 Estimate Phase Yield (Defect Removal Rate)

The quality manager guides the team in understanding phase yield (defect detection) concepts and helps them with estimating phase yield for each of the phases. Defects present in any phase are the total defects injected by the end of the current phase, less the total removed before phase entry.

Defects removed = (Defects present in the phase) * (Defects removal yield)/100

You will notice that the terminology used here is "defects removed" instead of "defects detected." The logic is that if a defect is found, it needs to be removed immediately in the same phase where it was found. There might be a few defects that are not possible to remove immediately in the same phase.

The major difference between using these terms "defects found" and "defects removed" is the mindset; the measurements and focus is not around just finding defects but to remove them. Also "defects removed" goes very well with "defects injected."

Once you start planning and tracking defects information, injection rate, detection rate, etc., you can quickly build up a good database and use it for future planning. We started collecting this data early in our TSP implementation phase and quickly, within 5 projects, we created a baseline and started using that information. Every time a project was completed the database would be updated.

If your team does not have historical data, you can refer to the data as shown in the following table. (This data is based on the experience we gained in 75 projects and set a high-quality bar for the teams to meet):

Phase	Yield	Comments
Requirements inspections	60%	Not counting editorial comments
High-level design inspection	60%	Team inspection
Design reviews	50%	Using design notation, templates and state analysis
Test case development	10%	Create test case before coding
Design inspections	70%	Using checklist
Code reviews	70%	Using personal checklists
Compiling	5%	Syntax errors/warnings
Code inspection	70%	Fagan inspection process
Unit test	65%	Write good unit test cases in design phase
Build and Integration Test	70%	
System Test	70%	
Acceptance Test	60%	

If the yield is 70%, it means the phase will be finding 70% of the defects that are present in that phase (this also includes defects that are injected in the current phase). Another way to look at this is in terms of the percent capability of the phase to detect defects. This is also a good benchmark to be used, and people can track their improvement in the area of phase yield over time (see Figure 12.3).

A typical question here is, how do we know how many defects are present in the current phase? It is not possible to know that until the project is finished. So, during project execution, the phase yield gets updated every time a defect is detected.

You will notice that the table here shows phases that typically find defects. It is not uncommon to find defects in other phases like design, code, etc. But, since the

TSP Quality Plan - Form SUMQ

Name: Team   Team: Dev Team   Assembly: SYSTEM   Date: 12/31/2007   Cycle:

Phase Yields	Plan	Actual		Phase Yield Planning Guidelines	
Planning		0%	Transfer Phase Yield Guidelines to Plan	Planning	0%
Requirements		0%		Requirements	0%
System Test Plan		0%		System Test Plan	0%
REQ Inspection		0%		REQ Inspection	70% Not counting editorial comments
High-Level Design		0%		High-Level Design	0%
Integration Test Plan		0%		Integration Test Plan	0%
HLD Inspection		0%		HLD Inspection	70% Using state analysis, trace tables
Detailed Design		0%		Detailed Design	0%
DLD Review		0%		DLD Review	70% Using state analysis, trace tables
Test Development		0%		Test Development	0%
DLD Inspection		0%		DLD Inspection	70% Using state analysis, trace tables
Code		0%		Code	0%
Code Review		0%		Code Review	70% Using personal checklists
Compile		0%		Compile	50% 90+ % of syntax defects
Code Inspection		0%		Code Inspection	70%
Unit Test		0%		Unit test - at < 5 defects/KLOC	90% For high defects/KLOC - 50-75%
Build and Integration Test		0%		Integration test at < 1.0 defects/KLOC	80% For high defects/KLOC - 30-65%
System Test		0%		System test - at < 1.0 defects/KLOC	80% For high defects/KLOC - 30-65%
Acceptance Test		0%		Acceptance test - at < 1.0 defects/KLOC	65% For high defects/KLOC - 30%

Process Yields	Plan	Actual
% Before Compile	0%	0%
% Before Unit Test	0%	0%
% Before Build and Integration Test	0%	0%
% Before System Test	0%	0%
% Before Acceptance Test	0%	0%

Defect Injection Rates (Defects Injected Per Hour)	Plan	Actual		Defect Injection Rates Planning Guidelines	
Planning	0	0.00	Transfer Defect	Planning	0

TSP Instructions | PlanGuide | QualGuide | Project | Team | Goals | Roles | SUMP | SUMQ | SUMS | Task | Schedule | LOGT | LOGD | Week | IRTL | IRWeek | DefectTypes | QPro/Part

Figure 12.3 SUMQ worksheet phase yield (defect removal rate)—blank.

TSP Quality Plan - Form SUMQ

Name: Team   Team: Dev Team   Assembly: SYSTEM   Date: 12/31/2007   Cycle:

Phase Yields	Plan	Actual
Planning	0%	0%
Requirements	0%	0%
System Test Plan	0%	0%
REQ Inspection	60%	0%
High-Level Design	0%	0%
Integration Test Plan	0%	0%
HLD Inspection	60%	0%
Detailed Design	0%	0%
DLD Review	50%	0%
Test Development	10%	0%
DLD Inspection	70%	0%
Code	0%	0%
Code Review	70%	0%
Compile	5%	0%
Code Inspection	70%	0%
Unit Test	65%	0%
Build and Integration Test	70%	0%
System Test	70%	0%
Acceptance Test	60%	0%

Transfer Phase Yield Guidelines to Plan

Process Yields	Plan	Actual
% Before Compile	81%	0%
% Before Unit Test	95%	0%
% Before Build and Integration Test	97%	0%
% Before System Test	99%	0%
% Before Acceptance Test	100%	0%

Defect Injection Rates (Defects Injected Per Hour)	Plan	Actual
Planning	0	0.00

Transfer Defect

TSP Instructions | PlanGuide | QualGuide | Project | Team | Goals | Roles | SUMP | SUMQ | SUMS | Task | Schedule

Figure 12.4 SUMQ worksheet on phase yield (defect removal rate).

formula includes defects injected in the current phase also, the calculation may not get the right answers. So, try to keep the planned phase yield to 0% for these phases. The actual yield might be more than 0%, and as you gather more data, in future projects it will be possible for you to estimate phase yield for these phases, also.

Here are the detailed steps on how to enter these numbers in the TSP tool.

Using TSP Workbook (TSP Tool)—**Enter Phase Yield (Defect Removal Rate) in SUMQ**

Purpose: Update the SUMQ sheet with the phase yield (defect removal rate). (See Figure 12.4.)

Person: Quality manager

Worksheet Name: **SUMQ**

How: The team refers to their historical data (or the quality guidelines) and decides on the phase yield (defect detection rate) for each of the phases. Click on the SUMQ worksheet and start entering information in phase yield section.

Location	Details
Assembly	In the top left section of the page you will observe a drop-down for Assembly. Ensure that the selection is on SYSTEM.
Phase yield	Scroll down toward the center of the sheet and go to the section named Phase Yield (just above the defect injection rate section). (See Figure 12.5.)
Plan	In the plan column, start entering information on phase yield for each of the phases. For the first TSP project, I would advise taking the quality guidelines and use them as is. Over time, once you have adequate data this information can be fine tuned. If you choose to use the data from the quality guidelines, click on the Transfer Phase Yield Guidelines to Plan. This will copy over all the recommended Phase Yield numbers to the appropriate cells. Once this is done, you can review each item with the team and ensure that the team understands it and agrees with the rates.

Note:
The TSP Tool suggests that the compile phase has a 50% phase yield. If you are using the latest development tools/environments, several compile defects are prevented. Therefore, 50% will not be practical to achieve. You should consider changing this to 5% (please refer to Figure 12.6)
Also, unit testing is showing 90%. I doubt if it is practical to achieve this number. Consider lowering it to something like 60–70%.
1. The quality plan is generated for the overall project.
2. You might be able to see quality data for individual assemblies; avoid planning for individual assemblies.

TSP Plan Summary - Form SUMP

Name Team

Team Dev Team

Assembly SYSTEM ▼

Defects Injected	Plan	Actual	Actual%
Planning	0.0	0	0.0%
Requirements	5.0	0	0.0%
System Test Plan	0.0	0	0.0%
REQ Inspection	0.0	0	0.0%
High-Level Design	8.3	0	0.0%
Integration Test Plan	0.0	0	0.0%
HLD Inspection	0.0	0	0.0%
Detailed Design	30.0	0	0.0%
DLD Review	0.0	0	0.0%
Test Development	0.0	0	0.0%
DLD Inspection	0.0	0	0.0%
Code	60.0	0	0.0%
Code Review	0.0	0	0.0%
Compile	0.3	0	0.0%
Code Inspection	0.0	0	0.0%
Unit Test	2.3	0	0.0%
Build and Integration Test	0.0	0	0.0%
System Test	0.0	0	0.0%
Total Development Defects Injected	105.9	0	0.0%
Defects Removed	**Plan**	**Actual**	**Actual%**
Planning	0.0	0	0.0%

I◄ ◄ ► ►I   TSP Instructions PlanGuide QualGuide Project Team Goals Roles **SUMP** SUMQ SUMS

Figure 12.5   SUMP worksheet on defects injected (plan).

After these data are entered, the TSP tool has all the information it needs around estimated defects in the product. It can guide the team on how many defects to expect in each phase and what the product quality will look like. Refer to SUMP sheet to see the estimated defects injected and removed in each phase along with the defect density.

TSP Plan Summary - Form SUMP

Name Team

Team Dev Team

Assembly SYSTEM ▼

Defects Removed	Plan	Actual	Actual%
Planning	0.0	0	0.0%
Requirements	0.0	0	0.0%
System Test Plan	0.0	0	0.0%
REQ Inspection	3.0	0	0.0%
High-Level Design	0.0	0	0.0%
Integration Test Plan	0.0	0	0.0%
HLD Inspection	6.2	0	0.0%
Detailed Design	0.0	0	0.0%
DLD Review	17.1	0	0.0%
Test Development	1.7	0	0.0%
DLD Inspection	10.8	0	0.0%
Code	0.0	0	0.0%
Code Review	45.2	0	0.0%
Compile	1.0	0	0.0%
Code Inspection	13.1	0	0.0%
Unit Test	5.1	0	0.0%
Build and Integration Test	1.9	0	0.0%
System Test	0.6	0	0.0%
Total Development Defects Removed	105.6	0	
Acceptance Test	0.1	0	
Product Life	0.1	0	

H ◀ ▶ H   TSP Instructions   PlanGuide   QualGuide   Project   Team   Goals   Roles   **SUMP**   SUMQ   SUMS   Task

Figure 12.6   SUMP worksheet on defects removed (plan).

12.5   Create and Review the Quality Plan

The quality manager leads the team in creating the quality plan based on the data entered in earlier steps and reviewing with the team to ensure everybody is on the same page and the plan is consistent, realistic, and is able to achieve the goals set by management and the team. The estimated defect injection and removal rates might need to be fine tuned to ensure they are able to meet management's goal.

Here is an overview of how the defects look. (*Note:* This is not available in the TSP tool; the table shown here is a sample for your reference.)

Phase	Hours in phase	Defects injection rate	Phase yield	Defects injected	Cumulative defects	Defects removed	Defects remaining	% defect free
Requirements	60	0.5			30	30	0	30	0.00
System test plan					30	0	30	0.00
REQ inspection			60%		30	18	12	2.55
High-level design	120	0.5		60	72	0	72	2.55
Integration test plan					72	0	72	2.55
HLD inspection			60%		72	43	29	8.66
Detailed design	200	1		200	229	0	229	8.66
DLD review			50%		229	114	114	24.84
Test development			10%		114	11	103	26.46
DLD inspection			70%		103	72	31	36.65
Code	200	2		400	431	0	431	36.65
Code review			70%		431	302	129	79.31
Compile	20	0.1	5%	2	131	7	125	80.24
Code inspection			70%		125	87	37	92.59
Unit test	150	0.1	65%	15	52	34	18	97.41
Build/integration test			70%		18	13	6	99.22
System test			70%		6	4	2	99.77
Acceptance test			60%		2	1	1	99.91
Product life					1			
Total				707		706		

Note:

The number of hours for some of the phases are not mentioned as they are irrelevant for defect injection rate (defects injected per hour).

From the table, you can get a sense of how the defects get calculated. This is very helpful in understanding the overall quality plan and how it fits in the big picture. At any phase, it would be very straightforward to get defect density. This gives a good understanding to the team members of how to find how many defects they are injecting and are finding in each phase. Also, how all of these contribute to the overall quality of the final product. From this table, they can see that they can impact the quality and prevent a lot of defects by following good process. They will appreciate the importance of review and inspection for all the work products.

As you can see if you follow the recommended defect injection rate and phase yields, you can catch 99.77% of the defects before the product gets out to user acceptance testing.

It is a key factor to note here that if the team follows good PSP practices in writing code and in reviews/inspection, it is possible to build a high-quality code (97.41% defect free) at the end of unit testing. With this plan, it is likely that you will have around one defect in production. If you want to avoid this, you will have to reduce the defect injection rate and increase phase yield for the unit testing and other phases towards the end of the project.

After the team estimates defect injection rate and phase yield, it becomes straightforward to calculate defects/KLOC for the project in each phase, number of defects removed in each phase, etc. This is essentially the quality plan. It may not be convenient for the team to review the quality plan just based on defect injection rate and phase yield (as they themselves have planned).

You can notice that the majority of the defects are found in reviews and inspection phases before the testing starts. These defects, if missed, might require substantial effort to find them in the testing phase. All the yields will show very high numbers; the testing phase can be completed fairly quickly with less effort, and you can be assured of having a high-quality product.

On the other hand, if reviews and inspection does not find an adequate number of defects (as planned in the phase yield), you will have more defects going into the testing phase and the project will get delayed. Also, even if you put a lot of effort in the testing phase and have the phase yield around 70%, you will still have few defects left. The majority of the project overruns I have seen are due to quality issues encountered in the testing phase.

I keep telling people, "*The testing job is not to find defects, but to ensure that there are no defects in the product.*" Essentially, engineers should not feel that quality is not their problem or responsibility. In fact, it is the responsibility of every engineer to ensure quality of the product—"right the first time" and/or find the defects as soon as possible after they are introduced.

To review the quality plan, the team needs to have detailed information about the actual number of defects injected and removed in each phase. The quality manager opens the SUMQ and SUMP worksheet and walks the team through it.

Scroll to the top of the SUMQ sheet and you will find defect density, defect ratio, inspection/review time ratio, and rates. (See Figures 12.7–12.9.)

Here are some of the quality plan review guidelines:

1. General
   a. Does the quality plan meet management goals?
   b. See if any of the rates needs to be adjusted to make it more realistic.

2. Review Defects/KLOC. This is the measure of defects found in the phase per 1000 LOC. This is a good indicator of the quality for the product up to the current phase. There are values for each and every phase. You don't need to worry about values in all the phases. Just focus on the following, and check to see if they are within reasonable limits.

  a. Unit test (< 5 defects/KLOC)
  b. Build and integration test (< 1 defects/KLOC)
  c. System test (< 0.25 defects/KLOC)

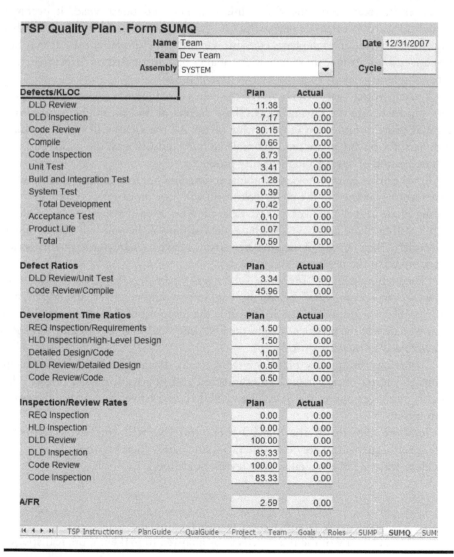

TSP Quality Plan - Form SUMQ

Name: Team   Date: 12/31/2007
Team: Dev Team
Assembly: SYSTEM   Cycle:

Defects/KLOC	Plan	Actual
DLD Review	11.38	0.00
DLD Inspection	7.17	0.00
Code Review	30.15	0.00
Compile	0.66	0.00
Code Inspection	8.73	0.00
Unit Test	3.41	0.00
Build and Integration Test	1.28	0.00
System Test	0.39	0.00
Total Development	70.42	0.00
Acceptance Test	0.10	0.00
Product Life	0.07	0.00
Total	70.59	0.00

Defect Ratios	Plan	Actual
DLD Review/Unit Test	3.34	0.00
Code Review/Compile	45.96	0.00

Development Time Ratios	Plan	Actual
REQ Inspection/Requirements	1.50	0.00
HLD Inspection/High-Level Design	1.50	0.00
Detailed Design/Code	1.00	0.00
DLD Review/Detailed Design	0.50	0.00
Code Review/Code	0.50	0.00

Inspection/Review Rates	Plan	Actual
REQ Inspection	0.00	0.00
HLD Inspection	0.00	0.00
DLD Review	100.00	0.00
DLD Inspection	83.33	0.00
Code Review	100.00	0.00
Code Inspection	83.33	0.00

A/FR	Plan	Actual
	2.59	0.00

⏮ ◀ ▶ ⏭   TSP Instructions   PlanGuide   QualGuide   Project   Team   Goals   Roles   SUMP   **SUMQ**   SUM

Figure 12.7 SUMQ worksheet project defects summary (plan).

TSP Quality Plan - Form SUMQ

Name	Team
Team	Dev Team
Assembly	SYSTEM ▼

Defect Removal Rates	Plan	Actual
Planning	0.00	0.00
Requirements	0.00	0.00
System Test Plan	0.00	0.00
REQ Inspection	0.20	0.00
High-Level Design	0.00	0.00
Integration Test Plan	0.00	0.00
HLD Inspection	0.25	0.00
Detailed Design	0.00	0.00
DLD Review	1.14	0.00
Test Development	0.38	0.00
DLD Inspection	0.60	0.00
Code	0.00	0.00
Code Review	3.02	0.00
Compile	0.33	0.00
Code Inspection	0.73	0.00
Unit Test	0.23	0.00
Build and Integration Test	0.01	0.00
System Test	0.00	0.00

Figure 12.8   SUMQ worksheet defect removal rates (plan).

3. Review Development Time Ratio in SUMQ and ensure all of these ratios are at least 0.5 for each of the following:
   a. REQ Inspection/Requirements
   b. HLD Inspection/High-Level Design
   c. Detailed Design/Code
   d. DLD Review/Detailed Design
   e. Code Review/Code

Process Yields	Plan	Actual
% Before Compile	81%	0%
% Before Unit Test	95%	0%
% Before Build and Integration Test	97%	0%
% Before System Test	99%	0%
% Before Acceptance Test	100%	0%

Figure 12.9   SUMQ worksheet process yield (plan).

4. Review Inspection & Review Rates. This is the measure of how many lines are reviewed/inspected per hour. If it is more than the recommended rate, you probably are not doing a thorough review and inspection, and should consider increasing the time spent in that phase.
   a. DLD Review (< 100 LOC per hour)
   b. DLD Inspection (< 100 LOC per hour)
   c. Code Review (< 200 per hour)
   d. Code Inspection (< 200 per hour)
5. Review A/FR ratio (appraisal-to-failure ratio).
   a. This is a good measure to see where the time is spent and to ensure that the team is spending more time in appraisal activities (reviews and inspections for design and code) compared to testing activities (unit testing and compile).
   b. Make sure it is greater than 2.
6. Review phase yield for each phase.
   a. Check the phase yield against the guidelines. Is it within reasonable limits?
   b. For places where the phase yield is significantly different from the guidelines, what are the reasons? Are these going to impact the final quality of the product?
7. Review process yield for each of the major phases and see if they are reasonable.
   a. % before compile (60% or more)
   b. % before unit test (80% or more)
   c. % before build and integration test (90% or more)
   d. % before system test (95% or more)
   e. % before acceptance test (97% or more)
8. Review defects injection rate for each phase.
   a. Check the defect injection rate against the guidelines. Is it within reasonable limits?
   b. For places where the phase yield is significantly different from the guidelines: What are the reasons? Are these going to impact the final quality of the product?
9. Review defect removal rates.
   a. This is the number of defects removed per hour.
   b. Check to see if they are reasonable.
   c. This is the place where you can see cost of finding defects. The higher the defects found per hour, the more savings there will be in finding the defects in those phases. As the number gets lower, it means the cost of finding defects in those phases is much higher.
10. Open SUMP worksheet and review the rest of the items in that worksheets.
    a. Time in Phase gives details about time spent in each of the phases. This gives a good overview of where the time is spent.

b. Defects Injected gives details of an estimated number of defects that are expected to be injected in each of the phases.

c. Defects Removed gives details of the planned number of defects that are expected to be removed in each of the phases.

11. Does the team have the processes, checklist, standards, etc., to be able to do effective reviews and inspection?

12. Is there any training needed to ensure high quality?

13. Any other issues that can impact the team's ability to deliver quality product on time.

Based on the team review, the quality plan may get updated and then finalized.

During these meetings the TSP coach should motivate the teams to understand the big picture on quality and how it is the responsibility of all the team members to ensure quality. If every team member cannot manage the quality of the work done for the product, they cannot rely on the test team to find defects for them. We all are human; it may not be possible to prevent all the defects, but we can use some of the practices to manage the defects effectively.

If the team can effectively manage their defects, they will have predictable results (cost, quality, schedule, etc.) and will be able to deliver a successful project. The key here is to understand the economics of defects—the cost (time and effort) of fixing defects. The defects can derail the project progress and might impact the organizational image and competitiveness.

To produce a high-quality product, the team needs to have people trained on sound engineering practices develop a quality plan, and measure and track quality at all the phases. With quality measures like defect injection and removal rate, the team can calculate the defects to be found in each phase and can very well manage quality of the product. This completes the quality plan.

12.6 Meeting Wrap-Up

Discussion Leader: recorder
Duration: 10 minutes
The TSP coach goes through the exit criteria for meeting 5 and ensures that all the necessary activities are done by the team.

The meeting recorder summarizes the meeting and performs the following actions:

■ Reads the list of action items, indicating the person responsible and the timeline for task completion. Ensures that all the team members are on the same page.

■ Documents the list of attendees and absentees.

■ Documents the time spent on each of the agenda items.

- Documents details of major discussion items.
- Lists all the major decisions made and the name of the people involved.
- Reads out the meeting report to the team members and confirms its correctness, completeness, and action item assignment (if any).
- Ensures with the team that there are no other action items.
- Documents the meeting notes and hands it over to the planning manager to file with the other TSP project notes.

This brings to end meeting 5. Make sure you take a backup of all the documents and the TSP tool.

Chapter 13

Meeting 6
Build Individual Plans and Consolidate

Meeting duration: About 2–3 hours, depending on project size and Team Software Process^{SM} (TSP^{SM}) experience. For teams that are well experienced in using TSP, around 2 hours.

The planning manager works with the team in creating individual plans and consolidates them to create a balanced team plan.

Meeting Agenda (Discussion Leader)

1. Meeting agenda and overview (TSP Coach)
2. Allocate tasks to team members (Team)
3. Produce individual plans (Team)
4. Load balance individual plans (Planning Manager)
5. Incorporate dependencies in the plan (Team)
6. Produce the team project plan (Planning Manager)
7. Meeting wrap-up and report (Recorder)

13.1 Overview

Most of the time, we end up making a team project plan. Are all the team members the same? Maybe not. Some have a different style of working, some people have different productivity, and so on. Each of the tasks is reviewed to ensure that it does not run more than 10 hours because if one does, it would be difficult to measure for earned value, and in some cases it might be too late to know if there is any issue.

TSP launch meeting 6 ensures that the team project plan is built using individual plans, and every team member has a chance to plan his/her tasks after taking into consideration their vacations and other activities. In this meeting each person will come up with a date when his/her work will get completed. Load balancing is done to ensure that team members complete their work in time to be shipped on schedule.

The TSP coach explains the process to the team, and helps the planning manager and team with the process understanding of creating individual plans. Detailed individual plans help the team in the following ways:

- Incorporate individual specific data around productivity, availability, etc.
- Each task will have clearly defined responsibilities (who will do which task, by when).
- Needs of the product are considered.
- Team will have balanced workload.
- Each team member would know what work is to be done and when.
- All team members can track their work precisely.
- The team can track the work that has been completed and what is pending.
- The team can measure their project status to a detailed level.

13.2 Allocate Tasks to Team Members

Once the overall top-down plan and quality plan is done, the next step is to create individual plans. There are multiple ways to get this done. It is advisable to involve all the team members in creating this plan.

The resource allocation is already done in meeting 4. In this step, check and see if each resource is allocated adequate tasks. This can be done by using Excel functions (like Auto Filter) to calculate number of hours that are required by each of the team members.

If the number of hours required by members is more than their available hours, they should reallocate the tasks to other team members who have some bandwidth. All the team members need to agree to the task allocations and should be ready to finish according to the timeframe.

The next step is to create individual TSP workbooks for each of the team members (see Figure 13.1). Here are the steps to create the individual worksheets.

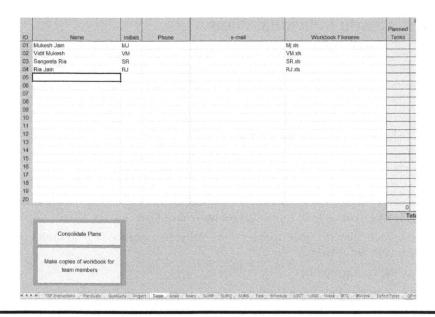

Figure 13.1 Make copies of workbook.

Using TSP Workbook (TSP Tool)—**Create Workbooks for Team Members**
Purpose: Creating TSP workbooks for each team member that they can use for making individual plan.
Person: Planning Manager
***Worksheet Name:* TEAM**
How:
Step 1: Click on the Task worksheet.
Step 2: Ensure that all the team members are listed and there is file name for each of them.
Step 3: Click on the Make Copies of the Workbook for Team Members button.
Step 4: You will get a dialog box to confirm the file created for each of the dialog box. Click Yes to confirm.
Step 5: Repeat step 4 for all the team members.
Step 6: Label the main file from which individual files were created as "master."

Note:
- After these steps are done, you will have TSP workbooks for each of the team members. They will be named as mentioned in the Team worksheet.
- Go to the directory where the files are created and ensure that all the files are created correctly.
- Do not rename these files. The file names need to be the same as mentioned in the Team Worksheet.
- If you click on this button again, it will overwrite the files, so make sure you keep backup copies of all the modified files and avoid clicking again on this button.

13.3 Create Individual Plans

Once all the TSP files are created, take a backup and distribute them to all the team members. Each team member creates an individual plan from this. There are two major steps involved in creating the individual plans:

1. Update Task List with their information.
2. Update Schedule with their availability.

Here are detailed steps on how to create the individual plan.

Using TSP Workbook (TSP Tool) — **Create Individual Plan**

Purpose: Each team member updates their individual workbook with their tasks and schedule information.

Person: Each team member

***Worksheet Name:* Task & Schedule**

How: Each team member opens their personal workbook and updates the task list and the schedule information. Follow these steps to update your individual plans:

Step 1: Remove tasks that are not assigned to you

1. Go to the Task worksheet.
2. Find all the tasks where you are not listed as a resource either primary or secondary (inspection). (Tip: You can use the Excel feature of Auto Filter and specify a condition Does Not Contain <your initial> in the resource column.)
3. Delete all the rows where you are not a resource. (Ensure that you delete all the rows from the Task sheet and not just the data.)
4. Clear the filter. Now you have only those tasks that you are responsible for or are doing inspection on.

Step 2: Update tasks that are assigned to you

1. Go to the Task worksheet.
2. For all the tasks that are assigned to you, ensure that the Engr. Value is set to 1.0 (except for the inspection tasks).
3. For all the inspection tasks where you are primary (author), ensure that you are allocated appropriately (usually 0.5 depending on how much effort you spend in inspection tasks as an author).
4. For the inspection tasks where you are reviewer, update the Engrs. Column appropriately (usually 0.5).
5. Review the productivity (rate per hour). Refer to the historical data (wherever available) and ensure that the rate is appropriately reflected (this would have been done in meeting 4, but just make sure you are comfortable with this. If you plan to change it, please inform the planning manager in advance.

6. Rearrange the tasks (by moving the tasks around) to ensure that they are in the order you are planning to execute the project.

7. Review tasks to see if there are any tasks that are more than 10 hours long. If that is the case, split them into multiple parts.

Step 3: Update schedule information

1. Go to the Schedule worksheet.

2. Refer to the availability numbers you have created in meeting 4.

3. Type your weekly availability numbers in the Schedule worksheet under column "Planned Hours."

4. After entering all the week's data, see what is displayed in the center top portion of the worksheet. If you see a red color text "Warning: Add Schedule Hours," you will have to add more weeks.

Step 4: Update Individual Plan

1. Once you have finished updating the tasks and schedule information, click on the Update Plan button on the Task sheet. This will update all the worksheets.

2. Refer to the Schedule worksheet and see when all of your tasks are expected to be completed.

Note:
Do not rename the individual Excel files. The name needs to be the same as mentioned in the Team worksheet.

13.4 Load Balance Individual Plans

Once all the individual plans are created, the planning manager and the team leader need to ensure that work is balanced fairly among the team members, and they can complete the project in about the same time frame. This is an important step to ensure that all the team members are having the correct amount of load, and the project will not get impacted if one of the person is heavily loaded with tasks and others have some bandwidth.

Here are detailed steps on how to create the individual plan.

Using TSP Workbook (TSP Tool) — **Load Balance Individual Plans**

Purpose: Ensure that each team member has about the same workload and is able to finish about the same time.

Person: Planning manager

Worksheet name: Schedule

How: Each team member reports the hours they need to complete the tasks that are assigned to them. The planning manager collects this information and balances the work load among the team members. Follow these steps to load balance individual plans:

(Continued)

(Continued)

Step 1: Find task load and completion date for each team member

1. Each team member goes to the Schedule tab.
2. Review what is displayed in the center top portion of the worksheet.
3. You will see—
   - Total Task Plan Hours
   - Total Schedule Plan Hours
   - Difference
4. The "difference" should have a negative number in it. That means you have adequate weeks for the project. If you see a positive number or if you see the red color text "Warning: Add Schedule Hours," you will have to add more weeks. Do that and click on Update Plan on the Task sheet before proceeding further.
5. Refer to the Cumulative Planned Value column and see where it becomes 100. Look at the Date column; this is the "expected completion week" for you to complete all your tasks.
6. Report the following information back to the planning manager:
   - Total task plan hours
   - Expected completion week

Step 2: Assess work load among the team members

1. The planning manager gets the schedule and workload information from all the team members and puts it in the following table:

Name	Task hours	Completion week	High/Low
Ria	240	03/17/2008	Avg
Raj	280	03/31/2008	High
Aman	300	03/31/2008	High
Krisha	190	02/25/2008	Low
Minal	210	03/10/2008	Low
Akshay	320	04/07/2008	High
Average	257	03/20/2008	

2. Find out average of task hours and average of completion weeks. For each team member, mark if their completion week is substantially earlier or later than average (2 or more weeks). If it is within 1 week of difference, that person's workload is balanced.
3. The workload (task hours) need not be close to average (especially for people who are going to be on vacation or who are allocated part-time to the project, etc.).
4. Follow the next step to balance the load.

Step 3: Rearrange tasks to balance the workload

1. Identify the person who is completing very late.
2. Ask the person to identify a few set of tasks (full components with all the relevant phases) that can be given to somebody else.

3. Try to make sure that the tasks that are selected, if they are moved, will bring the person's workload close to average.

4. Identify the person(s) that are completing early.

5. See who can take these tasks and assign the tasks to them.

6. While assigning the tasks, ensure that the person is capable and willing to do that task and, with those tasks, their workload and completion date will be close to the average.

7. Once the people are identified, open the workbooks of those individuals, cut the tasks from one workbook, and then paste them into another workbook.

8. Based on the tasks deleted and added in their workbooks, people will need to adjust their schedule information accordingly.

9. Click on the Update Plan button in the Task worksheet for all the workbooks and then repeat this process until the project plan is balanced.

13.5 Incorporate Internal Project Dependencies in the Plan

Once all the individual plans are balanced, the next step is to ensure that all the internal project dependencies are handled correctly, that is, if there are any project components that are needed before others can be developed, the appropriate individual should know about this and the plan needs to reflect this understanding.

Here are detailed steps on how to incorporate internal dependencies in the plan.

Using TSP Workbook (TSP Tool) — **Incorporate Internal Project Dependencies**

Purpose: The team need to be aware of all the internal project dependencies and the plans should take care of it so that the components are developed in the right sequence.

Person: Team members

Worksheet name: **Task**

How: All team members assess their task list and discuss their dependencies, ensuring that they will get the components when they need it. Here are the steps for the same:

Step 1: Team members review their task list and talk about any dependency they have on other components. They mention the week by which they need these components.

Step 2: The person who is developing a component checks the task completion week (Task Plan Date) and sees if it meets the expectation of the team member. If not, he/she needs to rearrange the tasks to be able to deliver in the week as requested by the other team member. If it is not possible to deliver by that week, the week is specified by when that component will be available.

(Continued)

(Continued)

Step 3: The person who needs this component can rearrange his/her task to a future week when the component is expected to be available.

Step 4: Repeat these steps until all the dependencies are discussed and tasks rearranged.

Note:

After every update, the team member needs to click on the Update Plan button in the Task worksheet to get the right picture of when the task is expected to be completed.

13.6   Consolidate and Create Team Project Plan

Once all the individual plans are balanced and dependencies take care of, you can go ahead and create the final team project plan. The planning manager leads the team in creating the team project plan.

Here are detailed steps on how to consolidate individual plans to create the final team's project plan (see Figures 13.2 and 13.3).

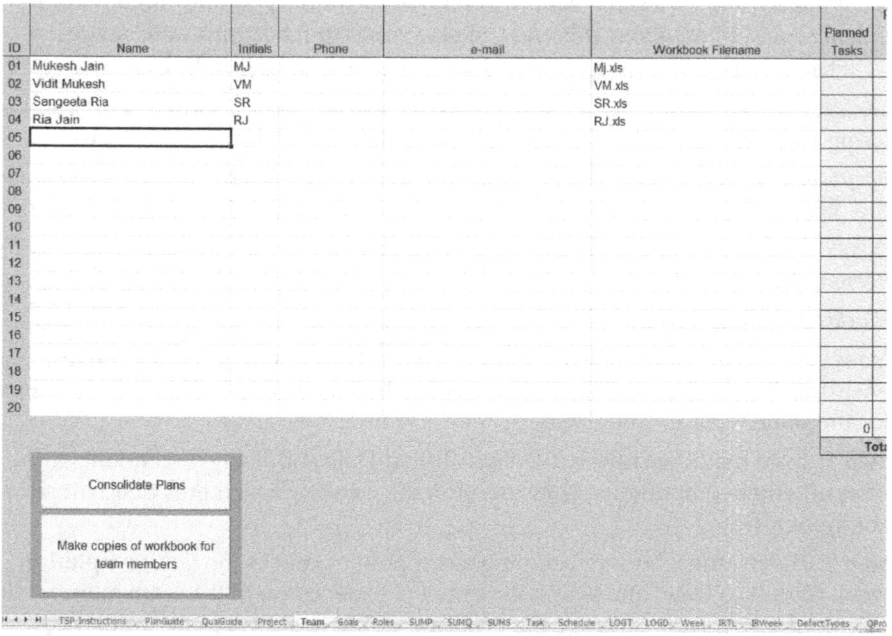

Figure 13.2   Consolidate individual plans.

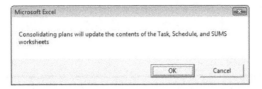

Figure 13.3 Consolidate plan confirmation.

Using TSP Workbook (TSP Tool)—**Consolidate Individual Plans and Create Team Project Plan**

Purpose: After all the individual plans are created, the planning manager consolidates all the plans to create the team's final project plan.

Person: Planning manager

Worksheet Name: **Task**

How: The planning manager copies all team member's individual plan Excel files in the directory where the master file is located. The detailed steps on consolidating the files are as follows:

Step 1: Open the file named master (this is the file which was saved after all the individual files were created).

Step 2: Click on the Team worksheet.

Step 3: Click on the Consolidate Plans button. You will get a confirmation dialog confirming your action "Consolidating plans will update the contents of the Task, Schedule, and SUMS worksheets" OK/Cancel.

Click OK.

It will try to locate the files in the same directory as the master file and open each file. Then it will copy all tasks and schedule data from all the Excel files (individual plans) as mentioned in the Team worksheet, consolidate the data, and update the master file.

After the consolidation is complete, the planning manager reviews the overall plan with the team to ensure everybody is on the same page. Open the Team worksheet in the master file and look at the top right side for the team's planned task hours and estimated week completion (see Figure 13.4).

Refer to the last task on the task list in the Master TSP Project file. Look at the "plan date." This is the week when the project will get completed.

Once the team agrees to the plan, the plan should be baselined. The planning manager opens the Master TSP Project file (ensure the macros are enabled), goes to the TSP tools menu on the toolbar, and clicks on Baseline. A message appears

ID	Name	Initials	Phone	e-mail	Workbook Filename	Planned Tasks	Planned Task Hours	Planned Schedule Weeks	Planned End Date	Predicted End Date
01	Mukesh Jain	MJ			MJ.xls	49	73.80819	9	2/25/08	2/25/08
02	Vidit Mukesh	VM			VM.xls	47	104.9028	9	2/25/08	2/25/08
03	Sangeeta Ria	SR			SR.xls	67	129.2796	8	3/3/08	3/3/08
04	Ria Jain	RJ			RJ.xls	39	120.8798	9	2/25/08	2/25/08
05										
06										

Figure 13.4 Consolidated team plans summary information.

asking for confirmation of the action: "Updating the baseline will replace the existing baseline date." Click OK. And now you have the project baselined. During meeting 9 or before the start of the project, if you need to make changes to the plan, make the changes and then baseline it again and overwrite the existing baseline. Once the team starts working on the project, the baseline should never change.

13.7 Meeting Wrap-Up

Discussion Leader: Recorder
Duration: 10 minutes
The TSP coach goes through the exit criteria for meeting 6 and ensures that all the necessary activities are done by the team.

The meeting recorder summarizes the meeting and performs the following actions:

- Reads the list of action items, indicating the person responsible and the timeline for task completion. Ensures that all the team members are on the same page.
- Documents the list of attendees and absentees.
- Documents the time spent on each of the agenda items.
- Documents details of major discussion items.
- Lists all the major decisions made and the name of the people involved.
- Reads out the meeting report to the team members and confirms its correctness, completeness, and action item assignment (if any).
- Ensures with the team that there are no other action items.
- Documents the meeting notes and hands it over to the planning manager to file with the other TSP project notes.

This brings to end meeting 6. Make sure you take a backup of all the documents and TSP tool.

Each individual should hold on to their files. These are the files they will be using for recording their data and reporting as they move forward.

Chapter 14

Meeting 7
Conducting Risk
Assessment

Meeting duration: About 1.5 hours, depending on project size and Team Software Process^{SM} (TSP^{SM}) experience. For teams that have good experience in using TSP, it takes about 1 hour.

This chapter gives guidelines around how the team can work together to identify issues and potential risks for the project, assess its impact, plan mitigation, and assign owner to track the risk.

The team leader leads the team in discussing project issues and risks that can impact their ability to deliver a successful project.

Meeting Agenda (Discussion Leader)

1. Meeting agenda and overview (TSP Coach)
2. Conduct risk identification and assessment (Team Leader)
3. Create risk mitigation and management plan (Team Leader)
4. Meeting wrap-up and report (Recorder)

14.1   Overview

Despite the best intentions, crises that lead to conflict with assessment plans often arise. Performing a conscious analysis of all the risks in a project helps the team know what might go wrong and plan for them accordingly.

Risk is the combination of the probability an event will occur and the adverse impact on the project if the event occurs. If you find that the combination of the probability of occurrence and impact to the project is very high, you should identify the event as a potential risk and put a proactive risk management plan in place to manage it effectively, and thus eliminate or reduce its impact on the project.

Risk is an integral part of any project, and it should be well managed. If the project team does not practice sound risk management, it may constantly be in a crisis mode, which will impact their ability to deliver the project successfully.

Typically, in software projects, where uncertainties are very high, risk management and mitigation are even more critical. Usually, risk on a small scale is acceptable to most of the project managers as its impact or consequent loss tends to be minimum. However, larger risks pose bigger dangers to the progress of the software project, and you need to manage them effectively. Risk management activities involve identifying potential risks, assessing them, assigning an owner to track the risk, and planning for contingent action if the risk materializes.

TSP Launch meeting 7 ensures that all the risks associated with the project's success are identified and discussed, and the documents and an owner are assigned to track it. It also ensures that risk mitigation plans are in place.

14.2   Risk Identification and Assessment

The first activity in risk analysis is risk identification. It helps you point out the potential risks for a software project across all phases of the project. Risks might evolve or change through the duration of the software project. Therefore, risk identification is an ongoing activity, and needs to be tracked and managed throughout the project. To identify potential risks for a software project, you can analyze the activities in the project, the software product description, and risks faced by the development team in similar past projects. This exercise allows you to identify the potential sources of risks to the current software project, assess the factor influencing the different inputs, and identify the phases in the system development life cycle (SDLC) when risk might materialize.

The team leader leads the brainstorming session with the team in identifying potential risks to the project. The project risk identification process usually considers the planned final product, project scope, project work breakdown structure (WBS), customer, management, team, technology, language, historical information around similar projects, and industry information to determine sources of risk, potential risk events, and risk symptoms. Use Excel file or whiteboard in recoding all the risks, and leave some room for doing risks analysis, assessment, and mitigation.

The team members or team leader should only evaluate any risks after they have all been identified in the brainstorming session. The focus should only be on identifying the risk. The main reason for separating risk identification and evaluation activities is that thinking about and approaching new risks, and evaluating identified risks, are totally different, and by combining them we may not be able to do a good job in dealing with either of them. In identifying potential project risks, all the team members will be thinking creatively about their experiences and expertise and exploring what could happen with their current project. In risk evaluation and assessment, these same people would be thinking differently and critically about the likelihood and impact of each risk on the project.

To trigger more ideas when identifying risks in the project during the brainstorming meeting, we adopted the approach of using major areas as *risk categories*. This helped us think through all the possible areas where the problem might occur.

There are essentially five components in this process:

1. Identify risk—team brainstorms on all the potential risks to the project and product.
2. Categorize risk—classify risks according to major risk categories as listed in the risk category table.
3. Risk assessment—give details about the conditions that can trigger the risk and what will be the possible impact to the project and product.
4. Quantify risk—assess the probability (frequency) of the risk and its potential impact on the project and product.
5. Prioritize risk—based on risk probability and impact, prioritize all the risks that can impact the project and product.

While leading or moderating the brainstorming session, encourage the team not to list typical or ordinary risks such as sickness, accident, and natural disaster. These can cause problems for almost any project, and there is not much that can be done to prevent them. The team should focus on true risks that are unique to the project. If the project is very much dependent on a person or is seriously vulnerable to natural disaster, the team should not ignore these risks.

Encourage everybody in the team to participate. One of the approaches we adopted was to go around the table and ask each person to list one risk. The moderator can classify each risk in the risk category. The only discussion allowed in this meeting is clarification questions around the risk. Nobody is allowed to challenge the risk, assess it, or discuss a solution.

This process continues until there are no more ideas left regarding project risk. People can then refer to the risks listed in the table and discuss if there are others that should be considered.

Risk category	Sources of risk
Man (People)	Project people, customers, end users, sponsors, stakeholders, skills, training, morale
Method (Process)	Development processes, project characteristics, cost, schedules, design, building, testing
Machine (Technology)	Security, development and test environment, deployment, support, operational environment, availability
Management (Organization)	Organization, politics, policies, management, rewards and reorganization, organizational focus and strategy, mission and goals, decision making, training, attrition, culture
Material (Requirements)	Requirements, specifications, tools, reuse, project dependencies, standards
Money	Budget, cost, resources
Environment	Legal, regulatory, compliance, competition, economic, technology, business

After the team members have identified all of the potential risks, the next step in the process is to evaluate each risk and assess its impact. To perform impact analysis, the team should think what would happen if that risk actually materialized. There are multiple impacts that any risk can have. There are multiple ways to assess a risk and its impact on the project.

There are several measures of risk impact that the team might consider—project schedule, project cost, product quality, etc. It is suggested that the team should consider evaluating risk's impact in terms of schedule consequences if the risk materializes.

While doing risk assessment, the team should review one risk at a time and discuss the magnitude of the risk impact, probability of its happening, etc., before it moves on to the next risk. All of these discussions need to be recorded in the following format:

Risk description	Risk category	Consequence	Probability (H, M, L)	Impact (C, H, M, L)	Schedule impact

14.2.1 Risk Impact

If you use schedule slippage as a measure, a high-impact risk will have significantly higher schedule slippage (in the order of several months to a year). Similarly, medium impact risks will most likely cause a project delay of a few weeks to a couple of months. A low-impact risk is one that will delay the project by a few days to a couple of weeks. This scale is typical for projects of 6 months to 1 year duration. For smaller project (2 months), a 2-week delay might be very significant, and the risk would be considered "high impact."

If there is any risk that has very critical impact on the project's success (i.e., over 100% schedule slippage, 100% cost overrun, etc.), you should consider using "C" to label the risk impact as "critical."

Considering all of these factors, the team enters C, H, M, or L in the risk impact column for each risk.

14.2.2 Risk Probability

A risk is different from an issue in that a risk has 1–99% chance of happening, and an issue is something that you know has happened or is going to happen (100% probability). So, essentially, every risk has a probability of happening.

The team brainstorms together to determine which risks are likely to affect the project, and the final product and key details about each risk. If there is 66% or more probability of a risk materializing, it is considered "high," that is, there is a two-third chance of the risk materializing. Similarly, for a risk with 33–66% probability, you can use "medium" (i.e., chances of the risk materializing is between one-third and two-thirds), and if it is less than 33%, you should use "low" probability.

14.2.3 Risk Priority Assessment

After all the potential risks have been identified and assessed for their impact and probability, the team will have a good understanding of the project risks. The next step is to quantify these risks into a table to ascertain their priority. One of the ways to do risk prioritization is to rank risks in order of their overall threat to the organization and, therefore, their priority for focus and action.

Sample Risk Prioritization Approach:

Probability/ impact	Low	Medium	High	Critical
High	M	M	H	C
Medium	L	M	M	H
Low	L	L	M	M

Essentially, the team looks at all the risk quantification numbers and orders them in the format to help in prioritizing the risks. The list of prioritized risks enables the team to commit resources for planning to the highest priority risks, and can make arrangements to manage it effectively.

14.3   Create Risk Mitigation and Management Plan

After the team completes risk identification and assessment, the next step is to plan mitigation actions for the few top-priority risks. The team leader leads the team in discussing risk mitigation and management plans. The discussion starts with reviewing each risk, and the team creates detailed plans for addressing the top risks, triggers, prevention, and potential solutions.

14.3.1   Risk Mitigation

Here is a suggested approach to create a risk mitigation plan:

- Avoid: Can we avoid the risk by changing project scope or approach?
- Plan contingency: Can the impact be reduced through a planned reaction in case mitigation is unsuccessful?
- Mitigate: Can the team do anything immediately to reduce either the probability or the impact of the risk?
- Research: Can we acquire more information about the risk before taking action?
- Accept: Can we live with the consequences if risk were to occur?
- Transfer: Can we transfer risk to other projects, teams, organizations, or individuals?
- Management advice: If the team doesn't know how to handle a risk, the risk can be raised with management to get its advice.

14.3.2   Risk Management

After the risk mitigation actions are planned, the next step is to assign an owner for the risk. The responsibility of the risk owner is to track the risk and risk triggers, and report the status in the weekly meeting.

The risk owner monitors risk metrics and triggering events to ensure that risk actions are working as per the plan. He or she is also expected to provide regular, detailed risk status reports for the project team and top-risk status reports to senior management and other project stakeholders.

Here is a sample form that can be used to track the risks.

Condition	*Consequence*	*Mitigation*	*Owner*	*Follow-up*	*Current status*	

The team leader should integrate all the risk mitigation and management plans with the standard project management processes to ensure that they are completed. Also, he or she should integrate risk management plan tasks into the project plan to track and report on a regular basis.

Senior management is always interested in understanding what the risks are for the project and what actions are planned to mitigate them. This is usually discussed in management meetings, and the team leader is expected to be ready with a plan for this purpose.

Here are the steps on how to get the issues and risks into the TSP tool (Issues and Risk Tracking Log—IRTL). (See Figure 14.1).

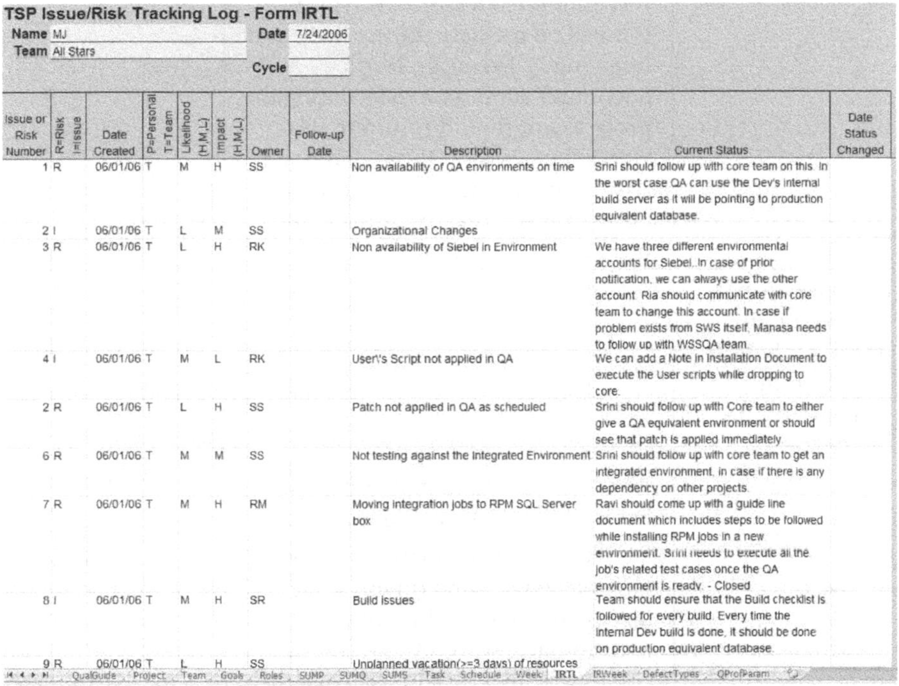

TSP Issue/Risk Tracking Log - Form IRTL

Name MJ Date 7/24/2006
Team All Stars
Cycle

Issue or Risk Number	R=Risk I=Issue	Date Created	P=Personal T=Team	Likelihood (H,M,L)	Impact (H,M,L)	Owner	Follow-up Date	Description	Current Status	Date Status Changed
1	R	06/01/06	T	M	H	SS		Non availability of QA environments on time	Srini should follow up with core team on this. In the worst case QA can use the Dev's internal build server as it will be pointing to production equivalent database.	
2	I	06/01/06	T	L	M	SS		Organizational Changes		
3	R	06/01/06	T	L	H	RK		Non availability of Siebel in Environment	We have three different environmental accounts for Siebel..In case of prior notification, we can always use the other account. Ria should communicate with core team to change this account. In case if problem exists from SWS itself, Manasa needs to follow up with WSSQA team.	
4	I	06/01/06	T	M	L	RK		User\'s Script not applied in QA	We can add a Note in Installation Document to execute the User scripts while dropping to core.	
2	R	06/01/06	T	L	H	SS		Patch not applied in QA as scheduled	Srini should follow up with Core team to either give a QA equivalent environment or should see that patch is applied immediately.	
6	R	06/01/06	T	M	M	SS		Not testing against the Integrated Environment	Srini should follow up with core team to get an integrated environment, in case if there is any dependency on other projects.	
7	R	06/01/06	T	M	H	RM		Moving integration jobs to RPM SQL Server box	Ravi should come up with a guide line document which includes steps to be followed while installing RPM jobs in a new environment. Srini needs to execute all the job's related test cases once the QA environment is ready. - Closed	
8	I	06/01/06	T	M	H	SR		Build issues	Team should ensure that the Build checklist is followed for every build. Every time the internal Dev build is done, it should be done on production equivalent database.	
9	R	06/01/06	T	L	H	SS		Unplanned vacation(>=3 days) of resources		

Figure 14.1 Issues and Risk Tracking Log—IRTL worksheet.

Using TSP Workbook (TSP Tool)—**Enter Issues and Risks Information in IRTL**

Purpose: Issues and Risk management is an integral part of project planning and needs to be tracked.

Person: Team Leader

Worksheet Name: **IRTL**

How: The team goes through the list of risks it has identified and enters them into the TSP tool.

Location	Details	Example
Issue or risk number	This number helps in referring to the risk or the issue. This is an autogenerated number. If this number is not autogenerated for you, enter the risk or issue number.	1,2,3 …
R = Risk I = Issue	Risk has a probability between 1 and 99%. Issue has a probability of 100%, that is, it is sure to happen. Enter "R" for Risk or "I" for Issue.	"R"
Date created	This is the date when the risk or issue was entered in this sheet. Typically, this will be the date during the launch (meeting 7). However, if you encounter additional risks during the project, you should return to this worksheet and add those additional risks. The risk date created should be always greater than or equal to the project start date in the TSP tool.	
The date format should be the same as that of the current settings of the machine.	10/23/1973	
P = Personal T = Team	The risk can be personal or the team's. Enter "P" or "T" accordingly.	"P"
Likelihood (H, M, L)	Likelihood is the probability of the risk materializing. Based on the team discussion, update this column appropriately with "H", "M", or "L". For issues, this column will have the value "H" (as the probability is 100% for issues).	"L" for low likelihood

Impact (H, M, L)	What is the potential impact of this risk on the project or the product? If the impact is going to be critical or very major, select "H" for a high-risk impact.	"H" if the project impact is going to be major on the schedule
Owner	Initials of the person who is assigned tracking responsibility for this risk. (Ensure that the same name is used as mentioned in the TSP team worksheet.)	"MJ" or "Mukeshj"
Follow-up date	Depends on the specific risk or issue. Follow-up might be needed around a date or frequently. Based on that, enter the date on which a follow-up is expected. This date is used as a reference for the risk owner and the team.	"Every Tuesday" or "March 18"
Description	Enter the detailed description of the risk or the issue. Give as much detail as possible. This will be referred to and used by the team throughout the project, and will also be used after the project is completed. You may know the details about the risk now, but after 3 months may not know what it was. So, giving adequate description is helpful.	"The development team will be using a beta technology, and any blocking bugs will delay the project"
Current status	The risk owner needs to update this column as and when the risk/issue status changes or more information is collected.	"Blocked due to 2 bugs in the beta technology"
Date status changed	Every time you update the "current status" field, update the "date status changed" field. This will give a good reference for people who are reading this log. It gives a good indication of how current the information is.	March 18, 2008

14.4 Meeting Wrap-Up

Discussion Leader: Recorder
Duration: 10 minutes
The TSP Coach goes through the exit criteria for meeting 7 and ensures that all the necessary activities are performed by the team.

The meeting recorder summarizes the meeting and performs the following actions:

- Reads the list of action items, indicating the person responsible and the timeline for task completion. Ensures that all the team members are on the same page.
- Documents the list of attendees and absentees.
- Documents the time spent on each of the agenda items.
- Documents details of major discussion items.
- Lists all the major decisions made and the name of the people involved.
- Reads out the meeting report to the team members and confirms its correctness, completeness, and action item assignment (if any).
- Ensures with the team that there are no other action items.
- Documents the meeting notes and hands it over to the planning manager to file with the other TSP project notes.

This brings to end meeting 7. Make sure you take a back-up of all the documents and TSP tool.

Chapter 15

Meeting 8
Prepare TSP^{SM} Project Launch Report for Management Briefing

Meeting duration: It takes about 1.5 hours, depending on project size, complexity, and the team's Team Software Process^{SM} (TSP^{SM}) experience. For teams that have good experience in using TSP, it takes about 1 hour. Actual slide preparation and review will take additional time (about 1 hour).

This chapter gives guidelines on how the team can work together to prepare for the management briefing in meeting 9.

The team leader leads the team in discussing what is expected from the team for the management briefing. It will review the project planning material created during the TSP Launch and create a presentation for the management briefing that covers high-level details about the project plan.

Meeting Agenda (Discussion Leader)

1. Meeting agenda and overview (TSP Coach)
2. Plan the management briefing presentation (Team Leader)
3. Create presentation (Team Leader)
4. Review presentation and prepare for management briefing (Team Leader)
5. Meeting wrap-up and report (Recorder)

15.1 Overview

The final management briefing meeting is a very important part of the project planning process (TSP launch). During this process, in meeting 1, management shares its goals and expectations from the project. Usually, an aggressive schedule is given to the team to work on.

During TSP launch project planning meetings 2–7, the team works hard to produce its project plan. The plan covers how the team can deliver the project and meet product goals, and it gives detailed information about the plan to management.

It is not uncommon to see that the team's plan may not meet all the desires of management, especially those around the schedule. For all the projects we have launched and coached, I found only 2 out of 75 projects that were able to create a project plan that was able to meet the management-proposed deliver date. It is very common to see that the majority of the TSP plans have longer schedules and might need more resources than was originally anticipated.

The difference between a TSP project plan and other project plans is that the chances of delivering a successful project is high with a TSP project plan because it covers all the aspects of the project in adequate detail. In the TSP project plan, the major emphasis is on getting it right the first time, and focuses on quality, effort, and planning helps in getting the project right from the beginning. In the case of other plans, the plan may be able to meet management's expectations and might sound promising, but it may not be able to deliver the results. I am not saying that the TSP plan will guarantee the project success; however, it increases the chances dramatically.

The team's project plan may not meet management's goals set in meeting 1. In fact, management doesn't really expect the team to meet all of the goals it has set. Anybody would love to get the project done "yesterday" with zero cost but, for all practical purposes, that is impossible. Nobody knows exactly how much time or resources are needed to deliver a project successfully. So, management allocates a few resources and sets an aggressive timeline for goals that it thinks the team can try to meet.

In fact, if the team's project plan is able to meet management's date, management would be surprised and might worry that the goals it set in meeting 1 were probably not aggressive enough. It might also think that it should have asked for an earlier date, as it cannot be a coincidence that the goal set by it was very precise and this is the best the team can do.

As you can see, this situation raises a lot of doubts. I am not saying the team should always have a plan that takes longer to achieve management goals. All these and other issues can be addressed in the management briefing meeting, and with the detailed plan, chances of running into such issues is comparatively less.

With all positive intent, the team works together and does its best to create an aggressive but realistic plan where they have given adequate thought around the goals and project challenges and come up with the rational plan.

In this chapter you will see guidelines on how to get ready for the management meeting and what kind of information needs to be presented.

15.2 Plan the Management Briefing Presentation

The team leader reviews the agenda items with the team for the management briefing meeting. He or she discusses the following with the team and gets an agreement regarding

1. Specific materials to be covered
2. What needs to be presented
3. Assign responsibility to team members for developing the material
4. Select presenter for presenting specific slides
5. Preparing the team for potential questions that can be asked by management

During the TSP launch process, the team creates several artifacts for the project plan. Usually, the team gets around 30 minutes to present its plan in the management briefing meeting. The team needs to prepare and present a complete and concise plan to management.

Here are some guidelines around what the management briefing presentation can cover:

1. Overview
   a. Meeting agenda
   b. Project objectives
   c. Project overview
   d. Proposed product details
2. Project team
   a. Names of team leader and team members
   b. Project roles assignments
   c. Team structure
3. TSP launch
   a. TSP launch process overview
   b. Listing of the launch products produced
   c. Brief summary of the work done in TSP launch
4. Goals
   a. Management's stated and implied goals
   b. Team goals
   c. Goal measures and tracking
   d. Comparison of the team's goals against management goals
5. Team's project plan
   a. Overview of the team's plan
   b. Development strategy
   c. Release plan
   d. Conceptual design (high-level architecture)
   e. Prototype plan
   f. Average task hours

      g. Overall size estimates
      h. Team's task and schedule plan
      i. Major milestones
      j. Resources
      k. Project dependencies
      l. Project schedule on Gantt-chart
      m. Help/support needed

6. Alternate plans (if any)
      a. Additional resource
      b. Longer schedule
      c. Shorter scope
      d. Other technology

7. Project quality plan
      a. Overall quality strategy
      b. Project quality plan
      c. Reviews and inspection plans

8. Risk management
      a. Project risks
      b. Risk assessment
      c. Proposed risk mitigation plan
      d. Risk owner, tracking, and management plan
      e. Help needed (if any)

9. Questions/comments

15.3 Create Presentation

The team leader works with the team and assigns tasks to the team members to create slides for management presentation.

It is recommended a template be used, so that you don't miss anything. The slides are assigned based on the team members' experience, expertise, and interest. All those assigned tasks for creating the slides need to understand the expectations and should be in a position to deliver the slides in time for the team review. Have graphs and tables as much as possible; it becomes easier for people to understand these. Focus on creating only a few slides for the presentation, and have additional supporting material in the appendix.

There should not be any major surprises in the presentation slides for the management and for the team. Make sure you cover the points that are discussed and agreed to by the team, and any major deviation should be notified to the management ahead of time. If you find any major issues while creating the slides, immediately bring those to team leader's attention and discuss the options.

As soon as the slides are completed, they need to be sent to the team leader, who will consolidate them and ensure they are consistent, correct, and concise.

15.4 Review Presentation and Prepare for Management Briefing

Once the presentation is ready, the next step is to review it with the team. The team leader leads the meeting, and a presentation dry run is done. This is done by the person who will actually present in front of management. Each person presents his or her slides as if they are being presented to before the management. The TSP coach helps the team in understanding how to do a short and sweet presentation such that management can get the relevant information in the shortest possible time, and the rest of the time can be used to discuss the plan with management.

If the team's plan is not meeting management's expectations, you should consider creating one or more alternate plans involving the following:

1. Additional resources
2. Changes in scope
3. Additional time/schedule
4. Multiple versions
5. Other technology

The alternate plans should focus on meeting at least the top main goals of management. This gives management multiple options and plans to choose from.

Typically, the alternate plans should have been created in meeting 4, but, in case it was not done, you should consider preparing it now. After the individual plans have been created, it is very time consuming to create a plan with additional parameters.

The team members work together to revisit the plan and make changes to one or more parameters and create alternate plans. Make sure the team keeps copies of the alternate plans.

Feedback is encouraged by everybody, and it needs to happen immediately on each slide (after it is presented). The moderator (or team leader) notes down the feedback, questions, comments, etc., on the slide and moves on. You may have some discussion on the slide feedback. You don't need to solve any problems immediately; you should continue the discussion on the presentation if anything to deal with can wait until the full presentation is completed.

After the review and dry run is complete, the TSP coach facilitates a session in which the team brainstorms to explore the possible questions management might ask on the project plan and what the possible answers are. This helps the team in preparing for the question/answer session with management. If needed, the team should update the presentation with additional information to answer some of management's questions.

15.5 Meeting Wrap-Up

Discussion Leader: Recorder
Duration: 10 minutes
The TSP coach goes through the exit criteria for meeting 8 and ensures that all the necessary activities are performed by the team.

The meeting recorder summarizes the meeting and performs the following actions:

- Reads the list of action items, indicating the person responsible and the time-line for task completion. Ensures that all the team members are on the same page.
- Documents the list of attendees and absentees.
- Documents the time spent on each of the agenda items.
- Documents details of major discussion items.
- Lists all the major decisions made and the name of the people involved.
- Reads out the meeting report to the team members and confirms its correctness, completeness, and action item assignment (if any).
- Ensures with the team that there are no other action items.
- Documents the meeting notes and hands it over to the planning manager to file with the other TSP project notes.
- It would be a good idea to run the presentation by a person outside the project to ensure completeness and correctness.

This brings to end meeting 8. Make sure you take a backup of all the documents and TSP tool.

Chapter 16

Meeting 9
Hold the Management Review

Meeting duration: It takes about 1 hour, depending on the team's and management's Team Software Process^{SM} (TSP^{SM}) experience. In case there is much discussion in the meeting (especially if the team is not able to meet management's goals), it might take a little longer.

This chapter provides guidelines on how to plan and run the management briefing meeting (meeting 9).

The team leader leads the management briefing presentation. There might be multiple team members presenting specific slides, but overall, the team leader should facilitate and moderate the meeting. It is strongly recommended that meeting 9 be scheduled well in advance (the meeting 9 date, time, and location should ideally be announced before meeting 1). This ensures management's availability and, during meeting 1, they would know when they will be meeting the team again to review the project plan.

Meeting Agenda (Discussion Leader)

1. Meeting agenda and overview (TSP Coach)
2. Management briefing of TSP project plan (Team Leader)
3. Plan review, discussion, questions, and changes (Team Leader)
4. Management's project plan approval (Team Leader)
5. Meeting wrap-up and report (Recorder)

16.1 Overview

Most of the time, the only item presented to management is the project schedule. This is not enough; management should have full information regarding the project plan. That's when it can add value and provide valuable feedback to the team. Management needs to know if the team would be able to meet its goals, when the team will be able to ship, what the risks in the project are and what the quality of the product will be. In case the team thinks it is unable to meet the management's goals for the prepared project plan, it will present an alternate plan.

TSP Launch meetings 9 ensure that management is informed about the project plan and the team gets a "GO" to start with the project. This helps in getting both management and the teams on the same page and with the same expectations.

16.2 Management Briefing of TSP Project Plan

The attitude of all the team members in the closing management meetings will largely determine how management reacts to the plan. The meeting success largely depends on the team's preparation and the way the meeting is conducted. The team leader needs to ensure that the team members are appropriately prepared for the meeting.

If possible, the team leader should encourage all the team members to attend the management briefing and clearly support the plan. This will give additional evidence to management that the plan is the entire team's, and not just the team leader's, and will reassure it that the team is confident in and committed to making the project successful. In the meeting, if management perceives that the team really tried to meet the date it had set but was unable to, it will be more receptive to the team's plan.

The team has worked hard for several days, thought through all aspects of the project, and created a thorough and achievable project plan. The plan may not meet all of the management's goals, but the team has tried hard to do so. The team leader wants to make sure that management understands the plan and agrees to it or gives feedback guidance before the team can move ahead with project execution.

The team leader starts the presentation by giving a brief overview of the project. He or she explains how much work the team has done in creating the plan, the overall planning process, work product produced, etc.

16.3 Plan Review, Discussion, Questions, and Changes

The management's objective is to get an assurance that the team has done its best to meet the project goals. Here is list of details that management typically looks for in the plan:

- Consistency and completeness in estimates, extra or missing tasks
- Basis and methodology for coming up with estimates, use of historical data

- If the plan is detailed enough to guide the team through the project
- What the alternate plans are that the team has considered
- How the team arrived at the schedule for the project, what are the options to accelerate the schedule, and at what cost
- Team's weekly task hours and how management can help to maximize weekly task hours of the team
- Project risks and mitigation plan, and how management can help
- How the team is planning to deliver a high-quality product
- Team's strategy for design, prototype, and reusing existing components
- Assess the team's confidence in meeting the plan
- Challenge the team to see if it can meet the plan

During the presentation, management may ask several questions, and it will be impressed if the team is prepared with answers and can provide additional detailed information. This indicates that the team has given adequate thought to the project plan, issues, and concerns. With all the team members present in the meeting, and additional backup material, the team demonstrates that it understands and supports the project plan.

Here are some tips on what the team can have as additional backup information:

- List of all the products, their estimates—size, effort, and basis for the estimates
- Overall task list for the project with estimated timeline
- Team's basis for task hours and how it maximizes its weekly task hours
- Additional alternative plans the team has considered
- How additional resource to the project would help the team
- How the team created the quality plan that can ensure a high-quality product
- What are the potential risks for the project and how the team plans to mitigate them
- Overall conceptual design for the product
- Team's strategy and plan for prototyping and reuse
- Team's confidence level on the estimates and what are the possible errors
- Project controls to ensure project is on track
- TSP coaching plan and TSP coach's commitment to the project

Management may recommend changes to plan and/or choose an alternate plan. The team should be receptive to the management's suggestions and recommendations. The team leader should understand what changes can be made and how that will impact the planned resources, work content, and overall plan. Depending on the changes management recommends, the team leader should ask for additional time (a few hours to a day) to review the recommendations and revise the plan appropriately.

16.4 Management's Project Plan Approval

The team's project plan is dependent on many estimates and assumptions but the team thinks this is the best plan that it can possibly produce with the given information at that moment of time.

At the end of the meeting, the team expects management to understand the project plan, to be comfortable in the knowledge that it is the best aggressive plan that the team can produce, and to know that all the team members are committed to meeting the plan and delivering a successful project. The team feels that the plan is aggressive and it will be happy if management approves it.

After the presentation and discussion are completed and management's questions are answered, the team leader should ask for management's approval of the team's project plan. Management may choose one of the plans or ask for some changes to be made to it. In any case, management should consider praising the team for its hard work on creating the project plan. It can formally approve the plan and set expectations regarding the communication rhythm for the project.

After getting management's agreement on and approval of the team's project plan, the team leader should close the meeting. He or she should end the meeting with a summary of the meeting's conclusions, any outstanding action items, who will handle each such item, and when.

16.5 Meeting Wrap-Up

The team leader formally thanks management for its time and feedback for the project plan. He or she then thanks the team and the TSP coach for their work for the past few days to create the project plan.

If the plan needs to be updated, the planning manager does that and sends out the details to the team and management and then baselines the plan again.

The meeting recorder summarizes the meeting and performs the following actions:

- Reads the list of action items, indicating the person responsible and the timeline for task completion. Ensures that all the team members are on the same page.
- Documents the list of attendees and absentees.
- Documents the time spent on each of the agenda items.
- Documents details of major discussion items.
- Lists all the major decisions made and the name of the people involved.
- Reads out the meeting report to the team members and confirms its correctness, completeness, and action item assignment (if any).
- Ensures with the team that there are no other action items.
- Documents the meeting notes and hands it over to the planning manager to file with the other TSP project notes.
- Reviews the list of comments and changes suggested by management and its assignments with the team to ensure everybody is on the same page.
- Backs up all the TSP project files.

Chapter 17

Postmortem and TSP^{SM} Process Review

Discussion leader: Planning manager
Duration: 60 minutes

After meeting 9 is over, the team conducts a postmortem for the Team Software Process^{SM} (TSP) launch and reviews the TSP process. The postmortem is important and necessary, as it provides a structured learning vehicle for the team where everybody is involved and, with the feedback mechanism, it completes the loop of any process for continuous improvement. This is also a good time for the team members to comment on the TSP coach's coaching style and effectiveness in guiding the team with the TSP launch for creating the project plan.

All the team members should participate in the postmortem and approach it with a positive attitude. There is always room for improvement, which can be achieved through feedback and comments. Any idea/suggestion is a good idea and should be considered; people should not be in a mode to attach to or defend any idea. Only with feedback can the team fine tune the process they use, because they are the best people to understand the process limitation, and they will be getting the most benefit if it is improved. Some people may just propose problem areas but have no solutions. That is ok; the purpose of the postmortem is not to solve all the problems in the meeting itself. A problems list is the starting point, and over time, the team can develop solutions to solve these problems. If somebody points out any "people issues," try to convert them into process issues and then try to solve them.

One of the expected outcomes of the postmortem meeting is the PIP (Process Improvement Proposal). The team brainstorms on what changes can be made to the TSP launch process that will help them in future launches and then they document them on the PIP form.

The planning manager reviews the TSP launch process and data with the team to ensure that all the TSP launch data are gathered and recorded in appropriate sections of the TSP tool and forms.

Chapter 18

Managing TSP^{SM} Teams

After the Team Software Process^{SM} (TSP^{SM}) launch and the project plan gets approved by management, the next step is project execution. The team needs to execute on the plan, manage their work, and deliver a successful project. Management of a TSP project is different from the management of a non-TSP project. Managing a TSP project needs understanding of the Team Software Process/Personal Software Process^{SM} (TSP/PSP^{SM}) methodology the team is using, and a manager should be able to coach the team on this. There is training available for managing the TSP teams, which can help managers to effectively coach the TSP teams.

During the project execution, the team will generate data. This needs to be captured at the right place to be able to manage the project well. All the data should be captured in the same TSP tool that was used for project planning in the TSP launch meetings.

18.1 Entering Project Data in TSP

When the team members are working on their tasks/activities, a lot of data is generated. If we do not capture this data, we are losing something. If we can't measure, we can't manage. In a TSP project, every team member logs their exact time for any activity. They also log interruptions, defects found in the work they have done, and the size of work product produced. This data collected gives a good insight into the project and helps the team in making decisions.

During the project execution several data need to be collected. Here is a summary.

1. Time (time spent on tasks, interruptions, task completion date, etc.)
2. Quality (defects found, defects details, defects injected phase, fix time, etc.)
3. Size (lines of code added, removed, modified, etc.)

18.1.1 Time on Task

All the time that is spent on the task is to be entered in the TSP tool. This time includes any reference/research activities, etc. (that are not covered by any other phase). Here are details about how these data can be entered in the TSP tool.

Using TSP Workbook (TSP Tool)—Add "Time Spent" on a Task Information

Purpose: While the team member is working on any of the assigned tasks, the effort spent on the task needs to be captured.

Person: Each team member

Worksheet Name: **LOGT**

How: The engineer should consider keeping the TSP tool Excel file open while working on the tasks. The accuracy of the time is important to be able to drive metrics about the project. Open the TSP tool (the individual team member's file) and click on the LOGT worksheet.

Location (Column)	Details
Task	This column has the name of the task that the engineer is working on.
	Refer to the task worksheet to see what task you are expected to work on in the current week. In some cases you might need to start working on a task that is expected in future weeks. In those cases, you should consider moving the tasks around.
	When you are ready to start working on the task, right click on the task and click on Open Task. Then select the task that you are planning to work on.
	When you select a task, the fields Assembly and Phase get their value automatically (based on the task).
	For an example, see the Login Page Detailed Design.
Date	This is the date on which the engineer started working on the task.
	Click on this column, and it will default to today's date (as per the computer's system settings). You can override today's date by typing in some other date (in case, you want to enter the data for an earlier date). It is highly encouraged that the team members should enter the data immediately as the task is done.
	For tasks that span multiple days, please refer to the notes section (e.g., 10/23/2007).
Start	This is the start time of the task (see Figure 18.1).
	Click on this column and it will default to the current time (in HH:MM:SS format, as per the computer's system settings).

Location (Column)	Details
	You can override the current time by typing in the time (in case you started on a task sometime back and forgot to enter the time). It is highly encouraged that team members should enter the data immediately as they are working on the tasks. For tasks that spans multiple days, please refer to notes section (e.g., 20:38:04).
Int.	This is the column to enter the interruption time while working on the task (i.e., the time you were interrupted while working on the tasks: phone call, coffee break, hallway conversation, etc.). You may be interrupted multiple times for the task. Total up all that time and put one interruption time per task (in minutes). In the comments, you can enter the type of interruptions (e.g., 20 for 20 minutes).
Stop	This column is the stop time for the task. Click on this column and it will default to the current time (in HH:MM:SS format, as per the computer's system settings). You can override the current time by typing it in (in case, you started on a task sometime back and forgot to enter the time). It is highly encouraged that the team members should enter the data immediately as they are working on the tasks. Having a stop time on a task doesn't mean that the task is over. It just mean that the task has been paused. So, essentially you might have multiple entries in the LOGT for the same task. For tasks that span multiple days, please refer to notes section.
Delta	This is an auto-calculated column. It represents the time spent on the task. Here is the formula used for calculation: *Delta = (End time − Start time) − interruption time*
Comments	Use this column for entering any comments for the task and interruption details.

Notes:

1. Always enable Excel macros before making any data entry in the file.
2. Consider closing the task entry in LOGT if you know you are going to be away from the task for a long period (anything above 1 hour), for example, lunch, meeting, training, etc. After you are back, create a new entry in LOGT for the same task and continue. For all the calculation purposes, all the time spent on the same task is summed up.
3. If the task spans multiple calendar days (e.g., you start a task late in the evening and finish after midnight), you should close the task entry just before midnight and create another task entry after midnight. This will ensure that the delta calculation is done correctly. *(Continued)*

(Continued)

4. In case you forget to start or end a task, you should make the entry as soon as you remember to. Make your best judgment on when the task started or ended. It is better to have some approximate data around the time rather than having no data.
5. If you are in Code Review phase and find some defects, when you fix those defects, the time should still be logged against the code review phase and not for the coding phase. This holds similarly for defects found in inspection, testing, etc. Once you move to the next phase, there should be no additional time recorded for the earlier phase for those components.
6. For various reasons, if you are not able to work on any tasks from the current week and are planning to work on future week's tasks, you should rearrange the tasks accordingly in the Task worksheet to reflect the tasks that you are working on in the sequence.
7. You can use the "Move completed tasks" option on the TSP tool as shown in the Figure 18.2.
8. Always take backup of all the files.

18.1.2 Defects Data Entry

While doing any task work it is likely that you will encounter defects. Defects can be encountered in any phase: development (design, coding) or quality control (review, compile, inspection, testing). Irrespective of where the defect was introduced (even if it is introduced in the current phase) and which phase finds the defect, all the defects need to be entered in the LOGD sheet in the TSP tool.

The defects found can be in your own work or somebody else's work. If it is in the work that you were responsible for, you should enter that defect in your sheet. If the defect is in somebody else's work, give the defect to that person and have him/her enter that defect in their personal TSP worksheet. All the defect data entry is entered against the assembly/subassembly phase and the individual.

TSP Time Recording Log - Form LOGT

Name MJ   Date 12/31/2007
Team Dev Team

Cycle
Hours 6.5

Assembly	Phase	Task	Date	Start	Int	Stop	Delta	Comments
SYSTEM	REQINSP	SYSTEM REQ Inspection	12/5/2007	15:11.46	10.0	16:42.34	80.8	Tea break, completed inspection
Login Module	DLD	Login Module Detailed Design	12/5/2007	17:45.21		18:53:11	67.8	Detailed Design completed
Login Module	DLDR	Login Module DLD Review	12/5/2007	19:00.13		19:41.23	41.2	Design Review completed
Login Module	DLDINSP	Login Module DLD Inspection	12/6/2007	12:32.33	5.0	13:15:04	37.5	Inspection done (phone interruption)
Login Module	CODE	Login Module Code	12/6/2007	22:31.33		23:59.00	87.4	Coding (stoped at midnight)
Login Module	CODE	Login Module Code	12/7/2007	0:01:13		1:16.26	75.2	Coding (continue after midnight)

Figure 18.1   LOGT—Enter time.

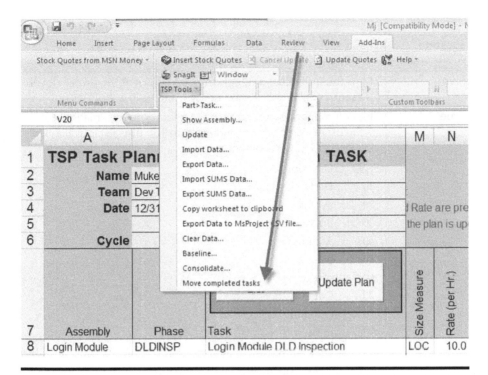

Figure 18.2   Move completed tasks.

Using TSP Workbook (TSP Tool)—**Enter Defects in LOGD Worksheet**

Purpose: While working on the task, as and when a defect is encountered, it needs to be entered appropriately in the LOGD worksheet.

Person: Each team member

Work sheet name: **LOGD**

How: While working on the product, as and when a defect is encountered, all the details need to be entered in the TSP tool–LOGD worksheet. Open the LOGD worksheet and enter defects information

Location (Column)	Details
Date	In this column, enter the date when the defect was found.
	Click on this column and it will default to today's date (as per the computer's system settings). You can override today's date by typing in some other date (in case, you want to enter the data for earlier date). It is highly encouraged that the team members should enter the data immediately as they find the defect while working on the task (e.g., "12/27/2007").

(Continued)

(Continued)

Location (Column)	Details
Num	This is the individual defect number (it is not at the project level). Use sequential number starting with 1 (e.g., 1, 2, 3 ...).
Type	This column is used for capturing Defect type information. Here is the list of defect types suggested in TSP (this list is available in the Defect Types Worksheet).

Type	Description
10	Documentation
20	Syntax
30	Build, Package
40	Assignment
50	Interface
60	Checking
70	Data
80	Function
90	System
100	Environment

	Based on your organizational or team's defect classification and/ or personal classification, you can modify the defect type list. Try to retain the high-level defect type structure (i.e., if you want to add few defect type that are minor variation of interface, create those defect types and give them a number between 51–59 and so on). Keep the defect list consistent across the project. Example of a modified defect types worksheet is given in Figure 18.3.
Assembly	Select the subassembly in which the defect was found (see Figure 18.4). If the defect lies in a combination of two assemblies, log the defect against the assembly where the actual physical code lies. If you do not own that assembly, give the defect to the person that is responsible for the code.
	Select the leaf subassembly while entering the defect information. Do not select any high-level assemblies (e.g., Login Page).
Injected	This column captures the information on where the defect was injected. Use your best judgment here to determine where the defect was injected. It is important to get this correct as much as possible. If you think the defect was due to poor requirements or missed high-level design component, enter the phase accordingly as "REQ" or "HLD," etc. (e.g., "REQ").
Removed	This column captures information on where the defect was found. For all practical purpose, in TSP, defect found and removed phase are considered the same. Ideally, the defect is removed in the

Location (Column)	Details
	same phase where the defect was found. Even if the defect is not removed in the same phase, this column should have the value where the defect was found/detected. Defect can be found in any phase: development (design, code) or quality control phase (review, compile, inspection, testing). It can also be found in the same phase where it was injected (e.g., "Code" or "Review").
Fix Time	The time (in minutes) it took to fix the defect. When you are working on fixing the defect, make sure you log the time in the phase where the defect was found, and in the LOGT entry, mention the defect number in the comments column. This data is useful for compiling aggregate information around the defect and the time it takes to fix a certain type of defect in certain phases, etc. (e.g., "30").
Fix Ref.	This column is a cross-reference field used to log the defect number that introduced this defect. If you determine that the current defect was introduced while you were fixing some other defect, enter that information here.
Description	Enter the description of the defect. Give as much detail as possible. Don't give just the symptoms. Try to give defect root-cause information in this column.

Notes:

• Enter all the defects in the LOGT, including defects found in compile, code, review, inspection, etc.
• Defects data helps you to improve your personal effectiveness and efficiency in the long run. Also, with this data you can gain insight into your product quality and can make decisions.

Type	Description
10	Documentation
20	Syntax
30	Build, Package
40	Assignment
50	Interface
60	Checking
70	Data
80	Function
90	System
100	Environment
81	Function Parameters
91	System - Performance
92	System - Security

Restore Defect Type Defaults

Figure 18.3   Defect types.

TSP Defect Recording Log - Form LOGD

Name	Version 1.92			Date	10/23/2006			
Team	All Stars							
				Cycle				

Date	Num	Type	Assembly	Injected	Removed	Fix Time	Fix Ref	Description
9/4/2006	1	80	B1D_10282 Code		CR	5.0		Default preference not saved
9/9/2006	2	80	B1D_10282 Code		UT	15.0		Deletion incorrect after search
9/19/2006	3	80	B2D_10283 Code		UT	5.0		Bug in UI for cR 15916: Listbox enabled for single select on clear
9/19/2006	4	80	B1D_16108 Code		CR	10.0		Country Logic miised in delete holidays
10/9/2006	5	80	B1D_10282 Code		IT	5.0		Incorrect varialbie used
10/9/2006	6	80	B1D_10282 Code		IT	5.0	5	Defect introduced while fixing other defect
9/4/2006	7	60	B1D_16019 DLD		DLDR	5.0		Used to case when to update the table, but this is not necessary
9/20/2006	8	50	B1D_6852 DLD		CODE	10.0		No pagination was showing the page numbers
9/19/2006	9	50	B1D_6852 CODE		UT	7.0		Row was saving wrongly in the database

Figure 18.4 LOGD—Enter defects data.

18.1.3 Task Completion

When you finish working on the task, you think you have done all you could do, and now you are ready to move the product component to the next phase, the task is considered complete. As soon as you complete any task you should close the task entry and enter task completion date on the task worksheet. Here are details about how to complete the task in the TSP tool.

Using the TSP Workbook (TSP Tool)—**Enter 'Task Completion' Information**

Purpose: When the task gets completed, it needs to be marked accordingly and the completion date entered.

Person: Each team member

Worksheet name: **TASK**

How: Just entering task data in LOGT is not enough. When the task is completed, it needs to be closed in the LOGT and the date should be entered in the Task worksheet. Open the Task worksheet, locate the task that you want to mark complete, and follow the steps as mentioned below:

Location (Column)	Details
Actual Date column	This column (column V in Task worksheet) is used for the engineer to enter the actual task completion date. Any task that has a task completion date is considered complete. This is the only way to mark any task complete. Locate the task, click on this column for "actual date," and enter the date of task completion (e.g., "12/27/2007").

Notes:

• As soon as the task is marked complete (see Figure 18.5), the task will no longer be available in the "open task" menu on the LOGT sheet.

- Once you have marked the task completed, do not unmark the task. If you have to work on the completed task for any reason (defects, incomplete, etc.), use the phase where you encounter and fix the problem, and log the time against that task phase.
- You can move all the completed tasks in the task worksheet to the top to clean up some area on the task worksheet.

18.1.4 Size Information

After you complete any task (move the product from one phase to another), calculate the size and enter the information in the SUMS worksheet. Size information keeps changing as the product moves, and the final size is only available after the product is complete and ready to ship. But to get a good understanding of the project health and status and to take meaningful action in time, it is required to have the size information available for the assemblies throughout the project. Even though the product may not be finished, as it moves to other phases, the size should be updated. If it is too much of a hassle to update every time it moves the phase, then make sure you keep the relevant information handy and enter the data every Friday.

The size information should only be updated by the person who is assigned as the owner of the subassembly in the SUMS worksheet. During TSP sheets consolidation, all other size information gets replaced by the information provided by the owner of the subassembly. If there are multiple people working on the same subassembly, you should have only one owner of the same in the SUMS and only that person should be changing the size information in the SUMS for his/her individual sheet (which eventually gets consolidated into the master TSP plan).

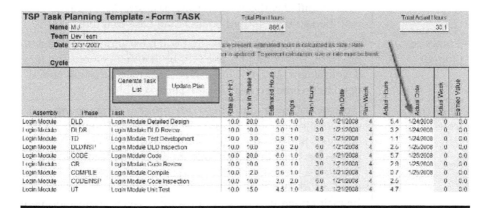

Figure 18.5   Task completion entry.

Using TSP Workbook (TSP Tool)—Enter Actual Size Information for Completed Tasks

Purpose: When the task gets completed, update its SUMS entry with the size information (see Figure 18.6). This helps to gauge the project progress, and the defect data can be used in conjunction with the size data of any assembly.

Person: Each team member

Worksheet name: **SUMS**

How: When a task is complete, the size data for the assembly needs to be updated. Even if the task does not fully complete the assembly work, but as and when the task moves through phases, the size data needs to be updated. Open the TSP tool file, click on the SUMS worksheet, navigate horizontally to the Actual Size section and enter details against the subassembly as mentioned in the table below.

Location (Column)	Details
Actual size (Base)	The base should only be used for existing programs that are leveraged for this project and developed outside of this project. If the program/document is developed in this project, do not include this in the base. Enter the size of the base program or documents that you have used in the project to enhance or make changes to it (e.g., 300 LOC base program size).
Actual size (deleted)	Enter the size (LOC or pages) that you have deleted from the existing (base) programs or documents. This is used in conjunction with the base size measure. You cannot have deleted without having any base size. The number in deleted column should always be less than base size.
Actual size (modified)	Enter the size (LOC or pages) that you have modified or changed from the existing (base) program or documents. This is used in conjunction with the base size measure. You cannot have modified without having any base size. The number in modified column should be less than base-deleted.
Actual size (added)	Enter the size (LOC or pages) that you have added to the base program. This column is used for both enhancement and new development. Any new lines of code or pages that are added need to be entered here for the subassembly.
Actual size (reused)	If you are planning to use any code/programs/documents as is without modifying or deleting anything, enter that size (LOC or pages) here. As the team matures with the PSP and TSP processes, this number should increase. People should start focusing on reusing a higher percentage of software from the previous release. The major benefit of reusing software is saving in development and testing time; it prevents many defects in the product, also.

Location (Column)	Details
Actual size (new and changed)	This is an auto-computed column. As you enter size data in the other columns, this column gets updated. This data is mostly used for further calculations in TSP. Please note that this column will only calculate new and changed size, and is computed as follows: Actual Size (New and Changed) = Added + Modified
Actual size (total)	This is an auto-computed column. As you enter size data in the other columns, this column gets updated. This column gives the final size total of the assembly or subassembly—the ultimate size measure of the final product. This column is computed as follows: Actual Size (Total) = Base − Deleted + Added + Reused

Notes:

- The size information should only be updated by the person who is mentioned as owner on the SUMS worksheet.
- If there are multiple people working on an assembly, they should send the size information to the person whose initials are mentioned on the SUMS worksheet.
- If this is not followed, the size information will be lost.
- Ensure that there is an owner mentioned for each of the assembly in the SUMS. If there is no owner name on the SUMS worksheet the size information will not get updated.
- As the size information is entered, it gets rolled up to their respective parent assemblies.
- The SUMS worksheet also has other rollup information for defects, time, etc.

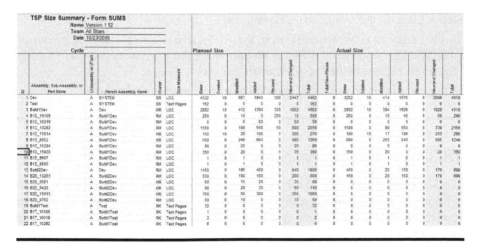

Figure 18.6　Size entry in SUMS.

Every team member is responsible for updating the file, taking backups of their personal files, and keeping it up to date into a central location. The individual files are needed for project data consolidation and further analysis and reporting.

18.2 Project Data Consolidation

Once all the individual plans are updated, all the engineers are expected to copy their personal files to a central location (as determined by the planning manager). Usually the day of the week is set and communicated for consolidation. I recommend using Monday morning as the deadline for uploading the latest files and Monday afternoon as the time for consolidation.

The planning manager leads the team in consolidating all the project plans onto the master sheet.

Here are detailed steps on how to consolidate individual plans to get a project status report.

Using TSP Workbook (TSP Tool)—**Consolidate Individual Plans**

Purpose: After all the individual plans are updated with the latest information, the planning manager consolidates all the plans to create the latest status update of the team's project plan (see Figure 18.7).

Person: Planning manager

Worksheet name: **Task**

How: The planning manager ensures that all team member's individual plan Excel files are in one single directory. The detailed steps on consolidating the files are as follows:

Step 1: Open the file named Master TSP Plan (this is the file that was saved after all the individual files were created and then consolidated).

Step 2: Click on the Team worksheet.

Step 3: Click on the Consolidate Plans button.

This will copy all tasks, schedule data, size, defects, task completion, etc., from all the Excel files (individual plans) as mentioned in the team worksheet and update the project status in the master worksheet.

At the end of this process, you should see a confirmation dialog box: "Consolidation complete."

18.3 Weekly Project Status Meetings

Weekly meetings are integral part of any project. In TSP weekly meetings are especially important because the team consolidates the plan and discusses the outcome, project status, and quality; resolves issues, etc., of the project; and decides how to proceed further.

ID	Name	Initials	Phone	e-mail	Workbook Filename	Planned Tasks	Planned Task Hours	Planned Schedule Weeks	Planned End Date
01	Mukesh Jain	MJ			Mj.xls	49	886.4167	11	3/10/2008
02	Vidit Mukesh	VM			VM.xls	42	731.3131	10	3/3/2008
03	Sangeeta Ria	SR			SR.xls	49	712.2714	10	3/3/2008
04	Ria Jain	RJ			RJ.xls	52	926.4167	12	3/17/2008
05									
06									
07									
08									
09									
10									
11									
12									
13									
14									
15									
16									
17									
18									
19									
20									
						192	3256.418	12	3/17/2008
						Total		Max	

Consolidate Plans

Make copies of workbook for team members

Figure 18.7 Project update: consolidate individual data.

The team leader sets up the weekly meeting and all the team members, team leader, and the TSP coach are expected to attend these weekly meetings. In the weekly meeting, the planning manager starts the discussion by presenting the project status. Use the "Week" worksheet to gather latest information about the project (see Figure 18.8).

The top portion of the week worksheet has the following summary data of the project.

TSP Week Summary - Form WEEK

Name	RPM		Date	7/24/06	
Team	All Stars				
Status for Week	8	Selected Assembly	Cycle		
Week Date	7/24/06	SYSTEM			

Task Hours %Change		Weekly Data	Plan	Actual	Plan / Actual	Plan - Actual	Project End Dates	
Baseline	653.1	Schedule hours for this week	77.5	54.0	1.43	23.5	Baseline	7/24/06
Current	609.5	Schedule hours this cycle to date	676.0	575.1	1.18	100.9	Plan	7/24/06
%Change	-6.7%	Earned value for this week	8.4	12.0	0.70	-3.6	Predicted	7/28/06
		Earned value this cycle to date	100.0	100.0	1.00	0.0		
		To-date hours for tasks completed	0.0	0.0				
		To-date average hours per week	84.5	71.9	1.18			
		EV per completed task hour to date						

Figure 18.8 Project status dashboard—week worksheet.

Weekly Data	Plan	Actual	Plan/Actual	Plan–Actual
Schedule hours for this week				
Schedule hours this cycle to date				
Earned value for this week				
Earned value this cycle to date				
To-date hours for tasks completed				
To-date average hours per week				
EV per completed task hour to date				

This provides many details to the team for understanding the status of the project and taking necessary action (if needed) to bring it back on track. This summary can also be used to report project status (see Figure 18.9).

The lower section of the week worksheet gives details of the tasks that were expected to be completed but are not yet. The team member responsible for the task gives reasons for the delay, and the team investigates to see if any help is needed.

If any engineer does not enter the task completion date, it will still show up as pending. It is common for the first few weeks to see these, and then all the team members ensure that their sheets are complete.

There are cases where some people need to work on future week's tasks before working on current week's task for business reasons or some dependency. In these cases, the current week task will show up as pending and overdue. Whenever any engineer needs to work on future tasks, he/she should move the tasks appropriately and click on Update Plan to ensure that they are working on the current tasks. They should, however, not change their individual schedule plan hours.

Figure 18.9   Project status task completed and due report—week worksheet.

TSP Schedule Planning Template - Form SCHEDULE

Name RPM
Team All Stars
Date 7/24/2006

Total Task Plan Hours 609.5
Total Schedule Plan Hours 688.5
Difference -79.0

Cycle

Date	Week	Planned Hours	Cumulative Planned Hours	Actual Hours	Cumulative Actual Hours	Planned Value	Cumulative Planned Value	Earned Value	Cumulative EV	Predicted Hours	Cumulative Predicted Hours	Predicted Earned Value	Cumulative Predicted Earned Value	Baseline Plan Hours	Cumulative Baseline Plan Hours	Baseline Plan Value	Baseline Cumulative Plan Value
6/12/2006	2	122.0	228.0	108.0	188.4	22.2	34.8	18.2	34.7			18.2	34.7	153.0	259.0	27.2	39.7
6/19/2006	3	107.0	335.0	101.7	290.1	18.7	53.5	17.2	51.9			17.2	51.9	106.0	365.0	16.7	56.3
6/26/2006	4	76.5	411.5	76.6	366.8	12.0	65.5	13.9	65.8			13.9	65.8	88.5	453.5	13.2	69.5
7/3/2006	5	86.0	496.5	69.9	436.7	12.5	78.0	10.5	76.3			10.5	76.3	80.0	533.5	12.4	81.9
7/10/2006	6	56.0	552.5	49.7	486.4	8.7	86.6	7.3	83.6			7.3	83.6	60.5	594.0	8.7	90.6
7/17/2006	7	46.0	598.5	34.7	521.1	5.0	91.6	4.4	88.0			4.4	88.0	56.0	650.0	5.4	96.1
7/24/2006	8	77.5	676.0			8.4	100.0					10.5	98.5	66.5	716.5	3.9	100.0
7/31/2006	9	12.5	688.5			0.0	100.0					1.5	100.0				

Figure 18.10   Project status: schedule worksheet.

The project schedule hours can be reviewed to see how much hours were planned and how much was achieved in the week. This gives adequate details, if the team is able to achieve weekly planned hours (see Figure 18.10).

The focus of the discussion in the weekly meeting is both to solve the problem (if any) and to prevent any foreseeable problems on the project.

18.4 Project Management with Data

Once all the individual files are consolidated into the master, all the data can be analyzed for the project. Some of the graphs and data can also be used in project reporting.

Open the master TSP plan workbook and click on Project Worksheet. There are multiple groups already created. Use the Chart controls to specific the week and use the drop-down menu to select the chart (see Figure 18.11).

18.4.1 Earned Value

On the drop-down menu in the chart controls section, there are three charts available for earned value: Cumulative, Per Week, and Trend. Select any appropriate

TSP - Project Summary

Name RPM
Project Ver 1.91
Team All Stars
Assembly SYSTEM
Version: TSP.20070123c. ©2007 J. Over.

Date 7/24/2006
Start Date 6/5/2006
Cycle
Today's Date
Override 7/24/2006

Time and Defect Log Controls
☑ Use Time Log   ☑ Use Defect Log

Chart Controls
Weeks 5   Max   Draw
Cumulative Earned Value ▼   Print

Cumulative Earned Value
Earned Value per Week
Earned Value Trend
Cumulative Plan vs. Actual Hours
Plan vs. Actual Hours per Week
Percent Defect Free
Cumulative Defects Removed by Ph
Defects Removed by Phase

Cumu

90.0

Figure 18.11   Project status review: chart controls.

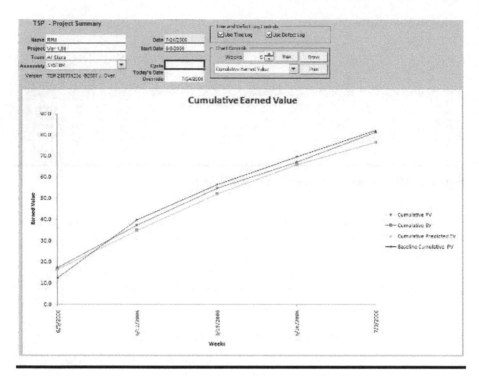

Figure 18.12   Project status review: cumulative earned value.

chart from the drop-down menu. For the specified period, it shows the graph for Baseline, Planned, Predicted, and Actual Earned Value. This information is useful to review the trend in earned value and take any appropriate action to correct it. In this particular example, you can see the cumulative earned value is very close to the cumulative plan value (see Figure 18.12).

In this particular example, you can see that the actual earned value per week is very close to the planned earned value for those weeks (see Figure 18.13).

18.4.2   Planned versus Actual Hours per Week

On the drop-down menu on the chart controls section, there are two charts available for planned versus actual hours per week, cumulative and weekly. Select any appropriate chart from the drop-down menu. For the specified period, it shows the graph for baseline, planned, and actual hours per week. This information is useful to review the trend in hours per week planned versus achieved, and take any appropriate action to correct it (see Figure 18.14). In this particular example, you can see the cumulative actual hours is slightly less than the cumulative plan hours. There is a pattern, the difference started in the first 1–2 weeks and stayed that way throughout. If no action is taken to rectify this, it will remain like this.

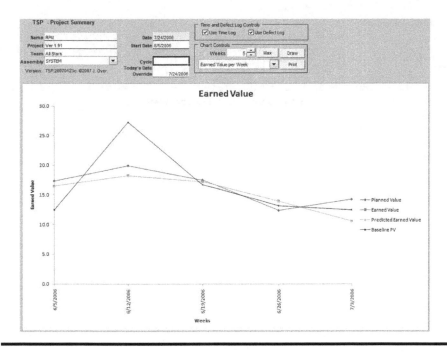

Figure 18.13   Project status review: earned value per week.

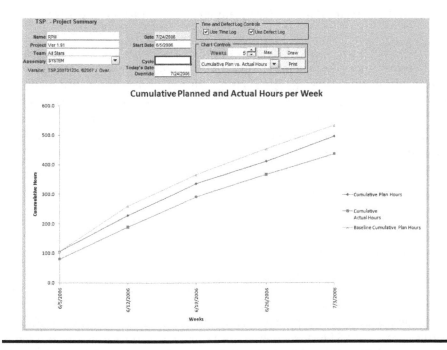

Figure 18.14   Project status review: cumulative planned versus actual hours per week.

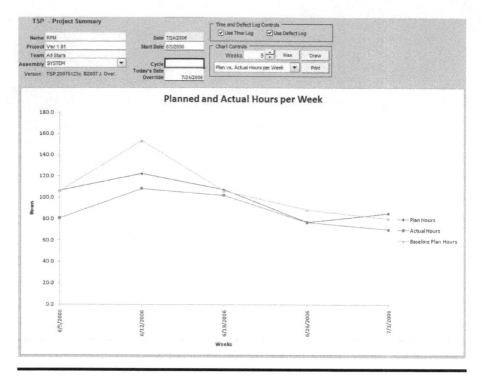

Figure 18.15   Project status review: planned versus actual hours per week.

In this example, the planned versus actual hours for every week can be reviewed and the weeks seen where the team was not able to achieve its planned hours (see Figure 18.15). A root-cause analysis can be done and action taken accordingly to catch up. As you can see, the team has never achieved more than the plan hours. If the difference is significant, it should raise a concern, which should be discussed in the team meeting.

18.4.3 Defects Metrics

With these charts, one can review defects density and defects removed (per phase and cumulative) for the whole project, any parent assembly or any subassembly (see Figures 18.16–18.19). This information is useful to review the overall defects in each of the phases—injected and removed—and take any appropriate action to correct it. Defect density normalizes the data, in case there is a significant variance in planned versus actual size.

In this particular example, you can see the cumulative defects removed (planned versus actual) for SYSTEM assembly. In the beginning, there were more defects found than planned, and after code review, actual defects found were less than the plan.

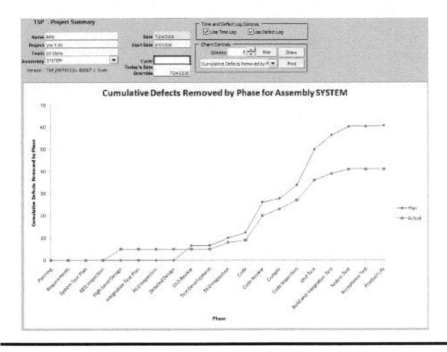

Figure 18.16   Project status review: cumulative defects removed by phase.

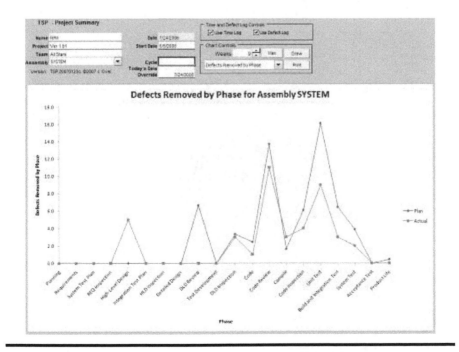

Figure 18.17   Project status review: defects removed by phase.

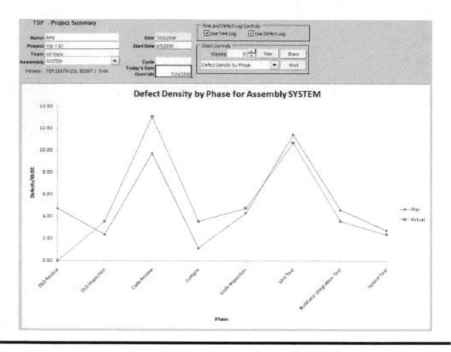

Figure 18.18   Project status review: defects density by phase.

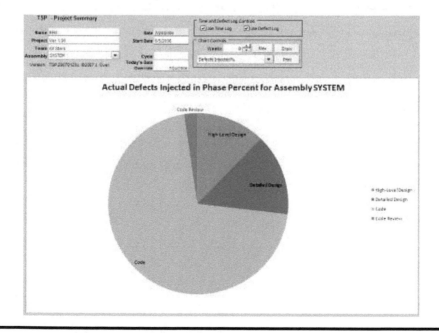

Figure 18.19   Project status review: actual defects injected in phase %.

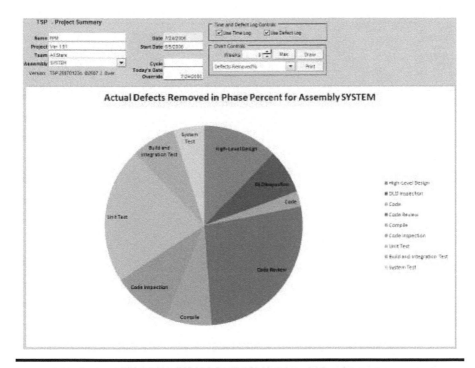

Figure 18.20 Project status review: actual defects removed in phase %.

This is possible for variety of reasons. There might be fewer defects injected or not enough attention is given to find all the defects. It is very tricky situation to be in. The best way to find the root cause would be to check the review rate and how many defects are found in testing. Check the other chart where the same defect removed information is shown per phase. This might give insight into any particular phase where the problem might be.

Please refer to Figure 18.20 to understand the breakup of actual defects removed. It shows the percent of defects removed in each of the phases. You can see that the team did not remove any defects in the design review phase and unit testing found fewer defects than what was planned.

18.4.4 Inspection and Review Rates

Inspection and reviews are an important part of the TSP project, and we need to ensure that it is done effectively. To get the best out of review and inspection, the design should be reviewed/inspected for not more than 100 pseudo codes per hour and not more than 200 lines of code. This ensures that the engineer gives adequate time to review/inspection. The chart helps us to review the review and inspection rate—planned and actual—for each assembly (see Figure 18.21). In this example, you can see the review and inspection rate are better than plan.

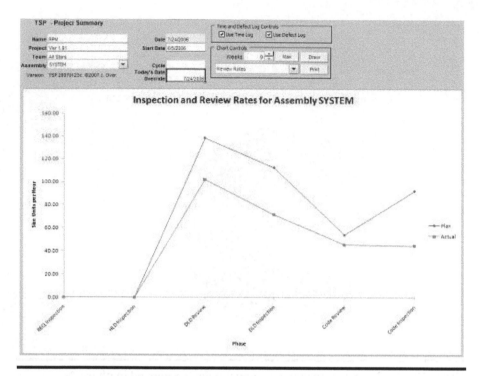

Figure 18.21   Project status review: inspection and review rates.

18.4.5   Phase and Process Yield

Phase yield is the effectiveness of defect finding phase. In the quality plan, the team plans for the percentage of defects they plan to find in each phase (see Figure 18.22). During project execution, they record all the defects information (injected and removed phase). The process yield looks at cumulative yield over several phases (see Figure 18.23).

In this particular example, you can see that the team was not able to achieve the phase yield as per the plan for code review and inspection. This should be a topic of concern and should be reviewed in the meeting.

18.4.6   Percentage Time in Phase

This chart is created based on the time that is recorded by each team member for each phase. This gives a good overview of where the time is spent on the project. In this example, you can see that majority of the time was spent in build and integration test. If you compare this graph with other graphs (phase yield), you will notice that one cause of the team spending more time in build and integration might

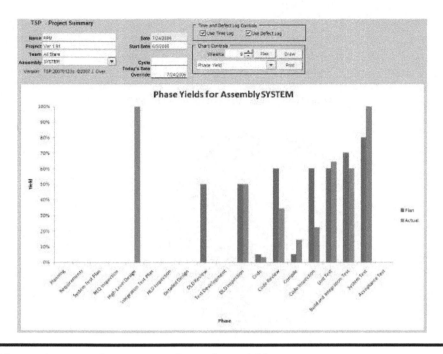

Figure 18.22 Project status review: phase yield.

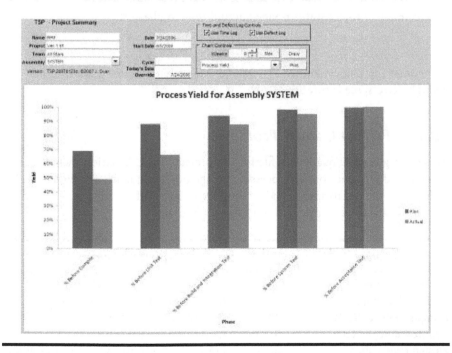

Figure 18.23 Project status review: process yield.

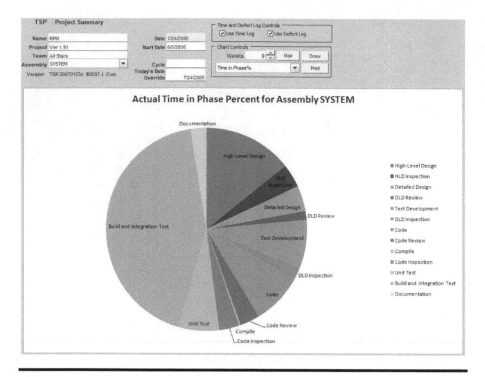

Figure 18.24   Project status review: actual time in phase %.

be because the phase yield for review and inspection was not good (did not find enough defects, see Figure 18.24).

18.4.7 *Project Quality Profile*

This chart gives you quality profile for the project. The calculation includes effectiveness and efficiency of the processes and the product quality (see Figure 18.25). This is also referred to as the Product Quality Index (PQI).

The details used for calculating PQI is as follows:

Parameter	Value	Description
Design/code time	100%	Design time as % of coding time
Code review time	50%	Code review time as % of code time
Compile defects/KLOC	10	Compile defects/KLOC
Unit test defects/KLOC	5	Unit test defects/KLOC
Design review time	50%	Design review time as % of design time

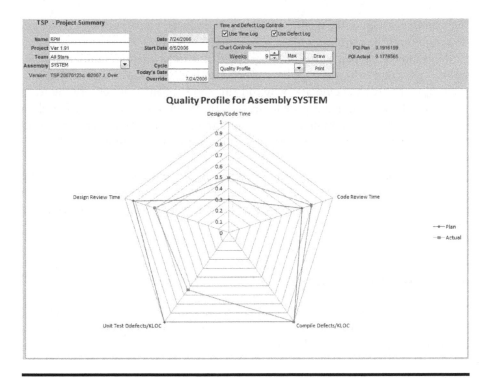

Figure 18.25   Project Quality Profile.

If the actual value for each of the parameters is equal to or better than what is mentioned, you get a score of 1 for that parameter. For values that are worse than the plan, you get less than 1 score for that parameter. At the end scores of all the 5 parameter are multiplied, and you get PQI. The Ideal PQI possible is 1. In practical terms, if your PQI is better than 0.5 you have a very high chance of delivering a high-quality product. In the spider chart, one can see what parameter is not meeting the mark, and focus improvement effort accordingly.

18.5 Project Reporting

Achieving a relatively accurate view into project status is a very challenging goal. It is very important for the team to know how they are doing at any moment of time. This helps them to identify potential issues and take appropriate action before it is too late to prevent any major disaster in the project. Data is captured on all the engineering activities done by the team. This data is consolidated at the team level. The consolidated data is compared against the plan, giving the team insight about how it is doing against the plan. TSP's Team Status Meetings help the team review their project earned value, quality of the work products, hours put in by the team, deviation from the plan, etc.

Slips usually happen a little bit every day. If the tasks are not granular enough, we may not know how much we have slipped until it is too late. So, for any slip in the project, the team should ask, why did this slip happen? Is it because the team member(s) did not put in adequate hours or is the task taking more time? Based on the analysis, we need to watch the parameters and take appropriate actions. If necessary, a replan needs to be done, and the ship date should be adjusted or features cut, etc.

A quality problem does not arise overnight. As a team, we need to monitor the quality of the product, defect injection rate, and defect detection yield compared to the plan. For the project to be successful, the key is to inject fewer defects and find defects early.

18.6 Our Experience

Here comes the interesting part: Once the project was in the execution stage, we started capturing data for all the activities. For each of the components, a majority of the measurements were in the following categories:

- Size
- Time (task hours spent, completion date)
- Defects (phase introduced, phase removed, time spent, type, etc.)

Within 2 weeks we started seeing meaningful graphs that gave a good view of the overall health of the project and projected completion date. Developers were little reluctant in the beginning to record time and defects, but after few weeks they were able to manage their work more closely and effectively.

In the beginning, we found that the majority of the people were not spending adequate (planned) time on self-review and inspection of the design/code. A majority of the modules code review was done in less than 34% of the allocated time, and the defects found in these phases were less than 10% of the plan. When asked about this, they said they had done the review and the time allocated was more than necessary. I had two options: (1) to ask them to spend more time, and (2) wait and watch until they fail. The choice was difficult, but then I thought, if I convince them to spend more time, they may do that without actually believing in the process and the output. I chose to go with the second option.

During the unit testing phase, they started seeing a lot of defects (in meeting 5), we had planned to catch 60% of the remaining defects in UT phase, around 16 defects. Actual number of defects found was 62, almost four times that. During the weekly meeting I asked the quality manager to present his analysis: people were not ready to agree that finding 62 defects in UT is a bad thing, and potentially we will have more defects in production.

I then showed the team, as per plan defect detection rate, we would have about five defects in production. This was an eye-opener for the team. They wanted to fix the problem as soon as possible. I asked them to stop everything and do a self-design and code review, and then do inspection again. This additional work meant the delivery date would slip. But the team was proactive and proposed to work on two weekend days to catch-up.

The code review process started. I could see people getting very serious about the checklist, process finding, and logging defects. We found a few more defects than we had planned for (planned 221, actual 234). Code inspection was seriously done, and we found 31 more defects. In UT we found only 3 defects. Now, the product went to Integration and System Test, and we found only 2 defects in this phase (planned 3). Develop and Test were working really hard to find more defects, but could not find even one.

Finally, the day came for Acceptance Test (AT) by the end users. The project was on schedule for AT. After 4 days of AT, we heard the good news: not a single defect was found in the product. And then it went live 2 days early. We monitored the product for 3 months. No defect was found in production (Planned 1 defect in AT + Prod). The whole team was happy, and the team got an award for excellent delivery. Lesson learned: Do what you have planned for and track it closely. Do course correction if needed.

Chapter 19

Coaching TSP^{SM} Teams

Coaching is one of the most important aspects of Team Software Process^{SM} (TSP^{SM}) project. The coaching job is not done after the training and the TSP project launch. In fact, the real coaching work starts after the launch.

19.1 The Importance of Coaching

To get the full value of TSP, the TSP coach needs to work closely with the project team throughout the project (at least for the first project). Without a TSP coach, there is a danger of the project team losing focus on the TSP, moving TSP to the "back seat," and/or abandoning it completely.

Coaching is not just for new teams; even existing teams need coaching. The investment in building TSP coaching expertise pays off very well in just a few projects.

Coaching is not just a TSP process and TSP tool, but one of the overall concepts of Personal Software Process^{SM}/Team Software Process (PSP^{SM}/TSP), helping each individual use these to their full potential to mature their software development process and deliver successful projects.

19.2 Individual and Team Coaching and Guiding in Right Direction

The TSP coach needs to coach mostly everybody on the project team: the team leader, planning manager, quality manager, other role managers, the project team, and all the individual engineers.

Usually the first few weeks need a lot of coaching for the team members to ensure that they understand the PSP/TSP principles and how they relate to their real work. Hopefully, some of it should have been covered in the PSP engineer training and the rest in the launch, but during the project they may encounter other problems, especially with the TSP tool (they might be using it for the first time). It is highly recommended to have a coach on site. If you happen to use a consultant coach or a remote coach, make some arrangements for the coach to spend some time with the team in the first few weeks.

Earned value based project management is used where the task is counted as completed only if it is done 100%. There is no credit given for any task that is partially complete.

The TSP coach reviews the data with the individuals and the team for the following:

1. Completeness
2. Consistency
3. Deviation from plan
4. Projected completion date
5. Quality
6. Improvements
7. Trends
8. Estimation accuracy
9. Process improvement proposal

Here are the things that are typically reviewed by the TSP coach for coaching individuals and the team.

1. **Earned value**—Planned versus actual work completed and projected earned value. What actions are planned to bring it back on track? The confidence level of meeting the committed date. Try to find out the root cause for deviation and suggest appropriate actions.
2. **Weekly task hours**—If this is significantly lower than the planned weekly hours, discuss with the individual, see why there is a deviation, and try to find out the root cause. See if it is a one time deviation or if there is a problem with the estimates. Also, see if the individual is recording the time appropriately and if there is anything else he/she is working on that takes up lot of time. The ultimate goal is to achieve the planned weekly task hours.
3. **Productivity rates**—Planned versus actual productivity rates should be reviewed to see if the rates are close to the planned one. It is very important to review this in a timely manner to assess the productivity rate and see if the individuals can complete the tasks in the planned time line.
4. **Percentage of time in phase**—During planning percentage of time is allocated to all the phases to ensure adequate attention and effort is spent on

the phases. You may not hit the exact percentage across the phases, but the overall distribution across multiple assemblies should be representative of the plan.

5. **Size**—Size is the basis of all the estimates, and the plan is impacted if the size estimates are significantly off. All the engineers are expected to enter the size details after the task completion or at least on every Friday. This will give adequate details to be able to gauge if the size estimates are accurate or grossly off. If you determine that the size estimates are no longer accurate for any reason, consider bringing this up in the weekly team meeting and discussing it for possible solutions.

6. **Defects**—Individuals can get full value for the TSP/PSP process if they follow the process religiously, log all the defects, and take appropriate corrective action to improve the quality of their deliverables. The TSP coach ensures that all the defects are logged in the correct place and have relevant information. In the initial period, the coach helps the individual in analyzing the defects and taking corrective action to prevent such defects. This needs to be monitored to ensure that overall the defects count is reducing and the engineer is not making the same type of mistakes/defects.

7. **Defect density**—Along with defects, monitoring defect density is equally important. Defect density is defects per KLOC. While the engineer is working on a project component, it is not uncommon to inject a few defects, and in other phases they probably get found and removed. As the defects are found, the defect density of those components gets updated and the engineer can see the quality of the product. To ensure timely feedback, it is required that all the team members update the size as soon as possible, complete one component at a time, and log all the defects in timely manner. The TSP coach reviews the defect density against the TSP guidelines and the plan, and coaches the engineer accordingly. In the initial period, the coach helps the individual in analyzing the defect density and recommends corrective action to improve defect density for other components. This needs to be continuously monitored to ensure that the defects density is reduced over time for each engineer.

8. **Unplanned tasks**—In any project it is possible to get unplanned tasks. There are four types of unplanned tasks:

   a. An additional task for the project component (that was missed in planning)
   b. A task from other team members of the same project
   c. Any nonengineering task on the project that was not anticipated
   d. Any other task not related to the project

   While it is important and required to work on the unplanned tasks, it should not adversely impact the engineer's ability to work on other committed tasks and schedule. If the engineer is getting a lot of unplanned tasks, you should ask him/her to talk to the team leader and see what can be done to minimize disruptions with unplanned tasks, and review the potential consequences of this on the planned tasks.

9. **Phase yield**—Phase yield is the capability of the phase to detect defects from the product components. As defects are logged in subsequent phases, the phase yield of all the phases gets updated (reduced) and starts reflecting actual phase yield. The final phase yield is computed only at the end of the project (after user acceptance testing is done). We don't want to wait until the end of the project to determine if the phase yield was achieved. Therefore, always monitor the phase yield to see if it is reasonable (significantly higher than the plan). If it is near the planned value and the project is still not in the final states (integration or system testing), you should be worried about the quality of the product, as the phase did not catch the required percentage of the defect. As a result, you should be encountering higher defects in the later phases of the project and or in production. This needs to be continuously monitored to ensure that overall the phase yield is improving as you move from one component to other components in the project for each engineer.

10. **Load Balancing**—If during coaching, you encounter one or more engineers lagging behind and may not be able to finish in time, you should recommend that they talk to team leaders for possible load balancing. It is always better to take action as soon as the problem is encountered rather than trying hard to catch up and ultimately cut corners or delay the overall project.

19.3 Improving Individual and Team Performance

The TSP coach can use the following guidelines to access the deviations and recommend appropriate action to bring the project back on track.

1. **One-time deviation** (special cause). Was this just a one-time event (e.g. sick, unexpected loss of work time, etc.)? These are usually the unexpected circumstances, are not predictable, and the likelihood of repeating this is comparatively low. A one-time action is recommended to bring the project back on track (e.g., working on one of the evenings or weekend, or reassigning one of the tasks to another team member, etc.).

2. **Natural variation** (common cause). If the planned task hours are 12 for the first week and 13 for the second week, we do not expect exactly 12 and 13 in actual numbers. There will be variation, and variation is part of life and is seen in everything. The variation should be random and should be on both sides (i.e., some weeks, actual are more than the planned and other weeks lower than planned, etc.). If you see variation on a single side, you should consider doing deep analysis and find the root cause.

3. **Incorrect estimation/bias** (significant difference and trend between the plan and actual data). If there is a significant difference between the plan and

the actual data, and the trend is on one side (usually the actual is significantly lower than the plan), it is clear that the estimates may not be appropriately done for the project or the person is having trouble meeting commitments. In any case, the root cause needs to be found and appropriate corrective action should be recommended. If the corrective action is to revise the estimates, see if this revision is to be done for just one individual or for all the team members. And if it is going to impact the project schedule, you should bring this into the weekly meeting and have people discuss it. If everybody agrees on the change, it needs to be discussed with the management.

19.4 Coaching the Team to Understand Their Own Data

For the first few weeks, the focus of the coaching is about the weekly meeting, TSP process, and correct and complete data entry. The TSP coach needs to participate in all the weekly team meetings, schedule 1:1 meetings with all the individuals for every week in the beginning, and then for every other week.

During individual coaching, the TSP coach reviews the individual data on time, size, and defects, and reviews his/her plan for improvement around the quality. The TSP coach can give some specific guidance around how the engineers can improve their process to deliver better results.

As the weeks pass by, the TSP coach coaches the team in understanding and analyzing the project data, and in taking action on items needed for improvement. Specific aspects to look for are: project plan versus actual plan, data consistency, updating the project plan in a timely manner, the role manager's tasks, risk tracking and mitigation, quality issues, etc.

Even though the TSP coach will be spending significant time on the project and meeting with each of the individuals, it is the responsibility of each of the team members to improve outcomes and keep the project on track. The TSP coach may not be expert in the technology or the domain, but have adequate expertise in TSP and data analysis that can help the team to continuously improve.

19.5 Summary

This chapter focuses on how the TSP coach can coach the team and individual members in reviewing their own data, continuous planning, and becoming more efficient to manage their work effectively.

Teams make a detailed plan; the accuracy of it depends on the historical data. If the execution is not as per the plan, it may not be able to deliver on the commitments. The important factor here is logging their work data, tracking progress, reviewing metrics, and taking corrective action at the right time to ensure the project is on track.

Chapter 20

Overview of Six Sigma

Six Sigma is a combination of a philosophy, framework, methodology, and road-map for improvement and metrics. The goal of Six Sigma is to improve customer satisfaction by eliminating variation and defects from the process. Six Sigma balances rigor and objectivity with speed and common sense.

The term *Six Sigma* is a statistical term for variation, and it refers to the ability of a set of processes to produce the desired output (within specification limit). Specifically, processes that operate at Six Sigma level produce less than 3.4 Defects Per Million Opportunities (DPMO). Six Sigma has an approach

Six Sigma originated at Motorola in the early 1980s with the focus on reducing product failures by 10 times over a 5-year period. Six Sigma is not a software development methodology nor is it a process definition. It is a general process/methodology for improving and optimizing processes and products. Six Sigma has many statistical tools that guide analysts in using scientific methods of analysis and driving appropriate improvements in the process and product quality. There are few elements of Six Sigma involved within the Team Software Process^{SM}/Personal Software Process^{SM} (TSP^{SM}/PSP^{SM}) methodology (e.g., regression analysis for estimation model).

Six Sigma Approach

- Focus on the end user and customer
- Drive cost down
- Integrate data into the decision-making process
- Identify and solve problems at the root-cause level
- Build infrastructure to encourage and support process improvement
- Breakthrough improvements

- Drive cross-functional teamwork
- Paradigm shift in mindset
- Build sustainability
- Integrate functions and disciplines
- Drive growth

Typical Six Sigma Roles

Executive Leadership	Includes top management and CEO. Responsible for setting up a vision for Six Sigma for the organization. Empowers Sponsor and Champion with freedom and resources to explore new ideas for breakthrough improvements.
Sponsor	A leader who allocates resources and supports Six Sigma initiatives. Nominates Champions and reviews the program.
Champion	Runs the Six Sigma program and implementation across the organization in an integrated manner. Provides direct support to project teams and is accountable for program success and results.
Master Black Belt	Identified by Champions. Highly experienced Black Belt for most difficult projects; acts as in-house expert Six Sigma coach for the organization, trains and mentors Black Belts. Time is devoted 100% to Six Sigma. Ensures integrated deployment of Six Sigma across various functions and departments. Focuses on identifying projects/functions areas for Six Sigma.
Black Belt	Leads complex improvement projects. Trained and skilled in rigorous statistical methodologies; leads project teams; full-time commitment is encouraged. Trains and mentors Green Belts.
Green Belt	Leads improvement projects (or sub-projects on a Black Belt team); skilled in problem-solving and statistical tools; part-time commitment.

20.1 The Need for Continuous Improvement

In TSP/PSP engineers collect lot of data around project execution, product quality, etc. TSP/PSP framework has some guidelines for improving personal process and product quality. However, it does not provide any specific guidelines or tools around continuous improvement.

Continuous improvement is important part of the PSP/TSP methodology, and if this is carefully done, you can achieve high levels of quality and mature the overall predictability of the project teams.

20.2 Solving the Right Problem the Right Way

20.2.1 Defects Are Inevitable

It is a fact that no software can be guaranteed 100% defect free. When everyone feels that software will have a defect no matter what we do, we stop taking action to prevent defects from appearing. In fact, defects are inevitable. However, if we *act* that way, we make it horribly true. Simply fixing the bug is not enough. Take a moment to figure out why the bug happened. If we analyze our mistakes and rethink the process, we can eliminate most of these mistakes. All processes have the potential for defects. Hence, all processes offer an opportunity for the elimination of defects and the resultant quality improvement.

Whenever you encounter a bug/defect, ask yourself:

- What assumptions were wrong?
- What rules did I break?
- How could I have detected this bug earlier?
- How could I have prevented this bug?

20.2.2 Fixing the Root Cause

Detailed root cause analysis (using Six Sigma methodology) of all the defects should be done on a regular basis (don't wait for project postmortem). Based on the findings of the analysis, appropriate process needs to be updated to ensure these kinds of defects do not occur, and if they occur, can be caught early. This will help the team to prevent these defects in future. When everybody starts sharing this data with other people, all the teams will be in a situation of preventing a majority of the defects, hence, doing it right the first time and shipping high-quality product on time.

We applied Six Sigma to the overall TSP launch process, defects analysis, and reduction and to improve productive hours. With Six Sigma analysis, our team was able to increase their available productivity to 25–27 hours per week (compared to their counterpart at the same level role and responsibility in the United States who have not more than 13 hours). Even if offshore productivity is considered 20% less with a high number of productive hours (double), we can easily see high value—not just productivity but also quality.

There are multiple Six Sigma methodologies, out of which two are the most popular: DMAIC (Improvement) and DMADV (Building).

20.3 The DMAIC Methodology

The key steps in the Six Sigma improvement framework are Define, Measure, Analyze, Improve, and Control. When a specific Six Sigma project is started, the goals related to customer satisfaction should be established and further divided into subgoals like cycle time reduction, cost reduction, or defect reduction. (This can be done with some of the tools in Six Sigma methodology).

Define	(D)	Zero in on a specific problem with defined return on effort
Measure	(M)	Determine current performance of process
Analyze	(A)	Validate key drivers of performance (root cause of problem)
Improve	(I)	Improved performance and validated realized results
Control	(C)	Implement controls to ensure continued performance

The Define stage for the Six Sigma project calls for baselining and benchmarking the current process. It also includes an assessment of the organizational/group change that might be needed for success. Once an effort or project is defined, the team methodically proceeds through the remaining phases of Six Sigma: Measurement, Analysis, Improvement, and Control.

The Six Sigma project improvement team works together, brainstorms, and identifies relevant metrics for the process and product, based on engineering principles and models. With detail data on processes in hand, the team can then proceed to evaluate the data for trends, patterns, causal relationships, special cause, common cause, root cause, etc. Usually the majority of the analysis for typical Green Belt projects can be done with a simple statistical tool. For more complex projects, you can do some experiments and modeling to evaluate/confirm hypothesized relationships or evaluate degree of influence of one factor over another in a process.

It is often necessary for the teams to iterate through the Measure–Analyze–Improve steps until they find the right set of root causes and are able to fix the majority of them. When the expected goal is achieved, control measures are then established in the process to sustain improvements.

When using Six Sigma, it is important to identify which process measures significantly contribute to the overall customer satisfaction, i.e., what are the vital few that impact customer satisfaction. The process and product quality is usually more sensitive to a few sets of factors than others. The analysis phase of Six Sigma can help identify the extent of improvement needed in each process substep in order to achieve the expected target/goal in the final product.

20.4 Using Six Sigma in Software

Six Sigma is more than a metric; it is a continuous improvement framework with a rich toolset, a philosophy to improve customer satisfaction, and a strategy to achieve business objectives. It is not specific to any industry. It is equally applicable to software. Wherever there is a process, Six Sigma can be used there to improve it. Software is a fairly new field, and software development has yet to attain maturity in terms of predictability (quality, cost, time, work-life, etc.).

There is a strong need to improve the software development process. Here are some key reasons:

■ Software is used in more and more mission-critical applications.
■ Foreign countries are taking up many software jobs.
■ Foreign governments are promoting software quality initiatives (CMMi).
■ The majority of the CMMi Level 5 organizations are in foreign countries.
■ The majority of costs (~65%) in software development projects are related to fixing quality issues.
■ The major cause of project failure is quality.
■ Software maintenance (fixing quality issues) is a business by itself.
■ Software development, maintenance, and acquisition takes up major portions of any IT budget.
■ Getting products developed in foreign countries is cheaper and can result in high quality.

The issue in software development process is not in the technology but in the way we measure, manage, and drive improvement. There is a mindset that needs to be changed. We often hear "Software will have defects—it's natural." If nobody moves to improve this situation, we will make it horribly true.

It's all about understanding change and applying it to the software development process. Here are some of the key aspects of change:

■ Change should be part of any process.
■ Any processes can be and should be measured.
■ There will be resistance to change—it is inevitable, learn to live with it.
■ Lead by example—change yourself to change others.
■ As you start measuring, you will start seeing positive results.

Why is software different?

■ Product complexity.
■ Metrics/measurements for software are different.
■ Software is an intangible product.
■ Most engineering teams adopt the Code–Test–Fix model.
■ Software development is still considered art/innovation.
■ Standard process is considered an inhibiting factor for innovation.
■ All the software development projects are different.
■ Process standardization for software has limitations.
■ Some best practices are available—but not used widely.
■ Subjective requirements—hard to measure success.

Six Sigma can very well be applied here to make software development more predictable and deliver successful projects (high quality, on time).

Here are the typical high-level phases in software development:

- Requirements
- Specifications
- Design
- Code
- Reviews/inspection
- Testing
- Deployment
- Maintenance
- Support

Each of these phases can be measured and improved using Six Sigma. The key here is to identify the right measures for the phase that impacts the overall project success and product quality, etc.

Here are the list of phases and some sample metrics/measurements that can be used as a starting point for driving any improvement using Six Sigma:

- Requirements (missed expectations, ambiguity, changes, etc.)
- Specifications (missed or ambiguous scenarios/goals, interoperability, performance, specification defects, etc.)
- Design (architecture, design defects, defects injected in earlier phases)
- Code (defects, defects classification, time spent/lines of code, rework %, root cause of defects, defects injection phase, defects fix time, etc.)
- Reviews/inspection (number of defects found, time spent, number of defects missed, etc.)
- Testing (number of defects found, defects injection phase, number of defects missed to the next phase, number found using automation, etc.)
- Deployment (issues encountered, code issues, availability, etc.)
- Maintenance (fixes, new feature requests, defects reported/fixed, time spent, code churn, etc.)
- Support (support calls, call category, major issues, average time spent on calls, major call driver, major time consumer, etc.)

Based on the problem area and measurements, an appropriate area can be chosen for improvement, and team can work accordingly to analyze and drive improvements.

I used Six Sigma for software development project in 2000. The first one was to improve the quality, completeness, and effectiveness specifications across the teams.

20.5 Project Case Study: Improve Product Specification Quality, Completeness and Effectiveness

We released a major version of one product and our customers/users reported several defects. Our customer satisfaction went down, support call volume spiked, and it was chaos. The immediate reaction from the management was "The testers did not do the right thing; they should have caught these issues." There was nobody to defend the test team, and the solution to the problem was just train the testers and add more testers to the team. Done.

I was a little hesitant to accept without data that it was the testers' fault. It is true that the customer first reported the issues—but we needed more data to prove where exactly the problem was. Otherwise, we might fix something somewhere else and think the problem was solved. The first step for me was to gather the information related to customer-reported issues. This was the Define phase. I collected all the information I could related to customer issues, support call records, etc. I did some measurements to validate some of the issues. The name of the project was "Improve team's ability to ship high-quality product." The project might sound very generic, but our difficulty was that we didn't know what the root cause of the problem was.

We knew the symptoms and were trying to collect more data. We collected data from testing team on all the defects reported, and the defects that were not fixed. We took copies of all the specifications and started doing our analysis. Our next step was to review the customers reported issues and see why their issues were missed. We started looking at the testing data. They reported few of those issues (about 18%), and they were not fixed for variety of reasons by the development team. So, we then talked to the development team. The reason they gave was that they were not asked to write those scenarios.

We were not trying to put the blame on somebody, but we wanted to know why these issues were not caught by the team. We then talked to the program managers who write the specifications. We were trying to map the issues to the scenarios in the specs. To our surprise, we found that the scenarios did not cover these. The issues were big enough (interoperability, performance, etc.) for us to further escalate our efforts. We collected more data on the usage of these features/scenarios, and surveyed around 2500 users. We found that majority of the users (82%) of them expected those scenarios to be supported and run. So, it was obvious that we missed them in the specifications and then in further phases.

Essentially, we were able to narrow down the root cause of the problem to the specification phase. We then did further exploration of the specification phase: how the specification is written, what are the inputs and templates, who are involved, who reviews, etc. We collected whatever data that was available. After going through all the specification process data and 2 weeks of analysis and brainstorming, we made recommendations on improving the specification process. Here is the list of items for change and all of them were adopted.

1. Have a defined spec process.
2. Create a specification template to cover the common issues people typically encounter.
3. Evangelize the usage of specification template and make it part of the process.
4. Define specification review and inspection process, involve team members (developers, tester, and usability) for reviewing the specification in time.
5. Create a traceability matrix for every specification; this matrix will trace all the requirements to specification, to code and test cases.
6. Get specifications reviewed by a few people from outside the team.
7. Have metrics in place for the specification process to ensure the process is followed, is efficient, and is effective.

After this process was implemented, we reduced specification-related defects by 85%, and the testing was more complete. The final product had 68% fewer defects than the last release. Our team got a "Quality Focus" award for the results achieved by improving the specification process using the Six Sigma methodology.

20.6 Mentoring a Six Sigma Project

You will not be able to get full value for a Six Sigma project without mentoring. People doing Six Sigma get basic statistical knowledge from the training. But they lack implementation details and situation-specific approaches. Mentoring provides guidance to the Green Belt or Black Belt to help them think outside the box, think breakthrough, etc.

Mentoring should not be a voluntary activity; there should be a commitment from both the sides to make the project successful. I recommend the approach of "teaching people how to fish," that is, instead of giving a solution directly, help the people understand the issue very well and coach them to find the solutions. I found that just asking questions helps; people are trained for and are capable of finding solutions; it's just that direction and some coaching will help.

Typically, an experienced Black Belt can mentor about five Green Belts and two Black Belts. The rhythm needs to be set to ensure the project is on track. The best way to get this done is to set up biweekly meetings for mentoring and reviewing the project progress.

Index

Milton Keynes UK
Ingram Content Group UK Ltd.
UKHW040110071024
449327UK00019B/953

9 780367 386375